The Stiftung Wissenschaft und Politik (SWP) is a foundation established in 1962 for the purpose of furthering analytic research into problems of international politics and security. Publicly funded, but politically independent, the SWP today maintains the largest research institute of its kind in the Federal Republic of Germany. The SWP receives almost all of the operating funds for the institute through annual non-project appropriations from the Federal budget. These are supplemented by grants for specific projects, obtained from private foundations in the Federal Republic and abroad. The SWP's professional staff, some 45 out of a total permanent staff of 120, is drawn from a variety of disciplines and professional backgrounds.
The research activities of the SWP seek to combine the requirements of general research in international affairs with the specific needs of policymakers. To that end, the institute develops its own research agenda, giving due regard to specific questions raised by *Bundestag* members or governments departments.
Results are usually disseminated in the form of non-classified studies and position papers. Many of these are intended primarily for the attention and specific needs of policymakers. Chief recipients are the *Bundestag* and its committees, the Chancellery, and various Federal Ministries.

Aktuelle Materialien
zur Internationalen Politik

herausgegeben von der
Stiftung Wissenschaft und Politik, Ebenhausen
Redaktion: Dr. Albrecht Zunker

Band 40/1

Klaus Segbers/Stephan De Spiegeleire (Eds.)

# Post-Soviet Puzzles

## Mapping the Political Economy of the Former Soviet Union

Volume I
Against the Background of the Former Soviet Union

Nomos Verlagsgesellschaft
Baden-Baden

Die Deutsche Bibliothek – CIP-Einheitsaufnahme

**Post-Soviet Puzzles** : Mapping the Political Economy of the Former Soviet Union / Klaus Segbers/Stephan De Spiegeleire (eds.). – Baden-Baden : Nomos Verl.-Ges.
(Aktuelle Materialien zur Internationalen Politik ; Bd. 40)
NE: Segbers, Klaus [Hrsg.]; GT
Volume 1. Against the Background of the Former Soviet Union. – 1. Aufl. – 1995
ISBN 3-7890-4042-8

1. Auflage 1995

# Table of Contents

# Preface

Klaus Segbers and Stephan De Spiegeleire

These volumes present some of the results of a large-scale project that was a rather unlikely event. During the past 18 months, more than 60 people contributed to this project – ideas, texts, data, money, nerves... Quite frequently, the whole endeavour seemed simply beyond feasibility. Nevertheless, the results are finally on the table.

This research undertaking would never have taken place without the assistance of the *Körber-Stiftung* in Hamburg, who had the courage to finance such a large, novel and unconventional project. We are especially indebted to Ulrich Voswinkel, and to Horst Roedinger, executive chairman of the *Körber-Stiftung*, for their generous support, both material and intellectual. Another tribute has to go to the *Stiftung Wissenschaft und Politik* (SWP) in Ebenhausen, where the project team was headquartered. We are extremely grateful that the SWP was willing to host our research even though the direct link with the main areas of its activities (foreign and security related issues) was not it was not always clear to everyone.

Finally, special recognition has to go to Rainer Lindner, who took care of the Ukrainian and Belarussian dimensions of the project; Nataliya Nosova, Elena Scheidt and Aleksandr Gadzhiev, who restlessly kept in contact with our project partners in the FSU; to Nick Allen, our English-language editor; to Mark Hatlie, Sharon Werning and Jane Prokop, who proof-read parts of the books; to Christine Kirschstein, who made it possible to combine the project with the day-to-day management of the East-European research unit of the SWP; to Christian Forstner, Christoph Baron and Gwendolyn Bellmann, who helped with the index, printout and formatting; and to Albrecht Zunker, the editor of this SWP Nomos-series, who never lost faith in the final product of the project. We are also indebted to the thoughts, suggestions, enthusiasm and other personal contributions of many other people involved in this project in many ways.

Even 'normal' edited volumes typically present formidable organisational challenges. Given the scope of this project, in terms of substance, volume, and the number and geographical dispersion of participants involved, we were extremely fortunate to be able to make use of the possibilities for international scientific co-operation and communication presented by the Internet. The pages of the books you have in front of you whizzed back and forth from Ebenhausen to many parts of the world a number of time, and without this new medium, this project clearly would have never been realised.

After some hesitation, we decided to translate all the Russian originals into English, in order to make them available to as large a group of people as possible. We worked with a couple of translator teams in Kiev and Minsk, whose translations were then proof-read and checked for consistency by Mr. Nick Allen from London, who invested much more time and energy than requested by the call of duty, and by the editors themselves, with whom the final responsibility for remaining inaccuracies or inconsistencies lie. Given the fact that neither of the editors are native speakers of that language, some of the final texts may appear somewhat sub-Shakespearean. However, we still thought it more important to make the works of these authors (many of which appear for the first time in English) accessible to a broad audience, and with that aim in mind, our main criterion was intelligibility rather than aesthetics. Wherever it was possible, we tried to simplify some quite complex Russian sentences into shorter and more digestible ones.

Finally, there are some purely editorial matters to which we would like to draw our readers' attention. We opted for British spelling, both for the English texts and for the transliteration of Russian words. We have tried to adhere to it consistently, with a few exceptions: Mr. *El'tsin* remains Mr. *Yeltsin* – as known from the papers and probably more comprehensible for most of the readers. For the same reason, the Russian capital *Moskva* appears as Moscow, *Rossiya* as Russia, and many other regions on *–iya* were also transliterated with the more common *–ia*. For the reader's convenience, we have included a small *glossary* in the 4th volume with explanations of some important recurring concepts or terms that may not be common knowledge to everybody. At the end of each volume, you will also find an *index* for that particular volume. All geographical maps in these volumes were prepared with the help of the *Geograph* program created by the *Merkator*-group of the Russian Academy of Sciences' Institute for Geography.

The *elite surveys* which are evaluated in chapters 3.9-3.11 were organised around a questionnaire which contained a list of interest groups which finally was agreed upon during a meeting with specialists from Russia, Ukraine und Belarus in Dagomys' in July, 1994. This meeting also played an important role in the overall conceptualisation of the project. The questions we asked about those interest groups were drafted by the project team and then slightly amended after Dagomys'. 40 experts (20 in Russia – mostly from Moscow, and 10 respectively in Kiev and Minsk) then filled out the questionnaire on diskette (basically in October and November 1994). The first results were presented at the project evaluation conference which took place in the SWP,

Ebenhausen, at the end of November in 1994. Although these elite opinion surveys were intended mainly for heuristic purposes, we did decide they may be of interest to enough people to include brief evaluations of them (in all methodological modesty). The editors intend to discuss the methodology in light of the first results, of critical comments and of the ongoing changes in the countries involved and plan to organise a second tour of this poll in 1996.

These books were conceived by us as an attempt to present the findings of our activities over the past two years to the international community of scholars, policy makers, policy analysts, but also the public at large. We hope and are confident that this systematic attempt at redefining politics in the post-Soviet space will provoke the interest of a broad audience, thus justifying the many efforts made by many people in realising these volumes.

# 1

# Systemic Transformation in Russia: A Critical Revision of Methods and a New Agenda

Klaus Segbers

The 'Great Transformation' in the former Soviet Union (FSU) impacts on Western societies and politics in multiple ways. That makes it necessary to understand its roots, forms, its direction and perspectives. Most analysts of this topic focus on the 'high politics' that seem to be visible and accessible – on presidents and their declarations of intent or their health, on parties, parliaments and administrations, on elections and constitutions. But it seems more than questionable whether this traditional approach is really a useful, enlightening and sensible one under the current highly unstable conditions. When states are not functioning properly, when politics are hard to organise, when statistics are questionable, when identities are unclear – in short, when the whole picture seems disturbed and when many accustomed approaches are falling visibly short, then it is not really advisable to stick to old-fashioned concepts of interpreting reality. So we thought about a different approach.

Something new had to be imagined: the historical processes in the FSU are too important for the OECD-states and beyond to be just ignored. Before we can even start to deliberate whether and how theses processes might be influenced with limited resources, it seems to be a good idea to return to some basic questions: if the state is not the only relevant actor and category of analysis, what territories, actors, groups and behaviours *do* really matter? It seems like a matter of great urgency to identify the basic levels and units of analysis, relevant structures, interests and agents involved in the transformations which started more than ten years ago, in March 1985 with the election of Mikhail Gorbachev as leader of the CPSU. The historic changes since then have had a major impact on the world – and vice versa. Only on the basis of a realistic view of developments up to and since then is it conceivable to reach sober interpretations, to develop reasonable expectations and to work out adequate policy options.

## 1 What Would It Be Interesting to Know?

What is of interest to whom in the post-Soviet expanse depends upon the context. A foreign correspondent in Kiev or Moscow, a bank employee in Düsseldorf or Detroit, a staff worker or planner in Brussels or Almaty, a social scientist in Ebenhausen, Novosibirsk or Santa Monica, a parliamentarian in Bonn, London or Simferopol' – they will all find different things of interest in various situations and contexts, or indeed not, as the case may be.

If we pragmatically hone this circle of potentially interested parties down to those who are affected by the developments at a professional or functional level, approximately the following central questions may arise:

- What connection exists between internal developments and internationally significant behaviour in the former Soviet areas of transformation? What are the determinants of visible foreign policy moves and behaviour?
- Which territories and actors (people, institutions, sectors, interest groups) in the areas of transformation[1] can or must be regarded as partners?
- Are our conceptual, methodological and theoretical instruments sufficient to properly evaluate fundamental developments in the areas of transformation?
- Are the societies of Western Europe trying to isolate themselves from the destabilising or hazardous consequences of transformations in Eastern Europe? If so – is that a realistic undertaking?
- If this is not the case, then what sensible and effective means of influence are available in the political, material, cultural, military and social spheres?

In addition to everything analysts know (or could know) about these systemic transformations, their origins, the forms and movements in which they manifest themselves, and their prospects, it may also be prudent to endeavour to make an inventory of the unknown. What, of the things we would want to know, are we as yet unaware of?

This interest in our own field of knowledge will undoubtedly continue to exist for a long time. If one agrees that for the majority of the constituent areas of the FSU the transformation will be a long-term process which cannot be artificially shortened, then it may be sensible to establish short and medium time horizons for which

---

**1** Since the category *state* is itself highly problematic (not only) in the FSU, within the framework of these considerations I will rather use this and similar neutral terms. For the general problem see Stephan *De Spiegeleire* in this volume; and Buzan, Barry. „The Level of Analysis Problem in International Relations Reconsidered," in Ken Booth and Steve Smith. *International Relations Theory Today*. Cambridge, 1995: 198-216.

prognoses and scenarios should be developed. At the same time, it is important to put current events and processes into perspective. Many developments appear quite different when they are set in a continuum of systemic changes rather than in the limited context of the moment.

Whereas this suggestion refers to the need for a methodical self-reassessment on the part of scientific observers, a further qualification is called for. Even if analysts were better and more advanced than is indeed the case today, their work could only be regarded as politically relevant if the dividing lines between science and policy advise, mass media, administrative departments and processes for policy formulation were flexible and organised in a co-operative manner. It is unclear whether it is at all possible under the present circumstances to set up effective and timely consultation procedures, or whether the mechanisms for formulating the day-to-day political agenda as well as the political structures and processes in the respective capitals function in such a way as to essentially preclude any effective interaction. This would indeed be the case if timely (re)action was unintentionally yet effectively obstructed and/or when internal political factors in western decision-making processes would conspire to block out truly reasonable insights and measures because of bureaucratic or other impediments.[2]

There also arise further questions on another level (which is not to be discussed at this stage), namely in connection with the rationality of particular decision-making processes and with the side effects of intervention (which are indeed hard to calculate). Policy decisions and their implementation often have other motives than to solve the problem which they are supposedly designed to address. Domestic, bureaucratic, personal and other motives play a significant role – also in Western chancelleries. Inputs and interactions in international relations are, it seems, more and more disconnected from the domestic political mechanisms, from the endemic rules of behaviour for the reproduction of political elites. And the other way around: domestic decisionmaking is more and more divorced from realities and necessities in international relations. So we should not nurture illusions with respect to the rationality of political processes in the West.

All of these problems clearly does not absolve policy analysts from trying to offer reasonable approaches to understanding change in Eastern Europe. The aforementioned issues are then a limitation of as well as a prerequisite to scientific

---

**2** A subject of separate examination would be the extent to which this applies to the question of opening Western markets to the competitive goods from Eastern Europe, and migration policy towards these countries.

progress as well as to the construction of a competent and pertinent educational and advisory capacity which could be incorporated into a responsive, realistic (analytically and politically) political strategy. Whether such a strategy is something to be realistically be expected in the foreseeable future is a question I would like to leave for our readers.

What we wanted to do with this project was to downplay 'high politics' and to stimulate thinking and research fuelled by simple questions such as: Who acts? What are the basic interests? What is the motor of change/development? What are the relevant spaces of action? What are the important social processes and dimensions? While this project is nothing more but a start and is limited in scope and reach, we hope it will nevertheless offer some new approaches and views, and will show and explore some directions of future analytical work.

## 2 Problems of Perception and Methodology

We should now address a more immediate problem which falls directly into the analyst's sphere of competence, namely the lack of analytical certainty, fluctuation of judgement and difficulty of perception.

The current weakness of categories and methods is evident. The historic changes in the world order after 1989 have in many ways not been understood. There is a great hunger for simple explanations and world views, none of which is remotely sufficient to explain anything more than its own inadequateness. This applies to a large proportion of the social sciences, and even more to transformation and international relations theories. John Lewis Gaddis's examination of the minimal prognostic capabilities of various formulated theories before the momentous events of 1989 was indeed impressive[3]. The happy-go-lucky principle of 'anything goes' in the post-1989 years, which produced a wealth of reciprocal, mainly exclusive attempts to embrace issues, reveals the extreme crisis of interpretation in the present day. From *The End of History* (Fukuyama[4]) to *The Clash of Civilizations* (Huntington[5]), from all relevant attempts to establish a new understanding to

3 Gaddis, John Lewis. „International Relations Theory and the End of the Cold War," *International Security* 17, no. 3 (Winter 1992/93): 5-58.

4 Fukuyama, Francis. *The End of History and the Last Man*. New York: Free Press, 1992.

5 Huntington, Samuel P. *The Clash of Civilization? The Debate*. New York, NY: Foreign Affairs, 1993.

*Aussichten auf den Bürgerkrieg* (Enzensberger[6]) – a veritable saturation with hypotheses of interpretation has occurred, which, taken as a whole, has produced little more than a new, yet equally confused overview of matters. It looks as though all macro-theories of the state of the world and its organising principles seem to have reached a dead end, at least temporarily.

Theories of international relations make, on the whole, little progress, although some efforts in certain segments are noteworthy.[7] At the same time, an easily accessible solution lies in a disorderly retreat to the tried and tested, to common sense, a solution which in some ways is attractive – and hazardous. The majority of the certainties that emerge out of this type of (mis)understanding crumble when confronted with empirical reality, which has been the case for a long time, and not just in the areas under transformation. Therefore, daring and highly imaginative thinking and experimentation appear to be a comparatively prudent investment in the future. This investment must be made – and much more actively than in the past.

New approaches are necessary more than ever. The traditional *Ostwissenschaft* has little alternative but to look for refreshment in real and partly more rigorous disciplines. Contributions from international relations theories like institutionalism and functionalism, critical theories and the world systems approach, and especially the discussion on adequate units of analysis can – and do – contribute a lot to understand East European transformations (cf. text 1.3).

Nontraditional economic models like political and new institutional economy and public choice approaches can – and do – contribute very much by focusing on the interplay between economics and politics, on institutional settings and frameworks rather than on organisations and norms; on bargaining mechanisms, on the rules of the game, on regulation modes (Aglietta) rather than on allegedly predetermined ideological systems. Such a reasoning corresponds neatly to the dynamic nature of the ongoing transformations. Theses models make it possible to apply concepts like that of the administrative market (Naishul', Kordonskii) or that of the economics of shortage and soft budget constraints (Kornai) to Soviet and post-Soviet conditions.

Another source of inspiration are multi-level and network theories. These can partly be found in the political science repertoire, but a better orientation can be

6 Enzensberger, Hans Magnus. *Aussichten auf den Bürgerkrieg*. Frankfurt am Main: Suhrkamp, 1993.

7 Hollis, Martin and Steve Smith. *Explaining and Understanding International Relations*. Oxford 1990; and Booth, Ken and Steve Smith (eds.). *International Relations Theory Today*. Cambridge 1995.

found in the historical *Annales*-school[8]. These models, which were developed by French historians, describe developments as taking place simultaneously on various levels, whereby the interconnections between levels and their mutual relationship are to be determined specifically. The concept of different time perspectives is here a basic one. Instead of looking exclusively on one set of data, events or processes, one can integrate developments which occur on various levels with different paces.

Also, chaos theories must be welcomed to better understand processes which are difficult to grasp with pure linear rationality. In a similar way, deconstructionist approaches can play an important role – not to get away from rational reasoning, from looking for appropriate terms for real events, but to effectively challenge conventional and overly limited, if not plainly wrong ways of reasoning and of labelling. To get rid of stereotypes often requires a visible decomposition of the old (see text 1.4).

Very important, of course, is finally the incorporation of quantitative social science methods into the field of East European area studies. The collection, storage, and interpretation of data do matter. Quantitative and qualitative methods can be matched in a fruitful way. Data bases, data processing, researches, polling, mapping and the like can enhance our understanding dramatically if these techniques are accompanied by state-of-the-art interpretations.

So, a combination of these enlisted approaches and analytical tools is required; not the construction of a new macro-theory, which, if tried, would be little more than an imitation. Interdisciplinary projects – like our Körber-undertaking – and the bringing together of Eastern and Western experiences and backgrounds (again as we did it) seems to be a promising way of studying the big changes underway in the FSU (but not only there). The focus then will be more on regulation, structures and institutions than on static or even value-determined systems; more on multilevel research operations than on ontological suggestions; more on deconstruction than on formal and hollow terminological conveniences; more on experiments than on the repetition of the extant approaches. Some of these orienting principles are, consciously or not, present in the work of the Russian, Ukrainian and Belorussian researchers presented in this book. Again, this is meant as a start, as an agenda rather than a final report on the state of transformation.

---

**8** See Bloch, Marc, F. Braudel, L. Febvre et al. *Schrift und Materie der Geschichte. Vorschläge zur systematischen Aneignung historischer Prozesse*. Frankfurt am Main: Suhrkampf, 1977; Burke, Peter. *The French Historical Revolution. The Annales School, 1929-1989*. Stanford, Calif.: Stanford University Press, 1990.

All what has been said above – the necessity to open up to various disciplines and to co-operative and multilevel work – concerns above all those researchers and scientists who, regardless of the discipline they may originally have stemmed from, have opted to focus their regional interests on Eastern Europe. In this context it must be emphasised more than ever before that Eastern European studies do not exist as such and certainly do not have not any special entitlement to empathy instead of methodical precision. It is far more appropriate to talk of special disciplines structured around particular regions and the current areas of transformation, which through their interdisciplinary nature may gain far more if they pursue a comparativist orientation.

Taken its specific – often very specific – stand, it is small wonder that the discipline *Ostwissenschaft* has been struck by a lively and emotional family conflict: a new *Methodenstreit* (conflict about methods). Traditionalists and revisionists, totalitarians and modernisers, empathic and social science approaches are talking to – or beyond – each other in strong language.[9] Of course, social scientists with their ability to work on highly mobile tendencies and agents and their principal ability to combine quantitative and qualitative techniques look better when addressing Soviet and post-Soviet tendencies than traditionalists subscribing to the notion that one cannot understand Russia with brains.

If one wants to search for examples for fresh and, at the given time, unconventional and highly fruitful schools and views on 'communism in operation', one must mention the Weimar national economists (like Friedrich Pollock), the British economists (E.H. Carr, R.W. Davies, Alec Nove), the Harvard Project after World War II (Bauer, Berliner, Inkeles), the Soviet Interview Project in the 70s and 80s (James Millar et al.), and to some extent also the green volumes of the U.S. Congress. These works and some other similar attempts at least tried to throw some comparatively unbiased light on the Soviet realities.

Yet we still conduct a considerable, overwhelming proportion of our debates in the terminology of an expired age. We talk of states, governments and their interests, of borders, democratisation and economic reforms, of the 'special path' of Russia and others, and so on. These are partly traditional terms, partly everyday expressions which, when utilised in a scientific context, must inevitably succumb to the weight of evaluation. The author's position is that most of these ciphers are not entirely

**9** For some impression see the contributions in Fleron, Frederic J. Jr. and Erik P. Hoffmann. *Post-Communist Studies and Political Science*. Boulder, Colo.: Westview Press, 1993. See also footnote 4 in Stephan De Spiegeleire's contribution to this volume.

wrong, yet they are no longer adequate and fall short of their intended effect. Essentially they are constructions which can be resorted to in the absence of better and more precise categories, which at the moment are only partially available or which have yet to be worked out.

In times of analytical uncertainty (deficiency of paradigms) and a high density of change on the plane of events, all global pronouncements about the intentions, interests and conduct/actions of states, governments and various societal groups (including self-appointed interest groups such as parties, associations etc.), have to be subjected to an even more sceptical appraisal than is the case for areas that are not under transformation. Such pronouncements must be especially verified in order to retain their validity.

That can be demonstrated with the so-called *problem of policy consistency.* The main point of reference for post-Soviet realities should be not 'internal stability' which might or might not be affected by developments in other spheres and which may or may not be a good phenomenon (depending on where and when it occurs), but the transformation process itself. The central topic, then, is the question of control and organisation of economic, social and political processes in general.

Today, there is no institution in Russia which is able to define, formulate and implement national interests in a similar way as, for example, in OECD-states. The relevant political and social interests are

a) much too fragmented,
b) basically driven by domestic concerns,
c) in a permanent flux.

This phenomenon as such is not new. The textbook-understanding of the traditional Soviet policy being conducted in a very homogeneous and highly effective manner is erroneous. The real history of Soviet decision-making from war-communism to the Five Year Plans, from the great construction projects to *uskorenie* [acceleration], from Brest-Litovsk to Afghanistan betrays a rather high degree of conflict and debates on many topics. Nevertheless, the competing interests did not block real decisions – in the 20s and 30s, and up to the 80s. This was one of the basic preconditions for stability in the Cold War and Détente-era, where a certain degree of internal integration and the observation of common rules of the game were working.

From 1987 onwards, with the transformation of all economic, social and political forms of regulation of the Soviet system under way, active and effective policies (domestic and external) of the successor states and other administrative spaces were basically paralysed. There were no agreed national interests in any meaningful sense, no operative mechanisms for decision-making on and implementing of policy strategies, little domestic use for most of the international and trendy topics and little international use for the permanent domestic uncertainties in the changing USSR.

The basically domestic character of the political agenda and the extreme difficulty for post-Soviet actors to come to terms with international topics and, consequently, the startling neglect of the world at large has been caused by the following changes in the configuration of traditional Soviet policy-determining factors:

- The fact that parts of the FSU turned from domestic regions into the (near) abroad. Accordingly, much confusion arose around non-fixed borders, visa regimes, banknotes, human and family relations across new borders, and the like.
- The multiplication and institutionalisation of spaces/territorial units, of interests and of actors. After the break-up o the USSR in 1991, a multitude of former administrative-territorial units declared themselves states, republics and the like.
- The clear and overriding priority of domestic and even idiosyncratic issues on the political agenda of basically all social and political actors, the reality of which is obviously hard to swallow for many Western observers who are permanently on the lookout for rational behaviour as they expect it, and for new grand designs and master plans, allegedly assertive or not.

The main operational modes for almost all FSU-actors are *vyzhivaniye* and *adaptatsiya* (surviving and adaptation), not design and influence. Beyond these immediate *concerns*, there is also a widespread lack of *intention* to organise politics as such, and to do something constructive at the nation-state level. So most post-Soviet elites act in a given context according to certain (but shifting) rules with the aim to position themselves in a fluid situation; they have no primary interest to build or shape a new world order or to resolve Balkan or demographic or ecological crises.

Indeed, of primary importance for Russian, Ukrainian and other actors are the access to and distribution of resources of all sorts, the proximity to centres of allocation of resources including the president of the RF (or other countries), and the rules according to which the power centre/s are established and reproduced are of basic interest.

Most of the views and interests connected with these central issues do not really matter for international affairs. As long as the domestic actors – including branches of the armed forces and *voennye okrugi* (military districts) – are preoccupied with domestic quarrels and rather disinterested in foreign topics as such, they do not find it worthwhile (i.e. it does not improve their relative domestic position) to get significantly involved in the Balkans, in NATO-affairs, not to talk about even less obvious topics. At the same time, however, just talking about these things may enhance the relative political weight of actors.

The interface between exclusively Russian spheres of activity (to accumulate capital and resources) and the rest of the world is only activated when really tangible interests are at stake: Will foreign banks be allowed to operate in Russia? Will foreign insurance companies be registered for post-Soviet spaces? What are the regulations for the export and import of commodities? How to get licences for the export of strategic raw materials? How can the vagueness of ill-fixed borders be converted into an asset? These are the kind of 'foreign policy' questions which *are* of real interest to the key actors, and where they try to exert real influence.

The consequence of this structure of interests is, of course, that it is not possible to define national interests in any meaningful and operative way. It seems that there is no chance to organise a coherent national consensus on national interests, be it by negotiation, ideology or by forced hegemony.

Accordingly, those interests which have an impact on foreign policy and which can be discerned have the peculiar character of vested and special interests – Russian banks, producers of aviation technology, oil and gas, etc. In other words, they are interests of the representatives of sectors, regions, and to some extent of the central bureaucracy. All of these follow their own interests which sometimes happen to be connected to the outside world – as is the case in Western systems. But contrary to OECD-countries, in the FSU there are no functioning mechanisms and agencies able to harmonise various and competing interests and to enforce viable compromises on the domestic pressure groups. The Russian (Ukrainian, etc.) state is not – yet? – in a position to play this role.

Instead of advocating and representing the interests of the nation-state, the Russian state only simulates (pretends to act in) this function. And Western politicians and the public accept this simulation with gratitude. Most of the actual Western political debates, like on regime-building, enlargement of the EU and NATO, seem to indicate an almost desperate Western search for partners in the East European countries who are able to act and who can be integrated into something. If one would accept here that the political actors there basically have other concerns (like accumulation, changes of the rules of the domestic games), and that most of the enlargement and anti-enlargement debates in the West are the latest and highest form of self-therapy of Western foreign policy elites, we could finally discuss the substance of politics instead of symbols and mantras.

Of course, the simulation in question is fuelled by the observation that foreign policy topics are being mentioned in the domestic quarrels in the RF: the official rhetoric (i.e. the declarations of the presidential apparatus, the MID, the Security Council on the Balkan crisis, NATO-enlargement, ratification of START, NPT etc.) is published in the Russian mass media and attacked by forces in the State Duma, the media and others. But more often than not, the (mostly) polemical debates are not about the core of the question, not on substance. In fact, they are frequently driven by the exchange value of the given question. Which leads us to our next point – the instrumentalisation of foreign policy topics for domestic purposes.

As objects for the inner-Russian debates, international political issues have a different value. The most trendy topics in this context are:

- The question of national strength and pride, which becomes more important as a symbol as the countries' actual strength is declining.
- The question of *westernisation* in the sense of rules of the game shaped by market regulations and pluralism of interests. While *westernisation* is becoming an ugly word, the basic orientation is hardly contested even by many communo-patriots, even when the pre-election campaign and the topic of national strength increasingly require a definition of Russian interests opposed to those of the West.
- The question of *Eurasianism*, which, as a school of thought, has its merits and traditions. But this idea has been misused and is now devalued as an instrument to bridge the economic capabilities and interests of liberal and patriotic fundamentalism in order to stress the specific nature of Russia which nobody really is able to define.

But all of these motives serve rather as referents for domestic battles and as reactive-defensive ideologems than as policy-regulating principles.

A last aspect I want to stress here is the obviously non-systematic character of many policy moves. An example for this is all the rhetoric aimed primarily at domestic counterparts. A striking example is, of course, the military intervention in Chechnya. In this case, certain civilian political figures in the entourage of Yeltsin talked the president and the military into this adventure for reasons which had little to do with either Chechnya, or oil, or security purposes, but far more with the president's weak showing in public opinion polls, with the coming elections and with the very personal worries of Yeltsin's closest collaborators.

This all said, it hardly seems possible to prove in a convincing way that there is anything close to a consistent domestic and foreign policy following clearly defined national interests in or of Russia.

This is not to say, however, that the inability to execute consistent policies does not imply that Russia cannot produce effects in the international arena. Being a permanent member in the Security Council of the UN, a member in many other international organisations and regimes, and being a country of this vast size caught in a difficult transformation process, it would be a miracle if there would be no repercussions beyond the Russian borders. The point is that most, if not all of them are not strategically conceived or pursued.

So, the problem of a – wrongly – suggested consistency of Russian policy at home and abroad is a good example of futile attempts to use old-fashioned approaches for explaining new and fluid phenomena.

Thus a new formulation and greater precision of theoretical and conceptual premises is called for when dealing with the constantly changing post-Soviet space. This is a crucial condition for a more realistic and professional analysis. However, as indicated above, there is still much to be done, particularly with regard to those who would turn to scientific work for enlightenment (be they politicians or journalists).

In connection with that, it is important to emphasise that analysts should be relieved of the burden of constant expectation so often placed upon them by outside parties with regard to their prognoses. In the short-term and from a superficial point of view, many aspects of events will tend to arise out of pure coincidence, will not be individually foreseeable and will, on reflection, not even be of particular significance. If and when, however, a prediction comes into fruition, the question remains open whether an appropriate reaction was forthcoming from those to whom it was originally presented.

Finally, it should be pointed out that transformation processes are only to a certain extent subject to internal and external control, possibilities for which are so frequently overestimated. Many things happen unexpectedly; the main currents which shape the surface of events, seemingly detached from any stream of logic, are only seldom directly accessible. Things happen or are developing at different levels simultaneously. For example, one could differentiate four spheres of activity: economic, social, political and international, and assuming that there are two sublevels within each of them – a factual one (events/policy moves) and a structural one (processes). So we get eight levels that often are not immediately connected with each other.

In other words, declarations of political actors on the one hand and actual political processes on the other are frequently disjointed. This also signifies that western and eastern observers must adjust and, if need be, reduce their expectations with regard to the prima facie rationality of the actions and the conduct of the post-Soviet actors.

From this it follows that the internal dynamics and inherent logic of political and social interactions in the FSU often stem from wholly different motives and calculations than those supposed by those on the outside. This observation is particularly pertinent when the remarks of individual politicians are identified with the national aspirations and interests of a (their) state, which can only happen at the cost of shutting out all other, often predominant, motives for such remarks. In even clearer terms, concrete policy in the FSU is not so much oriented towards western observers' requirements vis-à-vis understanding and categorisation but towards concrete interests. It is, or often seems to be erratic, muddled, off the point and yet at the same time relevant. But this behaviour is also mostly rational – just following different aims and concerns than suggested.

Accordingly, interests and behaviour are open to explanation once the relevant information is available, and perception stereotypes have been overcome. To apply social science methods thus does make sense.

This brings us to the problem of the desire for uniformity of judgement and evaluation; a quantity that is constantly sought but never found. Without a sufficient clarification of the underlying terms, the interests involved and the relevant actors and spaces, meaningful predictions are virtually impossible to produce. Even when these preliminary conditions are met, the result is often disappointing. As a rule there are no forthcoming 'yes' 'yes', 'no' 'no' responses but a coexistence of different conditions and, consequently, of evaluation. Findings concerning individual actors, measures, developments, etc., are only very rarely definite, unambiguous. The observer's perspective plays just as important a role as the setting of the temporal axis. Trends which have a stabilising effect at the present time can, in the long-term, give rise to unrest, and vice versa.

The more realistically and rationally these hurdles of judgement are regarded by observers, the more it is possible to avoid seasonal fluctuations of evaluation and opinion, which swing between euphoria and depression, and which often reflect the world views and convictions of the observers far more than the difficult and polymorphous reality of the post-Soviet spaces.

Actual possibilities for intervention and influencing events are, in any way, for the most part extremely limited – especially on a state-to-state level. So, one really should start with realistic interpretations.

## 3 What Are the Relevant Interests, Actors, Spaces and Modes of Their Behaviour?

One essential task to be addressed in the field of scientific political commentary is the development of methods to identify relevant spaces, objects and actors – i.e. levels and units of analysis. This task is by no means trivial in an environment which is characterised by notorious instability and such a density of surface change. The pure enumeration of traditional actors and their presumed interests and their patterns of behaviour is no longer adequate, and even leads one astray. Neither the respective governments of Gaidar or Chernomyrdin, nor the president and his entourage; neither the Russian Federal Assembly nor the State Duma and its fractions have definite, solid, consistently pursued 'interests', bearing in mind the numerous questions arising from day-to-day politics. Basic interests can be identified, but they 'drift' within a certain range of variance. Accordingly, the main players' interests have to be determined repeatedly.

Ideological orientations and declarations provide the weakest of all possible indications in the determination of real interests. Despite an initially radical monetary rhetoric, the Gaidar government was relatively moderate in terms of practical policy and did not execute a rigid 'shock therapy'. And, conversely, despite an evidently more professed belief in state interventionism, in 1994/95 Chernomyrdin's government enjoyed some success in macro-economic stabilisation, in containing inflation, reducing budget deficits and in privatising state enterprises.

Neither the Federal Assembly (the two-chambered Parliament), nor the government have developed institutional interests. It is rather the case that they are relinquishing the fields of competition for resources to other entities, the real actors and agents. As a matter of fact, these traditional state institutions are the very place where shifting coalitions between lobbies are formed which then represent state institutions for a certain period of time.

All these centres of power and influence, as well as interest groups follow specific rationalities and calculations which, however, cannot be grasped using such simplistic terminology as reform-friendly/hostile, co-operative/(neo)imperialistic and so on. There is also no specific 'Russian' policy with regard to other states..

Examples to support this are numerous: the fact that Abkhasian separatists received assistance from Russia does not mean that 'Russia' was directing 'Abkhasia' against Georgia. There is in fact a multiplicity of actors in the North Caucasus: the 'Confederation of Caucasian Mountain Peoples'; locally based Russian armed forces with their own commercial interests; various circles in Moscow which rest partly on geopolitical rhetoric, partly on corresponding geopolitical interests, and partly on the immediate intention of riding along on the surge of anticipated and incited patriotic opinions; and the mass media. Yet all of these actors fails to amount to a tailor-made and skilfully conducted 'Russian' policy. Simply by reaching outwards, Moscow's hand, which has only a very limited capability in its own realm, does not suddenly experience a miraculous increase in its power to define concise interests, to structure politics, and to calculate political strategies. The decision of the seemingly patriotic State Duma to vote against the treaty between Russia and Georgia (1994), which supposedly agreed with Russian interests, was highly instructive. Short-term animosities and manoeuvres against Presidents Yeltsin and Shevardnadze were weightier than the supposed long-term interest – if this interest is at all compatible with integration/re-integration.

The many voices from Moscow which could be heard in connection with the enlargement of NATO and the 'Partnership for Peace' programme, are also to be placed in the category of those requiring interpretation. At the beginning of April 1994, statements were forthcoming from both the president's close entourage and from the government which were unsurpassable in their colourfulness and contrast.

Many other events, decisions and behaviors likewise contributed to the broad picture of peculiarities which elude the courageous efforts of those who attempt to simplify matters. Many governmental decisions and presidential decrees are formal compromises with only temporary effect, soon ignored or altered.

The obvious cases of misappropriation of individual components required for the manufacture of nuclear weapons within the FSU and abroad are without doubt less a result of inadequate attempts at control by the Moscow centre than of the commercial interests and high-handedness of the management of the nuclear installations and of individual regions or local and military authorities. In the face of such a breakdown, how can Moscow as a Centre re-establish effective control of this and other policy fields?

Many more examples of inconsistent rhetoric and behaviour could be added. Post-Soviet policy is notoriously inconsistent, contradictory and fluid. That is because what makes political actors tick is not rationality and consistency in terms of national interests, but their relative standing in the all-encompassing race for positions, resources and the rules of the game.

In view of this confusion, one is faced with the urgent task of identifying those territories which actually do exist and function, the central interests in question, their representative structures, resources and operative capability. In identifying these elements, one should also be careful not to let oneself be deceived by formal areas of jurisdiction and of authority. The same is also true of the apparent and puzzling patterns of behaviour and opinions of societal groups, produced in reaction to the immense changes.

In attempting to define real, distinct and politically relevant territories/spaces and interests/groups, problems certainly arise. The same applies in trying to comprehend societal groups' potential to promote and obstruct the transition to self-regulation and in considering effective forms of adaptation and survival as a dormant social reserve for transformation. But there is, in my view, no alternative to start such an approach.

The main task therefore lies in identifying the real units and levels of analysis, in discovering the appropriate sources for explaining events and developments, and in examining the decision making processes and coalition building instead of accepting or assuming all of them in their traditional, common-sense and unverified state. Consequently, sound appraisals of the most important elite groups, their interests and potential will be possible. Using this background, parties, fractions and media can then also be placed in relation to the actual centres of power and pressure groups.

Likewise, the recognition of *politically relevant spaces and administrative units* is a central task. Various possible choices of the relevant units are available:

1 the *state* may be accepted as a satisfactory and individually relevant unit – if not, several variants arise;
2 *middle range administrative units* (republics, regions, districts) in the Russian Federation, the so-called subjects of the federation (89 in Russia, 26 in Ukraine);
3 the 11 *economic zones* and/or the 8 *inter-regional associations* (amalgamations of units from level 2);
4 *national units* (the former *autonomies,* now republics) versus *ethnically neutral units*, i.e., on the one hand the regions and districts named after an autochthonous ethnic group (such as Tatarstan, the Khanty-Mansiisk district; 21 units in all, now republics within the RF), on the other, regions overwhelmingly characterised by their 'Russianness';

5 *functional structures* formed by the above listed such as military districts (*voennye okrugi*) and Cossackdoms (*kazachestva)*, which have in fact already evolved into administrative entities, competing with federal and state administrations;

6 finally and from (2) through to (5) comes the *agglomeration level*, in particular four units – major cities (Moscow, St.Peterburg), capitals of the regions and republics, other towns, and the countryside which are relatively homogeneous in their existential and political consistency at each respective level;

7 further subdivisions are possible according to real economic characteristics, i.e., differentiation between donor and recipient regions; those which are self-sufficient and those which are import dependent; those which are situated in the core or at border regions.

8 Also to be mentioned are economic sectors which monopolise regions or the economic structure across neighbouring regions.

At all of these levels separate, politically meaningful and also internationally relevant interests and actors can be identified, some of which can be discounted with good reason and with regard to the context, while others cannot.

At present, the state as the formally most relevant politico-administrative unit level is acquiring an increasingly fictitious character, especially when confronted with expectations of effectiveness in most of the spheres of activity that are relevant for the transformation. This apparent extent of responsibility coupled with the erosion of organisational capabilities are to be taken into account analytically, probably best through attempts to typologically categorise regional and sectoral profiles. Russian scholars in particular have made good headway in this direction. Articles on these matters can be found in Vol. II.

In order to identify *interests*, as well as the structure and priorities of the political agenda in various politically relevant pressure groups and institutions, these groups must first be ascertained. Here the following criteria can help to narrow these down:

- *formal and functional channels* (ministries/ administrative structures/ representative committees and their corresponding jurisdiction and competence);
- *origin* of elites (former *nomenklatura*, generation groupings, chains of operation);
- *objects and commodities subject to rival claims* within and between elites, especially economic resources and rights of ownership;

- differences of *position and areas of transition between legal and illegal structures*;
- *range of interests*; ability to reach from local/regional to larger forum.

In the framework of this research project, the following means of subdivision has been developed, with which the various interest groups are to be approached[10]:

1 *Economic interest groups:* Primarily the agro-industrial complex and agricultural administrative structures (APK); the fuel and energy complex (especially oil and gas, TEK); the major groups of the military-industrial complex (VPK), namely the competitive aerospace sectors on the one hand and on the other the remaining, generally depressed, science-intensive sectors; the finance and circulation sector (banks, stock markets, trade chains, above all importers); the expanding field of private business (*novyi biznes*); the depressed, dying areas of industry; and the export-oriented sectors. Next to the principle of division into various sectors should be added the further criteria of the economic situation, survival prospects and proximity to the state (forms of property).

2 *State/ executive structures:* Above all, the presidential apparatus (administration, secretariat, Security Council); the governmental apparatus; the leading executive structures of the State Duma and the Federal Assembly.

3 *Social interests:* bodies of trade union leadership, religious hierarchies, illegal organisations, elite networks, ethnic elites, *obshchestvenniki* i.e., social activists and ideologists who do not have an organic connection to (a) or (b).

4 *Foreign interests:* the IMF, the World Bank and the IBRD as transnational actors, as well as foreign enterprises active in the FSU.

The media, parties, parliamentary fractions and similar groups are not yet independent, leading elements (units of analysis) in this model since they can to a considerable extent be classified as being derived from the listed interest groups. Their individual weight is not sufficient, their influence is largely representative or they merely serve as a vehicle for the personal ambitions of prominent individuals who are often well-known yet lack real influence, i.e., numerous party leaders.

In the case of the real interest groups as defined above, specific interest-based profiles and prospects for their realisation can be ascertained. A condition for this is the identification of the central thematic areas and tasks which really (and not merely in a declaratory manner) characterise post-Soviet politics.

---

**10** Compare the elite survey questionnaire for more details (text 3.9).

The following list identifies those activity fields which, according to our research, are truly determinant, regardless of everyday polemics:

1. *The definition and constant correction of macro-economic policy.* In this respect, successive governments can ultimately do little more than shift emphasis within the framework of an essentially fixed transformation course, both implementing market regulation by means of tightening budgetary constraints and simultaneously establishing an ever varying minimum level of state intervention. Inevitably, this results time and time again in a problematic stop-and-go effect in the transition to market regulation. The permanent state of tension which arises from this is perpetuated and is reflected not just in clashes between the presidential apparatus, the government, parliament, the various interest groups and the media, but also within the government, which itself consists of several blocks.
2. *The distribution of property rights and opportunities for the seizure of resources.* This concerns the competition between the variants of denationalisation (which could be clearly observed in 1994 during the clashes between the Committee for State Property – *Goskomimushchestvo* – and the Moscow City government), competition between political, social, regional and functional pressure groups and lobbies. Also affected is the balance of power between individual constitutional organs and numerous interest groups in the centre and the 89 subjects of the Russian Federation. The clashes over property distribution and seizure as well as its formalisation (legalisation), and ultimately the competition for the necessary key positions for this purpose, is (remains) possibly the greatest source of conflict.
3. *The relationship between political-territorial and national-territorial units of the RF and towards the centre* – whatever the centre may be at the time. During periods of transition these remain tense due to the relatively ineffectual, short-lived but probably politically unavoidable attempts at constitutional development. In view of the increasing weight of the regions or regional amalgamations, positional competition in the centre necessarily leads to the situation whereby the subjects of the Russian Federation are courted with various offers by the remaining power groupings in the centre (presidential structures, parliamentary leadership, governmental fractions) which weakens the overall cohesion of the RF. At the same time the regions themselves endeavour to influence these Moscow groupings. Treaties of the RF with certain individual component subjects, as in the case of Tatarstan (February 1994) and Bashkortostan (August

1994), are a sign that all attempts so far to create a comprehensive and lasting delimitation of competencies between various territories and the federal centre remain rather ineffectual. This did not change after the Russian military intervention in Chechnya. For these reasons, efforts to consolidate the federal budget are also open to question.

4. Effect, function and control of the *mass media.* It is above all to television that all political camps attribute considerable influence on the political attitudes and voting behaviour of the population. The days of exclusive state control are over. The printed media are predominantly dependent on sponsorship and it is primarily the economic lobbies which seek to gain increasing influence over the mass media, especially over television stations. The main two blocks of stabilisers – still around president Yeltsin – and chaots (all principal opposition groups) are the basic adversaries here.
5. *Relations between the successor states of the USSR*, which despite numerous meetings and declarations of intent remain chaotic. Of primary importance are Russia's relations with each individual state or quasi-state. The most difficult questions (partly of a practical nature, partly symbolic) arise from Russian-Ukrainian, Russian-Kazakh and Russian-Azerbaidzhan relations as well as from the task of defining 'Russia's interests' in the southern part of the CIS (border defence; presence of troops with and without peace-keeping mandates, above all in Georgia and Tadzhikistan; oil deposits and transportation routes (in and around Azerbaidzhan); and, in the Baltic states, Russian-speaking minorities.

Working from these thematic areas it is possible to ascertain the interest profiles of almost all the actors involved in the political process, primarily from a mixture of three components:

- Attitude towards possession of resources and property (regulated/deregulated);
- Stance on composition of the state (unitary/confederal);
- Position on relations to the world market (opening up/isolation)

In the framework of our research project, these values were accordingly ascertained in autumn 1994 by experts primarily from the areas in question. The results of these expert evaluations can be found in Vol. III of this compendium.

*Assertive potential* is estimated in a similar manner as interests. In this instance it is a question of the assessment of real influence, of 'political capital'. This includes such elements as mass popularity, the relative authority of elites, relations in the overall framework of elites ('contacts'), weight of particular structures (lobbies, parties, networks, media), financial capacities, social and political basis in society, proximity to economic and political decision-making centres, extent of particular dependence/independence on/from other structures.[11] Articles related to these question – interests, elites, pressure groups – are to be found in Vol. III.

At this point one must anticipate the objection that neither analytically nor politically, the West can refer to several dozen elite groups and territories at the same time. This is a pertinent observation. Nevertheless, one should not adhere by convenience or pure mental laziness to the fictitious, classical notion of single leading actors if it proves to be the case that they do not exist or if they are too heterogeneous or incapable of functioning. The development of a rational and selective FSU policy with a graded system of priorities is indeed highly conceivable. To this end, however, a realistic analytical basis is necessary.

The same also applies to the third major area, mysterious in many respects, in which a fresh assessment of our understanding is required, namely that of *social behaviour* and *societal moods*. Here, the main priority is to accumulate information about such areas as strategies of existence and survival, adaptation attempts, exploratory movements, strategies of obstruction and establishment/violation of regulations on the long and arduous road from 'society as an enterprise of the state'[12] to one based on self-regulation by social and functional strata, by individuals, and by various networks. This dimension basically remains overlooked or ignored in the transformation countries and by most Western observers.

The transition is necessarily linked to an increase in social differentiation, as groups of the poor and marginalised and the rich and privileged grow simultaneously. These processes are only scantily covered in official statistics which often contain manipulated figures, display irritating average values, undervalue the growing private sector and neglect secondary and additional incomes in rubles and western currencies.

Thus, the discrepancy between official data and general assessments of the economic situation on the one hand and people's evaluation of their own living conditions and the impression they make on visitors on the other, is astonishing. In this area a down-to-earth, balanced analysis is also necessary in order to be able to realistically assess the transformation processes. This can be achieved both through resorting to opinion polls as well as through special studies (for instance through recalculations of real income and standards of living). Materials concerning these questions are contained in Vol. IV.

**11** For criteria see *Novaya ezhednevnaya gazeta* 27 April 1994.

**12** Geyer, Dietrich. *Wirtschaft und Gesellschaft im vorrevolutionären Rußland*. Köln, 1975.

## 4 What Way Out of the Confusion? Which Information Do We Have at Our Disposal? Why the Körber-Project?

The philosophy of the Körber-project was to address these questions in an outspoken way. We do not think that our traditional analytical tools were sufficient to make sense out of the given situation in the FSU; nor do we think that we solved all problems connected with identifying new approaches. We basically tried three things:

- to apply new methods and views in order to find out how far they can take us;
- to assist researchers and observers in the FSU by working with them; and
- to propose new views to policy makers.

The conceptualisation of the project was not traditional, nor was it easy to realise. Conceptual political-scientific analyses, and differentiated, empirical preliminary work is not customary, especially in Germany. The difficulties and dangers described above which arise through the usage of standard terms and categories primarily (but by no means exclusively) in analysing the Eastern European areas of transformation, do indeed demand dramatically increased efforts. The empirical side then is not intended to be an alternative approach, but rather to foster more complete, complementary and stimulating results.

For this purpose, extensive concrete and (where possible) quantified information is essential (but, needless to say, not sufficient). Informational bases are continually improving. Apart from traditional printed sources and occasional trips to 'get a feel' for particular areas and atmospheres, many other information sources have become available. The information market is growing. Numerous centres, institutes and agencies offer analyses and interpretations. Above all, electronically transmitted, stored, processed and accessible data are increasingly available. . The main problem is no longer whether data are obtainable, but their organisation and management, ease and speed of access, data inquiry facilities as well as their safety and compatibility. In this field, the Körber project did some pioneering work, which unfortunately cannot be addressed in any more detailed way at this point.

When this informational basis is 'in tune' with a technical and organisational level, i.e., when a comprehensive and solid data bases are available , then questions concerning selection of information and interpretation of data can re-emerge more strongly in the forefront of attention and can be used for operative and concrete interests as well as for analytical purposes. To this end, conceptual efforts at the pinnacle of each particular relevant discipline are more than ever required. Here, analysts in the actual post-Soviet spaces are a first-rate resource, not only in the acquisition of raw data, but also in their evaluation and interpretation. These volumes are proof of that.

All this analytical work cannot succeed, of course, when it is imagined as clarification attempts just by some fresh-minded researchers of a new generation. Our proposed approach requires additionally something from our readers: at least some degreee of openness to alternative perspectives, a willingness to accept new views on subjects which seemed to be well-known and secure.

Furthermore, it requires a glance in the rear mirror: combined multilevel and multi-disciplinary approaches towards the starting conditions under which the changes started to occur; a reinterpretation of Soviet history; a new look at the reasons for the accumulated and multifaceted Soviet crisis; and, of course, at the *perestroika* are necessary.

A second basic aim of this research project was to assist young researchers in the three countries to communicate more effectively with Western partners and among each other – the last point being especially crucial. Common projects and activities among FSU-analysts are rare and difficult to establish, given their perception of competition and survival requirements.

Of course, we also hope that our approach and some of our findings have some impact in Bonn. Policy consultation is a very difficult business, and much depends on the political side. There are policy makers and policy planners who are ready to discuss methods and new approaches, but unfortunately this tends to be a minority.

Finally, there is the very important issue of Western expertise on the FSU-transformations. For many countries, regions and functional questions, we have a serious lack of expertise – even more so in the younger generation. While the situation may be slightly better in the US than in Western Europe, we definitely must encourage younger students of political and social sciences, of history and economics to get involved in this enterprise.

Even with this impressive range, the project and, accordingly, these volumes are not an encyclopaedia on everything in the post-Soviet space. We did not touch a couple of topics: parties, institutions and media for example, for reasons described above. But, there are also themes we would have liked to include: the life in and the behaviour of military districts as an often overlooked example of a certain functional-territorial independence from Moscow; religion and the question of values as a tool of identity and consensus-building in the society; the economic performance and macro-economic developments in the FSU – which seem such an important topic to us that we will publish five papers on this in a separate volume in the SWP working papers; non-governmental organisations (NGOs) as an example for self-regulation of certain societal groups. So, there are definitely answers to the question *What is left out?*, some of which we hope to tackle in the future in the framework of the second stage of this project.

## 5 Structural Problems in the Transition of Post-Soviet Society

In order to apply methods, to test approaches and to construct analyses in a sensible fashion, not only must one have a basic understanding of particular problems – actual or potential – but, above all, one must identify the structural problems of the transition in the post-Soviet societies.

The above-mentioned categorisation and accumulation of information must be linked with an appraisal of general and long-term framework conditions for the transformation processes in the FSU. It is possible to identify the following structural problems in the transition in most of the post-Soviet spaces as constituent components of such a framework of development conditions:

1. Having the form of both obstructions and breakthroughs, the changes are concomitants of a long transformation which is inevitably unstable and will remain so. Contrary and contradictory movements, confrontations and convulsions are not the exceptions to a generally organised transition – they are the rule. This is forever to be called to mind when the political excitements of the day suggest the presence of 'decisive battles'.
2. The transition to market regulation calls for an extremely difficult shift in the dividing line between two contrary and often mutually exclusive targets. On the one hand, there is the requirement of continued protectionism for economic objects which are (still) not competitive, of gradual shifts and political-tactical decisions regarding the sequencing and implementation of individual reform elements. On the other hand, there is a need to swiftly and drastically reduce state intervention; to relieve certain sectors of the economy, enterprises and also citizens of their dual role as both producers and consumers; and finally to resolutely harden budget constraints.
3. The old 'social contract' of the Soviet post-war period, whereby people exchanged their right to politically relevant dissent for guaranteed social protection and stability, was already eroding in the late 1970s when the traditional Soviet model of development was exhausted, with a corresponding reduction in

the resources and products which could be distributed. Since then it was not possible to devise any new social contract – there was no growth in resources, capital or trade which could be divided between republics, regions, sectors, enterprises and social groups. Instead, we are witnessing redistribution battles at the expense of those groups and regions with a lesser potential to assert themselves. Subsequently the social basis for the reform project shrinks politically, even when economic and social activities increase. This dilemma is expressed through social conflict, various forms of separatism and regionalism, as well as ethno-political conflicts and border disputes.

4. Functioning and effective infrastructure networks, i.e., transport routes and means, informational connections, health and education systems etc., are prerequisites for an effective transformation, for the integration into international co-operation patterns, as well as for mutual exchange relations in the post-Soviet spaces. In most parts of the FSU, however, these institutions are in a lamentable condition. Transport systems, railway lines, telephone networks, hospitals and schools are antiquated, overburdened and underfunded. In the foreseeable future, none of the successor states is in a position to produce the necessary means for the modernisation or replacement of the old and often hazard-ridden or non-effective facilities.
5. The forced modernisation in the FSU which is taking place under unfavourable internal and even, to some extent, external conditions, inevitably gives rise to forms of nationalism: new political-territorial units are established; spaces become economically and culturally homogeneous; cultural standards and languages are stipulated and asserted – often against the interests and regardless of the competencies of minorities in their own region and contrary to parallel processes and events in neighbouring regions. Nationalism is a phenomenon which is revealed as an inevitable aspect accompanying modernisation and yet which is simultaneously precipitated and organised from above. The product is a multitude of imagined ethno-communities simulating state functions and making disintegration an option on the political agenda.
6. The multiplication of the political-territorial units, interests and elites, which all have to act in response to intense internal pressure, makes it difficult and often impossible to organise, maintain or reconstruct what are in principle sensible forms of horizontal co-operation in the FSU. Many of the well-known political, economic, ecological and military conflicts are the result of the quasi-autistic behaviour of regional, sectoral or other elites.

It is virtually if not wholly impossible to influence all or even most of these fundamental conflicts from outside, let alone resolve them entirely. Nevertheless, a proper and realistic understanding of the mechanics of the specific transformations underway in the FSU is required to develop more adequate and sensitive political strategies for interacting with whatever units and actors are ready to do so.

## 6 The Structure of the Book

This book is organised in four volumes corresponding to four topical clusters: explaining basic approaches and methods as background of the project (Vol. I); the regional dimension with emerging geopolitical units (Vol. II); emerging economic, social and political interests, actors and elites (Vol. III); and the social dimension, i.e. the increasing distance between society and the state and, consequently, the development of various forms of survival and adaptation as phenomena of self-regulation (Vol. IV).

In the first volume we placed methodological articles which we hope will contribute to a more realistic understanding of Soviet and post-Soviet reality. *Stephan De Spiegeleire* puts the project's approach into a comparative perspective by relating our basic heuristic device, the rethinking of relevant units and levels of analysis, to the ongoing debate on this issue in the international relations literature (1.3). Without rethinking the Soviet past, it will be very difficult to develop an adequate understanding of the current transformations. *Sergei Medvedev*, a young researcher from the Russian Academy of Sciences‘ (RAS) Institute of Europe, attempts to reinterpret the Soviet Union and, consequently, Russia as a text, as a structure of signs. This leads not only to a possible reinterpretation of the USSR but to a change of perspective on other events (1.4). *Petr Shchedrovickii* is the director of the Moscow-based School of Cultural Politics. He describes dominant features of the development of the international system as the background for the historic changes in the FSU. *Raspad*, the collapse of the old imperial system, and transformation of the traditional features into something new are two sides of the same coin. He sees the administrative command system as the basic structure of the old regime, which finally collapsed under domestic and international (transnational) pressure to modernise the system (1.5).

*Simon Kordonskii,* political analyst and consultant in Moscow, presents the concept of the administrative market as a valuable tool to make sense of the old regulation mode as well as of the new proto-system. In this ‘market’ of acting and bargaining, sectoral and territorial principals are at work; administrative valuta (not yet money) is the currency; and the defence and enhancement of administrative weight is the basic aim of most operations (1.6). In another paper, Kordonskii applies this approach to the actual situation in the centre of power (3.7). *Vladimir Chervyakov* from the Centre for Political Conjuncture makes an impressive attempt to portray Soviet and post-Soviet history as a history of various forms of collecting and distributing resources by the state (1.7). This is the basis for an analysis and description of the interests and forms of the Russian national economic elite (3.13).

The regional dimension is one of the two main focal points of these books. Without a proper understanding of the territorial and territorial-political dimension, it is impossible to understand the post-Soviet spaces. *Sergei Medvedev* (2.1) explains the particularities of the Soviet regional structure, thus making it easier to understand basic components and mechanisms of the regional patchwork of Russia. Likewise, the independent analyst *Vladimir Kaganskii* (2.2) demonstrates the Soviet stamp on many regional-territorial developments today and focuses on the typical spatial organisation of the USSR. Some specific features of this organisation are explained in the articles of the head of the Working Centre for Economic Reform of the Russian government, *Sergei Pavlenko* (2.3). He describes the territorial structure, the stages of regionalisation in Russia, the interests of the elite groups involved in it, and the forms of legitimisation they use.

The Expert Institute of the Russian Union of Industrialists and Entrepreneurs (*Andrei Neshchadin* et al.) attempts to develop a typology of regional characteristics and patterns – economically as well as politically (2.4). The research team also presents and interprets voters' behaviour in elections and referenda at the regional level. *Il'ya Shkabara* from the RAS Institute of Geography's *Mercator* group (2.5) contributes a complementary survey of regional economies. He develops a typology that differentiates between depressed, stagnating, sluggish and stable regions. These approaches help to understand why certain regions, even in different geographical locations, have converging interests when they share certain social and economic characteristics. The same goes for *Aleksandr Kovalevskii's* paper on regional patterns and disparities of the privatisation process (2.8).

A very interesting attempt to assess the perspectives of regional disintegration in Russia has been worked out by *Andrei Treivish* and his colleague *Nikolai Petrov*, again from the *Mercator* group (2.6). They start with a determination of primary risks to the region seeking independence; go on to assess the secondary risks from the perspective of the Russian Federation; and finally establish the secondary risk for the region seeking independence. The intensity and distribution of risks is graphically represented on maps, which gives a very interesting impression of who might lose most when certain regions would try to opt out of the federation.

A special class of risk is addressed in *Emil' Pain*'s (who is member of the Presidential Council) and *Arkadii Popov's* piece on ethnic and regional conflicts in the post-Soviet spaces. They describe various types of ethnic conflicts in the RF and, subsequently, Russia's policy in and towards these conflict zones (2.7). *Sergei Tarkhov's* focuses on the factor space, more precisely what that requires in terms of transportation and infrastructure (2.9). This dimension always was of a dominant concern for all Russian and Soviet regimes, given the vast land mass, climate differences and differences in resources. *Mariya Lyashevskaya* (2.10) contributes an overview of the regional associations, unions of regions often suspiciously seen as cores of new independent entities.

After these papers that offer general interpretations of regionalisation in Russia, four case studies are presented: by *Vladimir Gel'man* and *Ol'ga Senatova* on the Vol'ga region (*Povolzh'e*, 2.11); by *Peter Kirkow* from Birmingham University on the Russian Far East (2.12); by *Mikhail Rozhanskii* from Irkutsk on Siberia in its historical and cultural as well as economic dimension (2.13); by *Ol'ga Vasil'eva* from Cheboksary/Moscow on the North Caucasus (2.14); and by *Grigorii Nemirya* from Donetsk on Donbass in Ukraine (2.15).

The last two pieces in the second volume on regions are from *Anatol Shvyatsov* on geography and ecology in Belarus, and *Nikolai Shulga* on federalisation and regionalisation in Ukraine. Both articles stress the importance of the regional factor for the two countries at the Western periphery of the FSU.

The third volume is on interests and interest groups. We definitely do not assume that groups carrying similar labels to their equivalents in the West work under similar conditions and have similar functions. The basic question we start with is what interests in those transitional conditions are relevant – relevant in the sense that they find organisational forms instead of being just declared, that they are powerful enough to be recognised – at least partly –, and that they can shape the rules of the game in terms of bargaining conditions, privatisation strategies, electoral procedures etc.

The first task in this volume is to identify those groups which qualify, under these criteria, as elite groups. Four papers (3.1-3.4) address this question: *Oleg Vite* and

*Vladimir Gel'man* (both from St.Petersburg and now working mostly in Moscow) try to identify criteria for distinguishing relevant interest groups (elites). *Sergei Pavlenko*, director of the government's Working centre for Economic Reforms, presents some theses on the new ruling class in Russia. And *Yakov Pappe*, a political consultant, enumerates those (economic) interest groups which are most effective in shaping economic and other policies.

After having defined, to some extent, what interest groups are relevant and how to distinguish between them, the focus shifts to the forms of exerting influence. *Vladimir Lepekhin* discusses the function and the role of – primarily economic – interest groups in the political process (3.5), while the analytical group from the Russian Union of Industrialists and Entrepreneurs' Expert Institute describes the phenomenon of lobbyism under late Soviet and Russian conditions (3.6). In another step, *Simon Kordonskii* attempts to apply his model of post-Soviet administrative markets (1.6) on the current political situation in Russia and to quantify administrative weights of numerous influential political roles and levels – often with names of the acting politicians attached (3.7). This structural-qualitative approach is followed by the political consultant *Mikhail Malyutin's* views on basic undercurrents in today's Russia's elites, which he differentiates between 'stabilisers' and 'chaots' (3.8).

The next cluster of papers includes the description and evaluation of the elite surveys which were conducted under the project's auspices. First, the questionnaires are presented which we handed out to our respondents (20 in Russia, 10 in Belarus and Ukraine, respectively). *Evkhen Golovakha* (Kiev), *Leonid Zaiko* (Minsk) and *Oleg Vite* (Moscow) who all had been involved in the project architecture, studied the data and the results and wrote the interpretation for the elite profiles and outlooks in their countries (3.10-3.12).

In a next step we asked specialists to describe the profile of certain interest (pressure) groups: the TEK/FEC, VPK/MIC and the agrarian lobby and their interests are developed in *Vladimir Chervyakov's* detailed analysis (3.13) of economic interests in Russia. This article rests on the theoretical approach on the distribution of resources he has developed in the first volume (1.7). In another contribution about the very influential energy sector and its leverage on economic and general politics, the TEK interests are studied by *Yakov Pappe* (3.14). The very interesting and fragmented MIC–dimension is outlined by *Vladimir Kolosov, Aleksei Krindach* and *Rostislav Turovskii* from the *Mercator* group (3.15). The so-called power structures/ministries, i.e. the army, special services and the interior ministry are analysed by *Mikhail Malyutin* (3.16). Then we present two papers on illegal structures and organised crime – often talked about in an alarmist fashion, but overlooked when it comes to the real influence of illegal groups, their origin in Soviet times, their political ambitions (*Ol'ga Kryshtanovskaya* and *Igor' Sundiev* – 3.17 and 3.18). The Cossacks in Russia, an interesting and controversial issue, are portrayed by *Mikhail Malyutin,* 3.19.

This volume concludes with two contributions on interests and elite groups in Belarus. *Ol'ga Zagorul'skaya* writes about the representation of various interests in her country (3.20). *Irina Bugrova* addresses actors and interests in Belarus (3.21). While these papers demonstrate that the process of the formation of elite groups is slower in Belarus (and in Ukraine) than in Russia, the first proto-elites are already on the political scene.

The fourth and final volume contains contributions on various dimensions of the societies' reaction to the changes underway. While many observers still assume that the population at large suffers dramatically from the transitions, fortunately many social groups and most individuals are gradually learning to adapt to the new social and economic mechanisms, to find niches, to earn money from various sources of income and, at least, to survive. This is, probably, the most encouraging and less expected development of social transformations after the disappearance of the Soviet regulation mechanisms.

In their article, *Evkhen Golovakha* and *Nataliya Panina,* sociologists from Kiev, describe strategies of adaptation and survival (not only) in Ukraine (4.1). *Viktor Voronkov* from St. Petersburg reflects on poverty in Russia – and comes to startling conclusions (4.2). This paper is matched by *Frank Fabel's* description of the activities of Russian self-help initiatives in St. Petersburg. The organisation he represents, *Deutsch-Russischer Austausch* [German-Russian Exchange], is active and effective in helping Russian initiatives of homeless people, drug addicts, soldiers' mothers, handicapped people and other actually or potentially marginalised individuals to organise themselves, to initiate projects and to establish networks of self-helping groups (4.3).

Similar to the poverty perceptions in the West, much alarmism has been produced in connection with allegedly forthcoming waves of migrants from Eastern Europe and the FSU. As a matter of fact, the dramatic emigration perspectives did not materialise, while the real problem turned out to be domestic migration in the FSU. This problem is the topic of *Kozlov's* paper on the geography of refugees (4.4).

Four papers address the ethno-national question. *Vladimir Kolosov* and *Andrei Treivish* describe the various ethnic areas in Russia (4.3). *Viktor Voronkov* writes on Russians as a community, discussing and rejecting numerous stereotypes of the 'Russians' and their 'Russianess' as something supposedly too specific, hard to understand with *ratio* and not eligible to many 'Western' forms of economic, social and political regulation (4.5). *Nataliya Panina* and *Igor' Chakvin* with *Tadeush Novogrodskii* address the topic of inter-ethnic relations and conflict in Ukraine and Belarus, respectively (4.7 and 4.9). Finally, *Anatolii Makarov* from Minsk tackles the question of social stratification in Belarus. (4.4).

Now, use these volumes as an offer to browse, to try out new views, to get upset, but also be ready to accept new ways of looking at the historic change underway in the FSU.

# 2

# Levels and Units of Analysis in Post-Soviet Studies

Stephan De Spiegeleire

## 1 Introduction

> [T]hose who are interested in understanding the inner logic of politics cannot forever ignore the opportunities for augmenting their thinking with formal constructs. Such constructs constitute too powerful an instrument of logical reasoning, and politics is too important a subject to leave its study to the often imprecise and logically flawed world of intuition, 'wisdom', and verbal analysis – to a domain in which the well turned word or eloquent phrase, however imprecise or illogical, carries the argument and dictates policy[1].
>
> Peter Ordeshook

This book was born out of a growing feeling of frustration about the methodological and substantive approaches in the analysis of both domestic and international developments in the post-Soviet policy space. As people who are called upon to provide the German government with in-depth analyses of the ongoing processes in the former Soviet Union and how they pertain to the West, it has become increasingly and painfully clear to us that the analytical frameworks (if such a term is applicable at all) that are used both in the policy world and in academia to explain the post-Soviet realities are woefully inadequate in many aspects.

In the first chapter of this book, Klaus Segbers has already offered a number of concrete examples in which the neo-realist categories that continue to dominate today's discussions on the post-Soviet space (such as 'the Ukrainian state', or 'Russian national interest'[2]) have demonstrably lost much of their explanatory

**1** Ordeshook, Peter C. *A Political Theory Primer*. New York: Routledge, 1992: 1.

**2** I will call these categories *neo-realist*, because this school of political thought has had and continues to have such a strong impact on foreign policy debates (especially in Russia and the US, but to a large extent also in Europe). Put briefly, neo-realism takes the nation-state as the primary unit of analysis in an anarchic international system. Because of the nature of that system, relative power is the key variable driving international politics, therefore leading to power. Particularly in this period of profound systemic (both international and domestic) flux, this should not come as a surprise. First of all, the *changes in the structure of the post-Cold War international system* certainly continue to play an important role in the declining utility of those categories. Leaving aside the issue of the relative usefulness of these neo-realist categories during the Cold War, it should be clear that many events in this post-Cold War era, even in the traditional temples of neo-realism such as foreign and military affairs, can no longer be sufficiently explained merely by using the category 'national interests', especially if these interests are assumed to be derived directly from the structure of the international system. Secondly, the fact that the Soviet successor states are undergoing drawn-out, multi-dimensional *systemic transformation processes domestically* should also throw some doubt on the continued prevalence of neo-realist categories. To what extent can these states that are struggling to discover their own geo-strategic, geo-political and geo-economic place in the world, to find new patterns of political aggregation for rapidly diversifying societal interests, to find a new *modus vivendi* between the different ethno-linguistic groups they encompass, to find more efficient ways of harnessing their economic potential, be expected to be able to define stable interests, let alone to have the administrative or coercive capacity to act internationally to further those interests?

If it is true that the old categories are becoming increasingly incongruous with the realities of the post-Cold War era (and the profound disorientation in the foreign policy establishments of virtually all governments certainly points in that direction), then one of the main tasks of the analytical community should, in our view, be to come up with new categories that do show more congruence with the empirical realities we observe. Throughout the course of this project, we have found it extraordinarily difficult to persuade policy-makers (as well most of our fellow-analysts) of the quintessentially *practical-political* importance of the seemingly purely theoretical questions we kept asking[3]. Although most of them probably share our dissatisfaction with the current categories, they are reluctant to join us in going back to the social scientific literature (which they perceive as being entirely irrelevant to their everyday concerns) to find some new questions and answers. It

endemic systemic instability. See especially Waltz, Kenneth N. *Theory of International Politics*. Reading, MA: Addison-Wesley, 1979.

3 I am hereby reminded of a the following caveat of Stanley Lieberson: "A theory that ignores existing evidence is an oxymoron. If we had the equivalent of 'truth in advertizing' legislation, such an oxymoron should not be called a theory" (Lieberson, Stanley. "Einstein, Renoir, and Greeley: Some Thoughts about Evidence in Sociology." *American Sociological Review* 56, no. 2 (February 1992): 4)

might therefore be useful to present one more concrete example of how one empirical reality in the field of foreign affairs can be interpreted very differently according to the analytical categories one chooses to use, and how the actual policy prescriptions will differ accordingly and, quite often, dramatically.

The presence of the Russian 14th Army in the Transdniestr region is seen by neo-realists as a typical attempt by the *'Russian state'* to *'project'* its *'force'* beyond its own '*borders*', either as part of some *'offensive'* larger '*neo-imperialist*' design or as a more *'defensive'* attempt to '*impose*' stability hegemonically in '*its backyard*'. We have grown so accustomed to these italicised terms, that we no longer stop to ponder the actual empirical validity of these very terms. And yet these categories have been culled from a very specific conceptual framework within which (and only within which) these abstract terms gain a precise operational content. In this case, for instance, these categories immediately suggest a classical 'realpolitik'al act by a 'strong' Russian state, which would supposedly call for a strong-handed Western reaction.

If one looks at the presence of this army from the point of view of the interests of the actual players involved, however, one immediately enters a different categorical framework, which at the same time also presents a radically different picture of the very same reality. First of all, one sees the economic interest of the 'army' itself (more accurately, a couple of brigades), which had been in an advanced state of decomposition when General Lebed' took over, and which rediscovered some semblance of stability afterwards. With this new-found stability, it was able to translate its presence on the ground into some concrete local political and economic arrangements that had definite economic benefits for the soldiers. These benefits would quickly disappear if the 'army' were to be relocated to Russia proper, as the experience with the troops that were withdrawn from Eastern Europe and Mongolia clearly indicated. Secondly, this more detailed look would also reveal an extraordinarily chaotic decision-making process, in which a local commander can ignore a direct order from his superior (the Minister of Defence) with virtual impunity after appealing directly to the President, without this having any political consequences for the Minister of Defence. One would also detect radical and open differences of opinion between the Ministry of Foreign Affairs and the Ministry of Defence, which are allowed to continue virtually indefinitely. At this level of analysis, therefore, one gets a dramatically different picture of an essentially very weak Russian state, which has lost control over many of the remnants of the old instruments of the Soviet state. Such an evaluation of the situation also presents the

West with very different (and almost far more difficult) policy challenges as well. In the case of Russia, which remains an enormous geopolitical unit with vast residual military (including nuclear) power, the strong-handed policies neo-realists would prescribe might from this perspective lead to the worst possible outcome.

Similar examples can be offered in virtually all spheres of public life in practically all countries of the former Soviet Union, and most of the papers in these volumes will bear witness to this point. We therefore submit that the analytical and methodological problems undergirding this project have so profound an impact on Western policy debates about the FSU that they can no longer be politically ignored. Most of the discussions both in the media and in policy circles continue to assume almost automatically that the classical unitary state approach remains the single most useful approach to explain the events in the former Soviet Union, be they economic reform, political changes, foreign policy (in)actions, or military developments. It is precisely the empirical usefulness of this analytical assumption that we wanted to challenge in this project, and we want to start presenting some new categories to get the developments in that part of the world in a better analytical grip.

Another important component of the frustrations that led us to set up this project is the continuing intercontinental gap between the North American scholarly community in this field and the European one. A description of the many differences between these two communities would transcend the scope of this paper, but anyone familiar with the situation will realise that the level of scholarly discourse in this field remains quantitatively, but especially qualitatively different between the two continents. It is hard to dispute that the American Cold War investments in human and physical capital in the area of social sciences in general, but also in the area of Soviet studies, have yielded impressive returns. The current infrastructure in this area in Europe therefore compares poorly to the North American one: it remains confined to some largely uncoordinated, fragmented efforts in a couple of countries with limited, antiquated and poor bibliographical, technological and methodological resources. In an era when a) the new geopolitical realities in Europe are presenting European governments with a whole range of new and urgent policy issues along its current Eastern borders; and b) the locus of decision-making in many areas is gradually shifting away from the national foreign policy establishments to a European Union, it is probably high time to start building up a 'European pillar' in the field of post-Soviet studies. This project was also conceived as a modest start in this endeavour.

## 2 Back to Social Science

In our quest for analytical assistance in coming up with new and more useful approaches and tools in analysing post-Soviet realities, our first instinct was to consult the academic literature in the field of post-Soviet studies. Unfortunately, we found that the field of Soviet/post-Soviet studies still seems predominantly preoccupied with its own failure to 'predict' the collapse of the Soviet Union, and has yet to emerge out of this debate with incisive new insights into the post-Soviet realities (or, for that matter, with any persuasive models of the Soviet realities). We had the impression that, just like the famous dictum about how soldiers always seem to be preparing to win the last war they fought, most of the Sovietologists in our field are still 'fighting' their own Cold War battles[4]. It is not our view that the Soviet

---

**4** For some taste of this debate, readers may want to consult: Alexiev, Alex. "After the Rubble, What?" *Problems of Communism* 41, no. 1-2 (January 1992): 117-120; Armstrong, John A. "New Essays in Sovietological Introspection." *Post-Soviet Affairs* 9, no. 2 (April 1993): 171-175; Bova, Russell. "Political Dynamics of the Post-Communist Transition: A Comparative Perspective." *World Politics* 44, no. 1 (October 1991): 113-138; Breslauer, George. "In Defense of Sovietology." *Post-Soviet Affairs* 8, no. 3 (July 1992): 197-238; Brumberg, Abraham. "The Changing 'Problems of Communism'." *Problems of Communism* 41, no. 1-2 (January 1992): 89-106; Chandler, Andrea. "The interaction of post-Sovietology and comparative politics: seizing the moment." *Communist and Post-Communist Studies* 27, no. 1 (March 1994): 3-17; Daniels, Robert V. "Is Sovietology Dead Too?" *New Leader* 74, no. 10 (9 September 1991): 7-10; Fairbanks, Charles H. Jr. "Introduction (Sovietology and the Collapse of Communism)." *National Interest*, no. 31 (March 1993): 5-9; Herspring, Dale. "Political Scientists and Sovietology." *Problems of Communism* 41, no. 1-2 (January 1992): 114-116; Jones, A. "Sovietology Is Not Dead, Long Live Sovietology." *Contemporary Sociology – A Journal of Reviews* 23, no. 1 (January 1994): 161-162; Katz, Mark N. "Analysing the Changing Foreign and Domestic Politics of the Former USSR." *Studies in Comparative Communism* 25, no. 2 (June 1992): 139-152; King, Charles. "Beyond Sovietology." *International Affairs* 70, no. 2 (April 1994): 291-298; King, Charles. "Post-Communist Studies and Political Science." *International Affairs* 70, no. 2 (April 1994): 291-298; Kubalkova, Vedulka. „The post-Cold War geopolitics of knowledge: international studies in the former Soviet bloc." *Studies in Comparative Communism* 25, no. 4 (December 1992): 405-417; Laqueur, Walter. "Intelligence and Secrecy: Sovietology Redux." *Society* 30, no. 2 (January 1993): 6-13; Malia, Martin „A fatal logic. (Sovietologists and the collapse of communism in the former USSR)." *National Interest*, no. 31 (Spring 1993): 80-90; Meyer, Alfred G. "Politics and Methodology in Soviet Studies." *Studies in Comparative Communism* 24, no. 2 (June 1991): 127-136; Meyer, Alfred G. "Observations on the Travails of Sovietology." *Post-Soviet Affairs* 10, no. 2 (April 1994): 191-195; Monas, S. "The 'National Interest' (American Sovietology and the Conservative Critique to Which It Has Been Subjected)." *TLS-The Times Litarary Supplement*, no. 4709 (2 July 1993): 17; Remington, Thomas F. "Sovietology and System Stability." *Post-Soviet Affairs* 8, no. 3 (July 1992): 239-269; Rutland, Peter. "Sovietology: Notes for a Post-Mortem." *National Interest* , no. 31 (March 1993): 109-122; Solomon, Peter H. Jr. "Against Premature Closure (An Open-Minded Study of post-Soviet Russia)." *Post-Soviet Affairs* 9, no. 3 (July 1993): 278-280; Tucker, Robert C. "Sovietology and Russian History." *Post-Soviet Affairs* 8, experience, or that the entire literature on the Soviet Union has suddenly become irrelevant. There can be no doubt, for instance, that the infamous 'path dependency' that we know from the neo-institutionalist literature is empirically, and therefore also theoretically, relevant to today's developments in that part of the world. What we do feel, however, is that many of main research questions that were driving the field in the past may retrospectively not have been the most useful ones. Although the field of Soviet Studies has yielded an enormous body of literature, we in fact still know disappointingly little about how policy was actually formulated in that system. We know, for instance, that the decisions in the field of the economy turned out to be economically inefficient, but the longevity of the system testifies to the fact that those decisions must have been politically efficient[5] for at least the key actors (i.e. not just the Politburo, but also the regional and functional groups that were represented in the Central Committee and in other decision-making bodies at lower and regional levels). This political equilibrium is as yet poorly understood, although that does seem to be the current research focus of many specialists in the field, both in the West and in the East.[6]

In contrast to the field of Soviet Studies, the broader social science literature proved to be a far more fertile feeding ground for categories, models and theories that could be usefully transposed to the realities of the post-Soviet policy space. It is becoming a convention in the field of political science to make use of a number of concepts and tools that have been borrowed from other social sciences. One of these emerging conventions is to think about the phenomena that we aim to explain in terms of dependent variables (the variables one is trying to explain) and independent

no. 3 (July 1992): 175-196; and Zwick, P. "The Perestroika of Soviet Studies – Thinking and Teaching about the Soviet Union in Comparative Perspective." *PS – Political Science & Politics* 24, no. 3 (September 1991): 461-467. For a good overview, see Fleron, Frederic J. Jr, and Erik P. Hoffmann (ed.). *Post-Communist Studies and Political Science: Methodology and Empirical Theory in Sovietology*. Boulder, Colo.: Westview Press, 1993.

**5** On the concept of political efficiency, see Barro, Robert. "The Control of Politicians: An Economic Model." *Public Choice* 14 (1973): 19-42; Inman, R. P. "On Setting the Agenda for Pennsylvania School Finance Reform: An Excercise in Giving Policy Advice." *Public Choice* 36 (1981): 449-474; Rose-Ackerman, Susan. "Inefficiency and Re-Election." *Kyklos* 33 (1980): 287-307; Wildavsky, Aaron. "The Political Economy of Efficiency: Benefit Analysis Systems, Analysis and Program Budgeting." *Public Administration Review* 26, no. 3 (1966): 292-310.

**6** See the works of Kordonskii (also in these volumes), Naishul, e.a.

variables (the variables one is using to explain changes in the dependent variables)[7]. The dependent variable of this project and, we would argue, of policy analysis with respect to the FSU in general, has essentially remained unchanged after the end of the Cold War. We are still interested in explaining what is happening in the post Soviet space in a number of issue areas that are of direct policy relevance to the West, i.e. mainly the political, economic, and security developments in those countries. The concrete manifestations of these policy preoccupations in these areas have changed since the end of the Cold War, but their actual nature remains the same. Especially in Europe, there is a fairly stable consensus that the events in the former Soviet Union continue to have a direct impact on the lives of all European citizens and on the development of European politics in general. Therefore, we remain vitally interested in trying to explain what is happening there as best we can, not in the least to be able to shape our own policies towards that area of the world in a more informed way.

By framing the issue in this way, we are at the same time also establishing the single criterion for successful modes of analysis: how well they explain the current observable realities in the post-Soviet space. It seems that for all too many scholars in the field of policy analysis, familiarity with certain established categories and analytical traditions remains the main criterion driving their research efforts. At the same time, theoretical consistency, elegance, and parsimony seem to be the overriding concerns in the research efforts of the more theoretically inclined scholars, who frequently prefer to avoid the intractability of actual political realities. Our approach towards these problems is more pragmatic: having observed the barrenness of the current (frequently non-theoretical) explanations, we are trying to 'put one step back' (to paraphrase Lenin) from some of the current policy debates in order to infuse our analytical efforts with some of the findings of social science theories. We do not do this for primarily theoretical purposes, but in the very concrete hope and expectation that these theories will offer us some additional analytical leverage over the approaches that currently continue to dominate the policy communities in Western Europe. In other words, our single criterion in this endeavour is analytical efficiency: how many of the observable empirical events that we are interested can be explained with a particular theory.

---

7 For a good overview of methodological concepts and problems in the field of social sciences, see Frankfurt-Nachmias, Chava, and David Nachmias. *Research Methods in the Social Sciences*. New York: St. Martin's Press, 1992.

## 3 A Tale of Two Paradigms

Without claiming to offer another critical overview of the field of Soviet studies[8], we found it useful to apply the now classic divide between the two basic paradigms in the social sciences to this field. On the one hand, there are a number of *rational choice explanations*, which try to explain events in the FSU as the result of the purposive actions of a number of actors that try to optimally match their particular aspirations with the means they have at their disposal, and that interact strategically with other actors that are engaged in similar maximisation exercises[9]. Because the term 'rationality' is so frequently misunderstood, it is important to underline that the actual concrete goals of the actors are essentially irrelevant: they can be egoistic or altruistic, idealistic or materialistic, short-sighted or far-sighted, intelligent or non-intelligent. The essence of these rational choice approaches is that the actions of actors can be modelled *as if* they were trying to maximise certain things[10], called 'utilities' (as a neutral term to cover as broad a spectrum of goals as possible) in the public choice literature[11]. One of the important implications of this paradigm (especially for policy analysts, who tend to focus on uniqueness, rather than on generalizeability) is that actors are seen as being interchangeable: any state or group

---

**8** See footnote 4.

**9** For some important contributions to the rational choice paradigm in political science, see Barry, Brian. *Sociologists, Economists, and Democracy*. Chicago, IL: University of Chicago Press, 1978; Harsanyi, John C. "Rational-Choice Modes of Political Behavior vs. Functionalist and Conformist Theories." *World Politics* 21, no. 4 (July 1969): 513-538; Riker, William H. *The Theory of Political Coalitions*. New Haven, CT: Yale University Press, 1962; Rogowski, Ronald. *Commerce and Coalitions: How Trade Affects Domestic Political Alignments*. Princeton, N.J.: Princeton University Press, 1989; Tsebelis, George. *Nested Games. Rational Choice in Comparative Politics*. Berkeley, CA: University of California Press, 1990.

**10** Therefore it is irrelevant whether the actors actually behave in a way that can be called 'rational', just like billiard players who execute their shots do not have to know the complicated mathematical formulae describing the optimal path of the ball (Friedman, Milton. "The Methodology of Positive Economics." In *Essays in Positive Economics*, Milton Friedman (ed.). Chicago: University of Chicago Press, 1953: 14-19), but still can be modelled 'as if' they knew those formulae.

**11** I will use the terms 'public choice' and 'new political economy' interchangeably to denote the field within social sciences that "seeks to analyze political processes and the interaction between the economy and the polity by using the tools of modern (neo-classical) analysis. It provides, on the one hand, an explicit positive approach to the workings of political institutions and to the behavior of governments, parties, voters, interest groups, and (public) bureaucracies; and it seeks, on the other, normatively to establish the most desirable and effective political institutions". Frey, Bruno S. "The Public Choice View of International Political Economy." *International Organization* 38, no. 1 (December 1984): 201.

within the state is hypothesised to make similar choices when confronted with similar challenges.

On the other hand, there are a number of what one could call *'non-rational actor'* approaches, which for various reasons deny that actors can be viewed as making those 'rational' calculations between means and ends. George Tsebelis has identified two distinctive classes of non-rationality[12]. On the one hand, there are non-rational *motivational explanations* that explain actions as resulting from actors' affective or impulsive motives (e.g. Tedd Gurr's 'relative deprivation theory' of revolutions[13]) which can be observed and analysed by the actors themselves and therefore also by observers. On the other hand, there are the *epistemological relativists*, who claim that there are certain critically important constructs between the actor and his actions which may be inaccessible even to the actors, and therefore also to the observer (e.g. Friedrich Engels' 'false consciousness', Sigmund Freud's 'inconscient pulsions', Pierre Bourdieu's 'habitus', or the various political culture approaches[14]).

These non-rational actor models have undoubtedly played an important role in Soviet studies. Among the most popular quotations in political 'causeries' on the former Soviet Union (and today's Russia), are undoubtedly Winston Churchill's description of Russia as a 'mystery wrapped in a riddle veiled in an enigma ' and Tyuchev's 'Rossiyu umom ne ponyat' ey tol'ko verit'? It should be pointed out that most area studies specialists typically emphasise the point that 'their' area is 'sui generis' and does not lend itself to 'simple' comparative or theoretical analysis. They suggest one needs a certain degree of empathic understanding, for which they claim to find the theoretical justification in the Weberian concept of 'Verstehen'[15], a form of explanatory understanding "that seeks to grasp the 'motivation' or the final cause of behaviour by 'placing the act in an intelligible and more inclusive context of meaning[16]". This interpretation of 'understanding' of social phenomena has lead

---

**12** Tsebelis, George. *Nested Games. Rational Choice in Comparative Politics*. Berkeley, CA: University of California Press, 1990: 21-22.

**13** Gurr, Tedd. *Why Men Rebel*. Princeton, N.J.: Princeton University Press, 1971.

**14** Barry, Brian. *Sociologists, Economists, and Democracy*. Chicago, IL: University of Chicago Press, 1978.

**15** Weber, Max. "Critical Studies in the Logic of the Cultural Sciences." In *The Methodology of the Social Sciences*, Max Weber (ed.). New York, N.Y.: Free Press, 1949.

**16** Dallmayr, F. R., and T. A. McCarthy. *Understanding and Social Inquiry*. Notre Dame, IN: University of Notre Dame Press, 1977: 21. Some analysts have, however 'recaptured' (quite plausibly) the Weberian concept of 'Verstehen' into the rational choice paradigm (Scharpf, F. W., and A. Ryll. *Core Games, Connected Games, and Networks of Interaction*. Cologne: Max-Planck-Institut für Gesellschaftsforschung, 1988: Tsebelis, George. *Nested* to a large hermeneutic tradition in the social sciences[17], which remains intellectually very vibrant, and which claims that social science is not "an experimental science in search of a law but an interpretive one in search of meaning[18]".

Although non-rational actor models were probably the dominant theoretical current in Soviet studies[19], the pendulum may now be shifting. Many of the most interesting studies about both the Soviet and post-Soviet periods to have appeared in the past couple of years are using some of the new methodological and theoretical developments in the field of positive political economy. A new generation of social scientists seems to be emerging who share with their predecessors a specific empirical interest in the post-Soviet region, but who no longer shun broad comparative studies that are theoretically inspired.

But it is obvious that the road ahead in this research direction remains a long and tortuous one. One of the main problems that we have confronted from our side, is that we still know disappointingly little about the new politically salient actors in the post-Soviet societies and polities. Before we can start mapping the emerging socio-political landscapes of these countries with some of the new methodological and theoretical tools that the 'new political economy[20]' offers, we need a far better understanding of the main actors who are presumed to be making those 'rational choices'. These volumes are in their very essence an attempt to deal with precisely this issue, which could be labelled the 'unit of analysis'-problem. In the next section, the intellectual antecedents of this problem will be briefly sketched.

---

*Games. Rational Choice in Comparative Politics*. Berkeley, CA: University of California Press, 1990: 44-45).

**17** Taylor, C. "Interpretation and the Sciences of Man." *Review of Metaphysics* 25 (1965): 3-51.

**18** Geertz, Clifford. *The Interpretation of Cultures. Selected Essays.* New York: Basic Books, 1973: 5.

**19** It should not be forgotten that area specialists have a definite 'corporate' interest in claiming special status for their region: if the study of that region requires not only certain linguistic or other area-specific qualities, but also psychological gifts of empathy, it obviously becomes much easier to shield off the profession from 'outsiders'.

**20** For the history of the term, see Arndt, H. W. "Political Economy." *Economic Record* 60 (1984): 266- 273. See also Inman, R. P. "On Setting the Agenda for Pennsylvania School Finance Reform: An Excercise in Giving Policy Advice." *Public Choice* 36 (1981): 449-474, and Ordeshook, Peter C. "The emerging discipline of political economy." In *Perspectives on Positive Political Economy*, James E. Alt, and Kenneth A. Shepsle (ed.). Cambridge: Cambridge University Press, 1990

## 4 First Steps First

We are not the first scholars in the field to call for more scientific rigor in the analysis of (and policy towards) the post-Soviet realities[21]. What we might be the first to do, however, is to focus systematic attention on some preliminary steps that have to be made before the field can engage in more rigorous theory-building. And although these preliminary steps may seem obvious, they are frequently ignored by analysts[22].

One of the first steps to be made in the scientific inquiry[23] into post-Soviet states is the step of *defining the universe of cases* one is trying to explain. It is impossible to propose any general advice on this matter, as it will depend to a large extent on the exact phenomena one is trying to explain. As a rule of thumb, however, it would almost certainly be unnecessarily restraining to confine oneself to the empirical evidence to be found in the couple of post-Soviet states. For most issue areas, more comparative material can be found (and therefore a larger *n*[24]), for instance in the similar historical experiences of systemic change (e.g. certainly from authoritarian to post-authoritarian systems[25], but also from feudal to post-feudal systems[26]). This is

**21** See the work of Matthew Evangelista, Alexander Motyl and Jack Snyder.

**22** The typical format of review essays about the 'state of the field' in Soviet studies starts out with a critique of the existing literature, goes on to demonstrate how that literature failed in its predictive and prescriptive tasks, ends with a plea for more social scientific rigor, sometimes accompanied with some concrete proposals.

**23** In this context, the recent work by King, Keohane and Verba (King, Gary, Robert O. Keohane, and Sidney Verba. *Designing Social Inquiry. Scientific Inference in Qualitative Research.* Princeton: Princeton University Press, 1994) is of great utility in, on the one hand, pointing out some basic rules to be followed by scholars in the design of social inquiry; but on the other hand also in 'legitimizing' rigorous qualitative (as opposed to quantitative) research methods.

**24** The small-*n* problem refers to the fact that for many issues social scientists are interested in, there are only a limited amount of comparable cases available, which makes scientific inference more difficult. Various strategies to overcome or remedy the small-*n* problem are discussed in King, Gary, Robert O. Keohane, and Sidney Verba. *Designing Social Inquiry. Scientific Inference in Qualitative Research.* Princeton: Princeton University Press, 1994: 217-228.

**25** For the transition literature, see a.o. Bates, R., and A. Krueger. *Political and Economic Interactions in Economic Policy Reform: Evidence form Eight Countries.* Oxford: Blackwell, 1993; Bermeo, Nancy. „Democracy and the lessons of dictatorship." *Comparative Politics* 24, no. 3 (April 1992): 273-292; Bermeo, Nancy. „Democracy in Europe. (The case for Eastern European democracies as contrasted with the political forces that undermined democracy in Germany and Italy) *Daedalus* 123, no. 2 (Spring 1994): 159-178; Bresser-Pereira, L. C., J. M. Maravall, and A. Przeworski (ed.). *Economic Reforms in New Democracies: A Social-Democratic Approach.* New York: Cambridge University Press, 1993; Centeno, Miguel Angel. "Between Rocky Democracies and Hard Markets: The Dilemmas of the Double Transition ." *Annual Review of Sociology* 20 (1994): 125-157; Collier, David and Deborah L. Norden „Strategic choice models of political change in Latin America." *Comparative Politics* 24, no. 2 (January 1992): 229-244; Di Palma, Giuseppe. *To Craft Democracies*. Berkeley: Berkeley University Press, 1990; Diamond, Larry, Juan Linz, and Seymour Martin Lipset. *Democracy in Developing Countries*. Boulder, Colo.: Lynn Reiner, 1989; Ekiert, Grzegorz. „Democratization processes in East Central Europe: a theoretical reconsideration." *British Journal of Political Science* 21, no. 3 (July 1991): 285-303; Geddes, Barbara. "Game Theoretic Model of Reform in Latin America." *American Political Science Review* 85 (1991): 371-392; Haggard, Stephan, and Robert Kaufman. *The Politics of Economic Adjustment*. Princeton: Princeton University Press, 1992; Hirschman, Albert O. "The Political Economy of Latin American Development: Seven Exercises in Retrospection." *Latin American Research Review* 22, no. 3 (1987): 7-36; Huntington, Samuel. "Will More Countries Become Democratic?" *Political Science Quarterly* 99, no. 2 (June 1984): 193-218; Huntington, Samuel. "How Countries Democratize." *Political Science Quarterly* 106, no. 4 (1991): 579-616; Karl, Terry Lynn. "Dilemmas of Democratization in Latin America." *Comparative Politics* 23, no. 1 (October 1990): 1-21; Kitschelt, Herbert P. "Comparative Historical Research and Rational Choice Theory. The Case of Transitions to Democracy." *Theory and Society* 22 (1993): 413-428; Lijphart, Arend. „Majority rule in theory and practice: the tenacity of a flawed paradigm. Rethinking Democracy: Institutionalism, Majority Versus Consensus, Civil Society, Religion, the Media." *International Social Science Journal* 43, no. 3 (August, 1991): 483-493; Linz, Juan. "Transitions to Democracy." *Washington Quarterly* (Summer 1990): 143-165; Linz, Juan, and Alfred Stepan. *The Breakdown of Democratic Regimes*. Baltimore: Johns Hopkins University Press, 1978; Linz, Juan, and Alfred Stepan. "Political Crafting of Democratic Consolidation or Destruction: European and South American Comparisons." In *Democracy in the Americas*, Robert A. Pastor (ed.). New York: Holmes & Meier, 1989; Mainwaring, Scott, Guillermo O'Donnell, and Valenzuela. *Transitions to Democracy and Democratic Consolidation: The New South American Democracies in Comparative Perspective*. Notre Dame: University of Notre Dame Press, 1992; Malloy, James M., and Mitchell A. Seligson. *Authoritarians and Democrats: Regime Transition in Latin America*. Pittsburgh: Pittsburgh University Press, 1987; Midlarsky, Manus I. „The origins of democracy in agrarian society: land inequality and political rights." *Journal of Conflict Resolution* 36, no. 3 (September 1992): 454-477; Moore, Barrington. *Social Origins of Dictatorship and Democracy: Lord and Peasant in the Making of the Modern World*. Boston, MA: Beacon Press, 1966; O'Donnell, Guillermo, Philippe C. Schmitter, and Laurence Whitehead. *Transitions from Authoritarian Rule*. Baltimore: The Johns Hopkins University Press, 1986; Przeworski, Adam. "Some Problems in the Study of the Transition to Democracy." In *Transitions from Authoritarian Rule*, Guillermo O'Donnell, Philippe C. Schmitter, and Laurence Whitehead (ed.). Baltimore: The Johns Hopkins University Press, 1986; Remmer, Karen L. "Redemocratization and the Impact of Authoritarian Rule in Latin America." *Comparative Politics* 17 (April 1985): 253-275; Remmer 91; Rueschemeyer, Stephens and Stephens 92; Rustow, Dankwart A. "Transitions to Democracy." *Comparative Politics* 2 (April 1970): 337-363; Smith, William C. "Democracy, Distributional Conflicts, and Macro-Economic Policymaking in Argentina, 1983-1989." *Journal of Interamerican Studies and World Affairs* 32 (June 1990): 1-42; Stallings, Barbara. "Political Economy of Democratic Transition: Chile in the 1980s." In *Debt and Democracy in Latin America*, Barbara Stallings, and Robert Kaufman (ed.). Boulder: Westview, 1989.

**26** It is remarkable that most of the so-called 'transition'-literature virtually ignores the experiences of 'Western' transitions from authoritarianism to liberal democracy, although the fundamental dilemmas were in many ways very similar to the ones faced by the post-Communist systems today: under feudalism as under communism, the economy was practically one of the most promising advantages of rational choice models, which, in contrast to the more interpretivist school, allows for more focused, structured comparisons between cases[27].

At the same time, however, one can also overcome some of the small-*n* problems by looking at a lower geographical level. In our case, this means the regions of the post-Soviet states, where one has a larger number of cases to test theories. There are also a number of other sub-national geographical units which may present interesting case-study material for a number of issue areas (e.g. the papers on ethnic areas, on Cossacks, or on military districts). Furthermore, one is not limited to geographical units – the quest for a larger *n* could also be expanded to encompass various functional units of analysis, either at the sub-state level (sectors, factors, etc.) or totally irrespective of geographical boundaries (e.g. the 'gas-sector' in the world as a whole).

This brings us to the second preliminary issue that has to be addressed before one can start building more rigorous (and hence also more useful to policy-makers) models of reality in the field of post-Soviet studies, and that is the issue of the most appropriate unit-of-analysis.

## 5 Levels and Units of Analysis

The unit of analysis problem is not a new issue in political science. Ever since the field started to orient itself more towards cumulative and rigorous theory-building, the issue has been hotly debated in what came to be known as the 'level of analysis' debate. From the very outset, the debate evolved around two different (but related) methodological issues. The first and most ardently debated one asked at which level

---

fully embraced within the political system, and the big hurdle of those days was how incipient markets could ever free themselves from the arbitrary political interference by the authorities. For an overview of some theories on how the feudal authorities themselves became the unlikely fathers of a market economy and how the tightly organized structures they had established presented a suitable setting for the rise of commerce, see e.g. Jones, E. L. *The European Miracle. Environments, Economies and Geopolitics in the History of Europe and Asia.* New York: Cambridge University Press, 1987: 85-103.

**27** Eckstein, Harry. "Case Study and Theory in Political Science." In *Handbook of Political Science*, 79-138. Fred I. Greenstein, and Nelson W. Polsby (ed.). 7. Reading, MA: Addison-Wesley, 1975; George, Alexander L. "Case Studies and Theory Development: The Method of Structured, Focused Comparison." In *Diplomacy. New Approaches in History, Theory and Policy*, Paul Gordon Lauren (ed.). New York: Free Press, 1979; Lijphart, Arend. "Comparative Politics and the Comparative Method." *American Political Science Review* 65 (September 1971): 682-693; and Lijphart, Arend. "The Comparable-Case Strategy in Comparative Research." *Comparative Political Science* 8 (July 1975): 158-177.

of analytical aggregation theorising about world politics could most fruitfully be pursued. The second one dealt with the problem of how observations and theoretical statements derived from different levels of analysis can be combined in theory-building.

In the field of international relations theory, the first debate about the level-of-analysis problem broke down the study of international politics into different levels (e.g. the micro- and macro-level), and asked which level offered most promise for reliable explanation and prediction[28]. Very quickly, however, the very term 'level-of-analysis problem' in the field of political science degenerated into little more than an taxonomic 'hook' that was used to categorise different strains of theorising on international relations[29].

Many different schemes have been suggested[30], but the most influential one still remains the trichotomy proposed in Kenneth Waltz' *Man, the State and War* as well

---

**28** Singer, J. David. "The Level-of-Analysis Problem in International Relations." In *The International System: Theoretical Essays*, 77-92. Klaus Knorr, and Sidney Verba (ed.). Princeton: Princeton University Press, 1961.

**29** This is certainly how most textbooks in international relations use the concept, albeit with varying degrees of sophistication. E.g. Russett, Bruce M., and Harvey Starr. *World Politics. The Menu for Choice*. San Francisco: W.H. Freeman and Company, 1981; Spanier, John. *Games Nations Play*. Washington, D.C.: Congressional Quarterly Press, 1993.

**30** See e.g. Greenstein, F. I. "Personality and Politics." In *Handbook of Political Science*, N. Polsby, and F. I. Greenstein (ed.). Vol. 2. Reading, Mass.: Addison-Wesley; Holsti, Kalevi Jaakko. *International Politics. A Framework for Analysis*. Englewood-Cliffs, N.J.: Prentice Hall, 1972; Jervis, Robert. "Models and Cases in the Study of International Conflict." *Journal of International Affairs* 44, no. 1 (1990): 81-101; Kaplan, Morton A. *Towards Professionalism in International Theory: Macrosystem Analysis*. New York: Free Press, 1979; Kaplan, Morton A. "The Hard Facts of International Theory." *Journal of International Affairs* 44, no. 1 (1990): 39-57; Levy, Jack S. "The Causes of War: A Review of Theories and Evidence." In *Behavior, Society and Nuclear War*, 209-333. Philip E. Tetlock, Jo L. Husbands, Robert Jervis, Paul C. Stern, and Charles Tilly (ed.). Volume 1. New York: Oxford University Press, 1989; Price, Douglas. "Micro- and Macro-Politics: Notes on Research Strategy." In *Political Research and Political Theory*, 102-104. Olivier Garceau (ed.). Cambridge, MA: Harvard University Press, 1968; Rosenau, James N. "Pre-Theories and Theories of Foreign Policy." In *Approaches to Comparative and International Politics*, 27-92. R. B. Farrell (ed.). Evanston, IL: Northwestern University Press, 1966; Rosenau, James N. *The Scientific Study of Foreign Policy*. New York: Free Press, 1971; Singer, J. David. "The Level-of-Analysis Problem in International Relations." In *The International System: Theoretical Essays*, 77- 92. Klaus Knorr, and Sidney Verba (ed.). Princeton: Princeton University Press, 1961; Tetlock, Philip E. "Methodological Themes and Variations." In *Behavior, Society and Nuclear War*, 334-385. Philip E. Tetlock, Jo L. Husbands, Robert Jervis, Paul C. Stern, and Charles Tilly (ed.). Volume 1. New York: Oxford University Press, 1989; Waltz 59; Waltz, Kenneth N. *Theory of International Politics*. Reading, MA: Addison-Wesley, 1979; Waltz, Kenneth N. "Realist Thought and Neo-Realist Theory." *Journal of International Affairs* 44, no. 1 (1990): 21-37; and Yalem, Ronald J. "The Level-of-as in his subsequent *Theory of International Politics*, where he distinguishes between the following three levels:

- the *first level*, which is the level of the individual decision-maker;
- the *second level*, which is the actual primary analytical unit in the international system, which for Waltz and most theoreticians today is the nation state; and finally
- the *third level*, which is the level of the international system as a whole, the level at which the primary analytical units interact with each other.

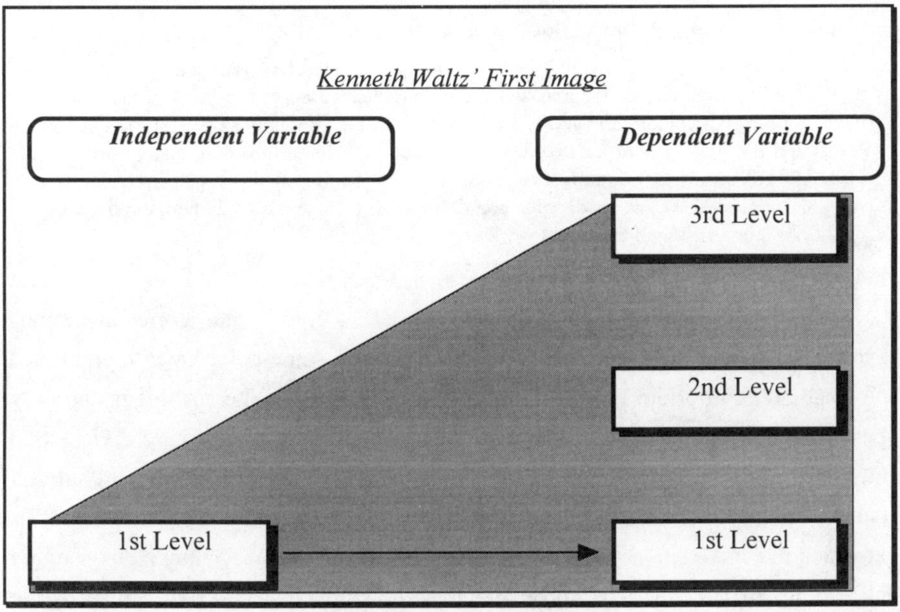


Both independent and dependent variables can be picked at any of these three levels. Waltz talked in this context about three 'images', to get across the idea that they are different 'perspectives' of 'looking at' world politics[31]. Thus, a 'first-image' explanation looks at the world from the point of view of the individual decision-maker (see diagram), e.g. uses a first-level independent variable (e.g. Truman's

---

Analysis Problem Reconsidered." In *The Year Book of World Affairs*, 306-326. London: Stevens, 1977.

**31** What is less frequently observed, however, is that the very 'level-of-analysis' debate clearly reflects the state-centeredness of the entire discipline of political science. Thus, even many of the critics who have argued that the systemic scholars' 'black-box' of the decisionmaking process should be dissected, go on to focus their attention primarily on the turf battles within the state's central decisionmaking agencies (e.g. the literatures on bureaucratic politics, or various applications of organizational theory on the study of world politics).

childhood experiences) to explain a second-level dependent variable (e.g. US policy towards Russia in the immediate post-W.W.II period[32]).

Various scholars have criticised and amended Waltz' three-tiered scheme and have proposed their own taxonomies with various levels at which world politics can be analysed. The most important point of contention in this debate, however, was the question at which level of analysis international politics could best be explained. Although this discussion remained one of the most lively ones in the field for a long time, its vigour seems to have subsided somewhat in recent years. In a recent overview of the field, Philip Tetlock came to the conclusion that

> [t]here are signs of growing tolerance among advocates of competing schools of thought. Many scholars now agree that the importance of any given level of analysis is not a constant but is likely to vary as a function of the configurations of variables at other levels and the type of questions we want answered... Different levels of analysis, in this view, do not represent mutually exclusive ways of looking at the world... The central research challenge is not to debunk competing levels of analysis but to improve the quality of theoretical and empirical work at one's chosen level[33].

The emerging synthesis of this debate therefore seems to be the suggestion that the field is gravitating towards a number of partial equilibrium stories at various levels of analytical aggregation[34], which will then at some point have to combined into a grand equilibrium theory of international relations. Whereas this is certainly (besides being an elegant and diplomatic solution to some of the sharp divisions in the field) a legitimate proposition, our experiences in the post-Soviet field suggest that the implicit continued acceptance of the nation-state as the key unit-of-analysis (at which the endogenous and exogenous stories would intersect) may be thoroughly misleading. In general, it is surprising that the implicit state-centred bias of the Waltzian taxonomy (but also in the emerging realist 'two-level game' synthesis[35])

---

**32** For an excellent example (and a good overview of social-psychological theories and how they can be applied to foreign policy analysis), see Larson, Deborah Welch. *Origins of Containment. A Psychological Explanation*. Princeton: Princeton University Press, 1985.

**33** Tetlock, Philip E. "Methodological Themes and Variations." In *Behavior, Society and Nuclear War*, 334-385. Philip E. Tetlock, Jo L. Husbands, Robert Jervis, Paul C. Stern, and Charles Tilly (ed.). Volume 1. New York: Oxford University Press, 1989: 339

**34** Putnam, Robert D. "Diplomacy and Domestic Politics: The Logic of Two-Level Games." *International Organization* 42, no. 3 (June 1988): 427-460: 430. See also the IPE state-centered literature surveyed in this paper.

**35** See especially Putnam's aforementioned essay. For some concrete case studies worked out on the basis of the original insights from Putnam's article, see Evans, Peter B., Harold K. Jacobson, and Robert D. Putnam. *Double-Edged Diplomacy: International Bargaining and Domestic Politics*. Berkeley: University of California Press, 1993. See also Andy Moravcsik's insightful introduction to that volume.

itself has so far gone largely uncriticised. We would submit that the privileged position of the 'state' has been undermined to such an extent and in so many areas of the world, that we have to start re-arranging even our categorical systems away from this state-centred bias (indeed possibly even away from the primarily geographical criteria which underlie all current taxonomies[36]).

The second (arguably more important) question about levels of analysis deals with the problem of comparing and integrating empirical and/or theoretical statements made at different levels of analysis. This problem was aptly described by Wolfram Hanrieder[37]:

> [P]ropositions derived from two different analytical environments, or levels of analysis [the reference is to internal and external dimensions of foreign policy – SDS], cannot be readily correlated because they are culled from different sets of empirical data and methodological assumptions.

In some way, levels of analysis can be seen as different slices of the political reality one is trying to explain. One of the first requirements of any kind of scientific inquiry is to reduce the complexity of that reality to more manageable dimensions. One of the ways in which this can be done is to cut up that reality into different analytical pieces along certain well-specified angles. One can, for example, cut up the reality of international politics in geographical slices, and try to explain what is going on on the basis of the picture one obtains from those 'slices'[38]. Or one can cut up today's Russia into different pieces along different axes: regional, functional, generational, cultural, etc.

The traditional 'slicing method' most theorists, analysts and policy-makers have been using is the one that cuts up the world in nation-states. There are, of course, other geographical 'cuts' that can be (and are increasingly being) used, both at

---

**36** Most critics of such schemes have criticized the *theoretical* primacy of one particular level (be it the individual, the state, the system,...) Yet very few people have criticized the fact that *geopolitical* units have enjoyed so much *taxonomical* predominance. Yet the consequences of continuing to frame international politics on the basis of these geographically-based taxonomic principles can hardly be overstated, for they are essentially of a mutually exclusive nature, and therefore almost definitionally contain the seeds of conflict. If one were to move away from exclusive geographical categories to also encompass other categories, then one would end up with many overlapping and crosscutting units of analysis which would totally alter the theoretical import of issues such as cooperation and conflict, or at least the way in which these issues are now being discussed.

**37** Hanrieder, Wolfram. "Compatibility and Consensus: A Proposal for the Conceptual Linkage of External and Internal Dimensions of Foreign Policy." *American Political Science Review* (December 1967): 975.

**38** Radiology here may provide a useful comparison: according to what issue one is trying to diagnose, one will use different radiological techniques (eg MRI, X-rays,...) to present that particular image of the body that will be most useful to the diagnostician.

higher levels of aggregation (e.g. groups of states – e.g. Europe, Latin America; international organisations such as ASEAN, the European Union, or the CIS), at lower levels (sub-national geographical units such as administrative units within states – regions or provinces; tribal or ethnic areas that do not represent administrative units), or at levels that cut across state borders (e.g. regional associations – e.g. the Rhineland area, the Black Sea area; the Baltic area); contiguous ethnic or tribal areas that cross state borders, such as the area inhabited by the Uighurs).

But one could take a different slice of that same reality which is based on functional rather than geographical criteria. The slicing could here be done on the basis of multinational corporations, or of religious communities throughout the world (Islam, Christianity, Orthodoxy, etc.), or of international factoral (e.g. the international 'proletariat'), sectoral (e.g. international cartels) or other functional (e.g. Pugwash) criteria, which cut across geopolitical boundaries and may present a radically different perspective on the same reality. The real 'level of analysis problem' now is how one can methodologically legitimately compare and integrate findings obtained from different slicing methods.

The fact that this problem is not as trivial as many political scientists seem to think[39] is well illustrated by what statisticians know as the 'ecological fallacy'. In a study of literacy rates, William Robinson discovered that at the regional level of analysis, regions with higher percentages of foreign-born people had higher literacy rates than those with lower percentages of foreign-born people. At the individual level, however, the opposite result obtained: native-born individuals were more literate than foreign born[40]. If one thinks of this problem in more prosaic terms as different pictures representing one object at radically different levels of magnification, it will be obvious to anybody that one cannot just compare what one sees on those different pictures as though they were isomorphic. The pictures *can* be compared (and natural scientists have discovered a number of statistical techniques of 'unbiased' ecological inference), but only if one 'converts' the observations to a common level of magnitude.

---

**39** Even King, Keohane and Verba seem to downplay the importance of this problem (King, Gary, Robert O. Keohane, and Sidney Verba. *Designing Social Inquiry. Scientific Inference in Qualitative Research.* Princeton: Princeton University Press, 1994: 30-31).

**40** Robinson, William S. "Ecological Correlations and the Behavior of Individuals." *American Sociological Review* 15 (1950): 351-357. The term 'ecological' is probably somewhat misleading; Robinson used it to denote the aggregate level of analysis. The main

Similarly, cross-level inference from different levels of analysis in political science is fraught with many dangers[41]. Many scholars in this field frequently come to the conclusion that variables at different levels of analysis are important for their particular research problem, and just indiscriminately throw them all together into their explanations for certain events, which is certainly methodologically dubious. As was already pointed out, many of the events that are occurring in the post-Soviet states may acquire very different meanings according to which 'image' one chooses to view them from. The papers in this book certainly do move between different levels of analysis (the nation-states involved, regions, sectors, factors, etc.) and therefore clearly illustrate this problem. At this stage, we can do little more than drawing our readers' attention to this problem, hoping to stimulate some further discussion on it.

We see the role of these volumes within this debate in the field as being essentially twofold: 1) to offer the reader a number of different 'slices' of the new post-Soviet reality, which will be presented as 'thick' descriptions of a number of key political actors in these post-Soviet states; and 2) to start a discussion on how these different pieces of this new emerging multi-dimensional puzzle can be put together. In order to give the reader some theoretical tools to start putting these complex puzzles together, we will in the remainder of this chapter try to present a number of strains of literature that frequently have nothing to do with the FSU as such, but whose analytical insights may be of use to shed light on many of the problems addressed. It is hoped that the interested reader will use the selected literature references to find further analytical assistance in dealing with some of these issues.

## 6 Some Pointers to Relevant Bodies of Literature

In this section, we want to offer a couple of pointers to some bodies of recent literatures, both empirical and theoretical, one might find useful in digesting some of the materials we are presenting in these volumes. This selection clearly does not aspire to be exhaustive. The main intention is to expose people from the policy-world to some ideas and approaches out of the social sciences that they might find

---

inference of the Robinson article was that using aggregate analysis to reason about individuals is a fallacy.

**41** On this topic, see also Lieberson, Stanley. *Making It Count: The Improvement of Social Research and Theory*. Berkeley: University of California Press, 1985.

useful in trying to make sense out of the new complexities of the post-Soviet political reality.

A first body of literature is the international political economy literature. This literature has many different strands, but a couple of them may be particularly useful to the analysis of post-Soviet societies and polities, not so much because of the actual topical or geographical areas they deal with, but primarily because of the analytical approaches they present.

## 6.1 Units of Analysis in the IPE Literature

### *6.1.1 The Domestic Structures Literature*

First of all, there is a frequently cited literature on domestic structures, which uses 'state strength' (more specifically the weak state/strong state dichotomy) as an independent variable in explaining states' foreign economic policies (although the idea could also be used for other policy areas such as military policy, general foreign policy[42], etc.). As introduced by Stephen Krasner in an IPE classic edited by Peter Katzenstein, the concept refers to

> [T]he power of the state in relation to its own society. This power can be envisaged along a continuum ranging from weak to strong The weakest kind of state is one which is completely permeated by pressure groups. Central government institutions serve specific interests within the country, rather than the collective aims of the citizenry as a whole... At the other extreme from a state which is completely permeated by political pressure groups is one which is able to remake the society and culture in which it exists; that is, to change economic institutions, values, and the patterns of interaction among private groups[43].

In that same volume, various advanced industrial states are placed along that continuum, with France and Japan[44] being closer to the strong pole of the continuum

---

**42** Theodore Lowi was one of the first ones to plead for a literature which seeks to "destroy any claim that foreign policy-making is a fundamentally different policy-making system, or one that is in any considerable way insulated from domestic political forces".

**43** Krasner, Stephen D. *Defending the National Interest. Raw Materials Investments and U.S. Foreign Policy*. Princeton, N.J.: Princeton University Press, 1978: 57; 60. Ikenberry, Lake and Mastanduno claim that there is a general consensus that the United States possesses a weak state (Ikenberry, G. John, David A. Lake, and Michael Mastanduno. "Introduction: Approaches to Explaining American Foreign Economic Policy." In *The State and American Foreign Policy*, G. John Ikenberry, David A. Lake, and Michael Mastanduno (ed.). Ithaca, N.Y.: Cornell University Press, 1988: 11), and they quote Nettl, J. P. "The State as a Conceptual Variable." *World Politics* 20 (July 1968): 559-592 and Katznelson, Ira. "Rethinking the Silence of Social and Economic Policy." *Political Science Quarterly* 101 (June 1986): 307-325.

**44** Zysman, John. "The French State in the International Economy." *Between Power and Plenty: Foreign Economic Policy of Advanced Industrial States*, Peter Katzenstein (ed.).

and the US closer to the weak pole. The popular perception of especially Russia but also of a number of other post-Soviet states today remains that they are fairly 'strong' states, in which a number of central decision-makers (typically called 'Kiev', or 'Moscow', or 'the Kremlin') are able to devise and implement coherent strategies in various policy areas. Most papers in these volumes portray countries that differ significantly from this picture, having multiple centres of decision-making, both in a geographical (e.g. the regions) and a functional sense. In that sense, most contributors to these volumes would probably agree with the statement that the post-Soviet states are closer to the weaker pole of this strong state/weak state continuum.

This weak state/strong state dichotomy has been criticised from a number of different angles: for leaving out the politics (e.g. logrolling) behind the domestic structures[45], for being irrelevant to the actual ability of states to implement policies[46], for not lending itself to comparative study[47], for being of limited utility in the analysis of a single case[48], or for leading to tautological arguments[49]. Yet the

---

Madison: University of Wisconsin Press, 1978: 255-293; Pempel, T. J. "Japanese Foreign Economic Policy: The Domestic Bases for International Behavior." *Between Power and Plenty: Foreign Economic Policy of Advanced Industrial States*, Peter Katzenstein (ed.). Madison: University of Wisconsin Press, 1978: 139-190.

**45** Gourevitch, Peter. "The second image reversed: the international sources of domestic politics." *International Organization* 32, no. 4 (1978): 903.

**46** Ikenberry, John. "Conclusion: An Institutional Approach to American Foreign Economic Policy." In *The State and American Foreign Policy*, G. John Ikenberry, David A. Lake, and Michael Mastanduno (ed.). Ithaca, N.Y.: Cornell University Press, 1988.

**47** Milner, Helen. "Resisting the Protectionist Temptation. Industry and the Making of Trade Policy in France and the United States during the 1970s." *International Organization* 41 (1987). Also a critique of strong state/weak state from a comparative perspective.

**48** Ikenberry, G. John, David A. Lake, and Michael Mastanduno (ed.). *The State and American Foreign Policy*. Ithaca, N.Y.: Cornell University Press, 1988:11. Others state more explicitly that the relative strength of even a single state can vary according to issue-area (Krasner, Stephen D. "United States Commercial and Monetary Policy: Unravelling the Paradox of External Strength and Internal Weakness." In *Between Power and Plenty: Foreign Economic Policy of Advanced Industrial States*, Peter Katzenstein (ed.). Madison: University of Wisconsin Press, 1978: 64 and 66; Krasner, Stephen D. *Defending the National Interest. Raw Materials Investments and U.S. Foreign Policy*. Princeton, N.J.: Princeton University Press, 1978; Zysman, John. *Governments, Markets, and Growth. Financial Systems and the Politics of Industrial Change*. Ithaca, N.Y.: Cornell University Press, 1983: 297).

**49** Lake, David A. *Power, Protection and Free Trade. International Sources of U.S. Commercial Strategy, 1887-1939*. Ithaca, N.Y.: Cornell University Press, 1988; Haggard, Stephan. "The Institutional Foundations of Hegemony: Explaining the Reciprocal Trade Agreements Act of 1934." In *The State and American Foreign Policy*, G. John Ikenberry, David A. Lake, and Michael Mastanduno (ed.). Ithaca, N.Y.: Cornell University Press, 1988:

idea continues to possess a certain intuitive appeal that can at the very least be used to undermine the traditional dominance of the nation-state as the primary unit of analysis. First of all, it probably remains a fairly useful descriptive tool to compare the ability of various states to implement certain policies, and this not only in the field of foreign economic policy. Thus, there can be little doubt about the fact that in a large number of issue-areas, most post-Soviet states are probably discomfortingly weak from this point of view. A comparison of the post-Soviet cases with the cases that have already been analysed in this literature (the US, Britain, Japan, West Germany, Italy, France) may therefore be quite revealing. Thus, John Zysman has suggested three variables that can be combined in one measure of a state's ability to implement policies that could be checked for the post-Soviet cases[50]. In another example, Krasner has referred in his categorisation of the US as a weak state to some historic reasons for the fragmentation of power and authority in the American political system[51], which could once again be compared to the histories of the newly independent states in the FSU.

But beyond these opportunities for comparative analysis, and just as was the case for the US debate on this weak state/strong state dichotomy, the most important pay-off of such a debate would be not so much to find out whether a particular state is actually weak or strong, but rather to focus the attention of scholars away from the virtual exclusive preoccupation with the central decision-making instances of a state into a more structured-focused discussion of the underlying actors within those societies and the actual dynamics of decision-making. And although the literature on domestic structures is predominantly analytical and not prescriptive, it should be pointed out that the strategic interaction with 'weak' states indubitably present

---

94. Put simply, the problem is that one cannot use the variable of state strength to explain the ability of a state to implement certain policies.

**50** Zysman, John. *Governments, Markets, and Growth. Financial Systems and the Politics of Industrial Change*. Ithaca, N.Y.: Cornell University Press, 1983: 300. The three variables are 1) mechansims of recruitment into the national civil service; 2) degree of centralization of the civil service; and 3) the extent of independence from legislative oversight.

**51** Krasner, Stephen D. *Defending the National Interest. Raw Materials Investments and U.S. Foreign Policy*. Princeton, N.J.: Princeton University Press, 1978: 62-64. The salient points here are the absence of a traditional society ("American society was born modern", therefore no need to break the backbone of traditional society); the absence of a territorial threat (therefore no need for centralized political authority); and the historical material abundance with high levels of equality. It will be obvious that the Russian historical experience has been the precise mirror-image of the American one.

different challenges from the ones we were used to with the 'strong' states[52] such as the Soviet Union.

If one then does decide to take a closer look at the main 'actors' underneath the state-level that a) have fairly clearly identifiable interests, that b) have the resources to influence actual policy actions in a wide number of issue areas, and that c) are demonstrably active in the 'weak' post-Soviet states, then one can once again fall back on some useful suggestions in especially the international political economy literature.

### *6.1.2 Sectors*

Since most of the literature on sub-state actors has emerged in the field of political economy, it should not come as a surprise that sectoral approaches enjoy so much popularity in the scholarly literature, both in the second image and in the second-image reversed tradition.

In the *second-image* vein, various authors have tried to analyse different (economic) policies as the result of the strategic interaction between various sectors of the domestic economy. Put broadly, the idea is that sectors in an economy have different policy preferences on various issue-areas that they try to translate into actual economic (but sometimes also more general domestic or even foreign) policy through various forms of lobbying. Most of the endogenous[53] tariff theories, for instance, take this approach. Following E.E. Schattschneider's depiction of the infamous Smoot-Hawley tariff of 1930 as 'pressure groups run amok'[54], they describe the various interest groups that have a stake in a certain tariff, their respective positions, the bargaining process that takes place between them and the decision-makers, and the actual policy outcome as a the result of a this bargaining process between those various sectoral interests[55].

The model that emerges from this literature is a typical neo-classical one with, on the one hand, a demand for protection generated by various rent-seeking[56] industries;

---

**52** De Spiegeleire 94.

**53** These theories are called 'endogenous' because, contrary to the systemic approaches which assume the preferences of the main analytical units (i.e. the nation states) to be determined extraneously, these approaches try to explain these preferences from 'within' though rational maximizing behavior by the main actors within the unit.

**54** Odell, John S. "Understanding International Trade Policies. An Emerging Synthesis." *World Politics* 43 (October 1990): 139-167:141.

**55** Schattschneider, E. E. *Politics, Pressures and the Tariff.* New York: Prentice Hall, 1935.

**56** See the paragraph on Rent-seeking in this piece.

with, on the other hand, a potential supply of protection by the state (with rational politicians that are interested in maximising the probability of re-election, or campaign contributions, and that at the same time have control over various redistributive resources); and finally with the actual policy (e.g. a tariff, or an export subsidy) as an equilibrium outcome in this market for protection[57]. When markets shift, the positions of the various industries may change, which will lead to changes in political coalitions, and ultimately to changes in government policy.

In this tradition, for instance, James Kurth has presented an explanation for various domestic and foreign policies that is based on the industrial 'life cycles' of textiles, steel, and automobiles (the traditional sequence of successive dominant sectors in most industrialised countries) for the last two centuries in the major European countries as well as for the United States[58]. One part of Kurth's story (which may actually be of particular relevance for the ever-popular parallels between Weimar Germany and today's FSU), for instance, dissects the changed political preferences of the leading economic sectors in Germany before and after Word War II[59], and explains how these preference directly affected economic but also foreign and security policies.

First of all, it should be pointed out that such endogenous policy theories, which have remained largely confined to the field of political economy, could easily be transposed to other issue areas. Foreign or military policies could also be conceptualised as equilibrium outcomes of the strategic interaction between various sectoral constituencies[60]. This general model can then, secondly, also readily be applied to the Soviet and post-Soviet cases. Some Russian scholars, for instance, have developed an 'administrative market' explanation for the Soviet political system which shows a remarkable affinity with the PE models that have been used

---

**57** For one of the most complete models of such a politico-economic market, see Magee, Stephen P., William A. Brock, and Leslie Young. *Black Hole Tariffs and Endogenous Policy Theory. Political Economy in General Equilibrium.* Cambridge: Cambridge University Press, 1989. This work also has excellent thematic bibliographies before each chapter.

**58** Kurth, James. "The Political Consequences of the Product Cycle: Industrial History and Political Outcomes." *International Organization* 33 (1979): 1-34.

**59** Because the German steel industry in the 1920s did not have a large domestic market for steel (as did Britain with the emerging domestic automobile sector and the demand for railway steel throughout the British empire), it had little other options available but to support those political groups who favored rearmament, revision of the Versailles Treaty and tariff barriers angainst imported steel from Western Europe. After the war, however, there now was a German 'civilian' market for steel, which led to different political preferences as well.

**60** Hintze, Weber.

primarily for the industrialised world, and most of the contributions on interest groups in these volumes are implicitly based on these models.

The post-Soviet states are probably particularly good test cases for some of these approaches, especially because of the historical political importance of economic sectors in the Soviet economy[61], but also because of the patent current weakness of those states, which makes them particularly vulnerable to capture by various well-organised economic sectors. The best political commentators from the quality Russian newspapers[62], for instance, implicitly (or sometimes even explicitly) use this general approach to analyse the day-to-day developments of the tumultuous Russian political scene. Most contributions to these volumes also illustrate the political salience of the economic sectors in today's Russia[63], and some focused comparisons between some of the Western case studies and the post-Soviet ones will certainly enrich this entire literature.

Secondly, there is also a *second-image reversed literature* on sectors, which explains how various sectors are affected by the international terms of trade or by other international systemic variables. Gourevitch, for instance, has described in a number of his works how various 'domestic' political dependent variables (such as regime type and coalition patterns) are affected by 'international' independent variables such as war, economic crises or world market forces[64]. Particularly Alexander Gerschenkron's work on the importance of the timing of industrialisation for the particular domestic structures that had to 'carry' industrialisation[65] has been widely used in comparative analysis, and also shows much promise for the post-Soviet-cases.

---

**61** Through the importance of the branch-ministries, for instance. See e.g. Lehmbruch 94.

**62** Especially *Kommersant-Daily*, *Segodnya*, and until recently *Novaya Ezhednevnaya Gazeta*'s weekly 'IQ' supplement, but also some observers from *Izvestiya* and *Nezavisimaya Gazeta*. Unfortunately, there are only a few Western observers of the post-Soviet states who use the same categorical schemes, prominent among them, however, are the *Economist* and the London *Financial Times*.

**63** See especially the papers by Chervyakov, Gel'man, Kordonskii, Lepekhin, Pappe, and Vite.

**64** Gourevitch, Peter. "The second image reversed: the international sources of domestic politics." *International Organization* 32, no. 4 (1978): 882-912; Gourevitch, Peter. *Politics in Hard Times. Comparative Responses to International Economic Crises*. Ithaca, N.Y.: Cornell University Press, 1986.

**65** Gerschenkron, Alexander. "Economic Backwardness in Historical Perspective." In *Economic Backwardness in Historical Perspective*, Alexander Gerschenkron (ed.). Cambridge, MA: Harvard University Press, 1963.

A systematic comparison of the position of the main sectors of the post-Soviet economies within the international division of labour, for instance, would demonstrate the preferences of these sectors with respect to many important issues that currently face those countries (and indirectly also with respect to some of those countries' policies). It is clear, for instance, that those branches of the Soviet Union's hypertrophied military-industrial complex which have found an exit onto the international market will have very different economic, but also political preferences, than those that are non-competitive and are therefore relegated to a shrinking domestic military market. These internal divisions can also help to explain why the once so omnipotent military-industrial complex has systematically lost most of the budgetary struggles it engaged in over the past couple of years. From this point of view, some of the papers in these volumes on a number of economic sectors, as well as parts of the results of the elite surveys may provide valuable insights into the political preferences of some of the key players in today's post-Soviet polities..

### *6.1.3 Factors*

The role of factors of production (such as capital, labour, or land) as units of analysis in international politics has a long and distinguished pedigree, within the Marxist school of thought, but also in modern trade theory (e.g. the Heckscher-Ohlin model) and the political models that are based on them. 'Classes', defined as groups of social agents that are characterised principally by their place in the production process, have always been a well-known basic unit of analysis in Marxist analysis[66], which saw the struggle between capital and labour as the main societal cleavage of advanced capitalism and predicted that the system itself would collapse under the strains of these contradictions. Various strains of the early literature on democracy, for instance, focused centrally on the alleged problematic relationship between social class and democracy[67]. And still today, social class remains, in the words of Rueschemeyer, Stephens and Stephens, an 'extremely powerful explanatory tool' in the social sciences[68].

'Factors' of production also play a key role in standard modern international trade theory. In the Heckscher-Ohlin model of international trade, factor endowments are the primary determinant of trade: relative price differentials across countries are

**66** Poulantzas, Nicos. *Pouvoir politique et classes sociales*. Paris: François Maspero, 1968.

**67** Held, David. *Models of Democracy*. Stanford: Stanford University Press, 1987.

**68** Rueschemeyer, Dietrich, Evelyne Huber Stephens and John D Stephens. *Capitalist Development and Democracy*. Chicago, University of Chicago Press: 1992.

primarily attributed to differences in national resource endowments. The model predicts that a country will export those commodities based on the factor which is relatively abundant (and therefore cheap) in that country, whereas it will import commodities which are produced with the relatively scarce factor. A country with a relative abundance in capital (e.g. a strong industrial sector), for instance, will tend to export capital-intensive commodities; whereas a country with a relative abundance of land will tend to export agricultural products[69]. In a logical extension of this model, known as the Stolper-Samuelson theorem, it was shown that protection benefits the owners of the locally relatively scarce factor, whereas free trade benefits the holders of the factor with which a country is abundantly endowed[70].

This model has a number of obvious political consequences which have started to be explored by some political scientists. Chief among those, Ronald Rogowski has opened an interesting line of comparative analysis that may also be usefully transposed onto the post-Soviet cases[71]. In another typical second-image reversed analysis, Rogowski argues that the preferences of various groups within a state can be inferred from that country's factor ratio (the relative abundance or scarcity of certain factors of production, typically land, labour and capital). Consequently, he is able to predict that increasing openness (as is occurring in most post-Soviet economies) will differentially affect various constituent groups within a state, and he is furthermore capable of identifying winners and losers, and of predicting the ensuing cleavages and coalitions along factoral lines.

Germany in the 19th century, for instance, was poor in capital and in land, but rich in labour. This lead to the emergence of the infamous coalition between 'iron and rye' (i.e. between land and capital) pushing for protectionism, while labour was pushing for more open markets. The US in the 19th century, on the other hand, was rich in land, but poor in capital and labour. This lead to a cleavage between protectionist capitalists and workers against free-trade oriented land-owners, in other words not along the traditional Marxist class lines, but along urban/rural lines.

The power of Rogowski's argument is that it is a purely deductive rational-choice theory with concretely specified predictions, and therefore (at least in principle)

**69** See e.g. Carbaugh, Robert J. *International Economics*. Belmont, CA: Wadsworth Publishing Company, 1991: 62-69.

**70** Leamer, Edward A. *Sources of Comparative Advantage: Theory and Evidence*. Cambridge: MIT Press, 1984.

**71** Rogowski, Ronald. *Commerce and Coalitions: How Trade Affects Domestic Political Alignments*. Princeton, N.J.: Princeton University Press, 1989.

fairly easily testable. One could try, for instance, to analyse the factor ratios for the different post-Soviet cases (either at a national or even more interestingly at a regional level) and see whether they systematically yield the political alignments predicted by Rogowski[72].

*6.1.4 Enterprises*

Another unit of analysis that has been used in the IPE literature is located at an even lower level of analytical aggregation, as it deals with the primary unit of economic activity: the enterprise. Especially multinational corporations and the role they play in the domestic politics of developing countries have become a heavily investigated topic in the IPE literature[73] that provides some interesting comparative material for the post-Soviet cases. At the same time, the role of multinationals in the industrialised world is now also being systematically researched. Helen Milner, for instance, has argued that the increasing role of US multinational firms with increasingly strong international ties explains why American trade policy in the 1970s did not become as protectionist as in the 20s, and this despite the fact that the main pressures were very similar[74]. The (slowly) increasing international exposure of certain Russian firms could therefore be hypothesised to have similar effects on their preferences with respect to Russia's role within its international environment. At the same time, Milner also demonstrates the importance of intra-industry differences, which is also an important consideration for some of the post-Soviet cases, as some of the papers in the volumes illustrate.

But a number of scholars have also demonstrated the importance of individual domestic firms, this especially in certain areas of military policy. Thus James Kurth

---

**72** In his own work, Rogowski already applied his model to the Soviet case, which he codes as rich in land and labor during the interwar period, and rich in land, fairly rich in capital and poor in labor after the war. Therefore, he would predict a coalition of land and labor against capital during the interwar period (which fits the actual developments reasonably well), and a typical class conflict situation after the war (which is more problematic). Evangelista has taken issue with Rogowski's coding of the post-war Societ Union as labor scarce, although his case study of the energy sector in the early 90s essentially validates Rogowski's predictions.

**73** See e.g. Barnet, R. J., and R. E. Müller. *Global Reach. The Power of Multinational Corporations*. New York: Simon and Schuster, 1975. For an interesting overview of prospective research avenues in this area, see Lall, S. "Multinational Enterprises and Developing Countries – Some Issues for Research in the 1990s." *Millenium – Journal of International Studies* 20, no. 23 (June 1991): 251-255.

**74** Milner, Helen. "Resisting the Protectionist Temptation. Industry and the Making of Trade Policy in France and the United States during the 1970s." *International Organization* 41 (1987).

has presented some telling evidence for the importance of US defence firms in US defence procurement procedures. He has shown empirically how various US decisions to buy certain weapon systems during the Kennedy, Johnson and Nixon Administrations seemed less inspired by strategic, bureaucratic or political (electoral) considerations, than by the interplay of these with the imperatives of keeping production lines open at the most important defence companies[75]. Similar considerations also play a role in the decision-making processes of other countries, whereby it is frequently difficult to determine the exact causality of the argument: do politicians use these companies to justify their strategic or political calculations, or is the companies who exert pressure on the politicians to translate their economic priorities into strategic aims at the national level? Or do both processes take place simultaneously? Leaving these questions aside, it is obvious that explanations for certain policy initiatives probably compel the analyst to go all the way down to the level of the enterprise.

Although weapons procurement may be a particularly visible example for the importance of domestic enterprises in military policy, there is ample empirical evidence that they are not absent from the other areas of foreign policy. Especially in American Politics, corporate lobbying is a well-studied phenomenon, and political action committees (PACs) are one of the main sources of income for individual Congressmen and for the political parties as a whole. This applies even more so to the case of the former Soviet Union, where the (regional and/or national) monopoly position of certain enterprises combined with the social function they fulfilled under the communist system has given these enterprises (and their managers, many of whom have acquired national and even international prominence) a formidable amount of bargaining leverage over the political leadership. Some of the regional papers in these volumes are again very illustrating from this point of view.

### *6.1.5 Regions*

If there is one level of analysis that is conspicuous by its relative absence from the IPE literature, it is certainly the sub-national geographical level of analysis (hereafter: regions). All of the literature discussed so far deals with sub-national actors, but only those of the functional variety, and not of the geographical one. It is truly striking how both the literatures on comparative politics and on international

75 Kurth, James. "A Widening Gyre: The Logic of American Weapons Procurement." *Public Policy* (June 1971): 373-404; Kurth, James R. "Why We Buy the Weapons We Do."

relations has virtually ignored what Ivo Duchacek called 'the territorial dimension of politics'[76]. Yet it is well documented at the empirical level that 'regions' are not only another geopolitical space within which many of the units that have been discussed so far are active and can be analysed (i.e. that they can be used as a level of analysis), but that they are also important political actors at the national level in their own right (i.e. that they are also units of analysis at the state-level of analysis on par with functional subnational actors[77]), and this in a number of different issue areas.

There exists, for instance, a fairly well documented literature on the role played by the individual states in the United States of America, and to a lesser extent also on the federal units in other countries. Robert Stein, for instance, has also used a 'market'-analogy to illustrate the interaction between national and sub-national actors. He distinguishes between supply-side and demand-side factors. Supply-side factors are the characteristics and objectives of central decision-makers. The basic idea here is that central authorities use their redistributive competence to translate their particular utility functions into reality. On the demand-side, the sub-national actors also have sets of preferences which they would like to see realised through various lobbying activities[78]. Thus, students of American politics have for instance observed that federal grants to US state governments tend to increase in periods before elections; that federal administrations tend to reward their own electoral constituencies (which was not uncommon in the former Soviet Union either); and that influential congressmen are able to secure greater federal spending for their constituencies[79]. Similar tests could be made for the post-Soviet states and are likely to show similar results[80]. Also the fascinating work done by Robert Putnam on the

---

*Foreign Policy*.

XX **76** Duchacek, Ivo D. *The Territorial Dimesnion of Politics Within, Among and Across Nations*. Boukder, Colo.: Westview Press, 1986.

**77** Or, as one scholar has put it less reverently, „just one more interest group in the 'policy soup'". Krane, Dale. „American Federalism, State Government and Public Policy: Weaving Together Loose Theoretical Threads", *PS: Political Science and Politics* 27, no. 2 (June 93): 187.

**78** Stein, Robert M. "The Allocation of Federal Aid Monies: The Synthesis of Demand-Side and Supply-Side Explanations." *American Political Science Review* 75 (1981): 334-343.

**79** For an overview of the literature, see Rich, Michael J. "Distributive Politics and the Allocation of Federal Grants." *American Political Science Review* 83, no. 1 (March 1989): 193-213.

**80** Whereby it should be pointed out that an (inconclusive) initial attempt to do this by Daniel Treisman was severely weakened by the obsolescence of his data.

Italian regions[81] offer many promising research ideas for students of Russian regionalism.

*6.1.6 The State*

The increased emphasis which we are trying to put on sub-state actors is not intended to deny the continued relevance of the actual state bureaucrats (typically and euphemistically called 'state actors'), also (maybe even especially) in the post-Soviet states. Whereas most of the actors described so far were on the demand-side of the creation of a policy, one also has to examine the supply-side, which in this case are the actual policy-makers and the bureaucrats behind them[82]. These state actors, who also have their own interests that are partially independent from the underlying societal interests described so far, have been the subject of a number of systematic investigations, this time not only in the field of foreign economic policy but also explicitly in the field of foreign policy.

Especially the so-called 'bureaucratic politics' literature has played an important role in this respect[83]. Of all the literatures reviewed in this overview, this is probably the one which is better-known in policy-circles and therefore requires less explanation. The main idea is that people's stances on policy issues are primarily a reflection of their institutional affiliation ("where you sit is where you stand"), a fairly intuitive idea that spawned many illustrations in a number of different issue

---

**81** Putnam, Robert D. *Making Democracy Work. Civic Traditions in Modern Italy*. Princeton: Princeton University Press, 1993.

**82** There are a number of rational choice models for the supply of government policies, which all share the assumption that bureaucrats are selfish utility maximizers, but put different elements into their actual utility functions (just re-election, or also other pecuniary or non-pecuniary goals). The seminal contributions here are Downs, Anthony. *An Economic Theory of Politics*. New York: Harper and Row, 1957, Niskanen, W. "Bureaucrats and Politicians." *Journal of Law and Economics* 19 (1976): 617-643 and Tullock 65.

**83** Allison, Graham T. "Conceptual Models and the Cuban Missile Crisis." *American Political Science Review* 58 (September 1969): 689-718; Allison, Graham. *Essence of Decision. Explaining the Cuban Missile Crisis*. Boston, MA: Little Brown, 1971; Allison, Graham T., and Morton H. Halperin. "Bureaucratic Politics: A Paradigm and Some Policy Implications." *World Politics* 24, Supplement (March 1972): 40-80; Art, Robert J. "Bureaucratic Politics and American Foreign Policy: A Critique." *Policy Sciences* 4 (1973): 467-490; Halperin, Morton H. "Why Bureaucrats Play Games." *Foreign Policy* 2 (April 1971): 70-90; Halperin, Morton H. "The Decision to Deploy the ABM. Bureaucratic and Domestic Politics in the Johnson Administration." *World Politics* 25, no. 1 (October 1972): 62-95; Halperin, Morton H. *Bureaucratic Politics and Foreign Policy*. Washington, D.C.: Brookings Institution, 1974 and Krasner, Stephen D. "Are Bureaucracies Important? (Or Allison Wonderland)." *Foreign Policy* 159-179.

areas for a number of countries, and could certainly also be replicated in the post-Soviet cases.

At about the same time Allison was opening a new research agenda by looking at the bureaucratic politics behind a state's decision-making process, a number of scholars were also trying to 'bring the state back in' to the field of comparative politics, which had in their assessment shifted too much towards societal actors (called the 'demand-side' in Ikenberry's words) while underestimating the power of the state as an independent actor (the 'supply-side'[84]). Krasner, for instance, described how the United States was able to act as a wholly autonomous actor in the field of raw materials, this even against numerous special interests, by using its special position to reframe issues and change the political resource distribution of societal groups[85]. In the same vein, Skocpol showed how autonomous state actions are possible even in a 'weak' state such as the US and she used the New Deal policy to illustrate the point. In their wake, a number of scholars have applied the new 'statist' paradigm to various issue areas ranging from revolutions to state-building and –disintegration[86].

In the late 1980s, then, a number of authors in the field of international relations theory picked up this theme from the comparative politics literature and started an attempt to develop a synthesis between the still dominant neo-realist literature focusing on systemic variables on the one hand, and the (re)emerging literature emphasising the role of societal actors in foreign policy on the other hand. Robert Putnam, for instance, argued in an important article that the entanglements of domestic and international variables could be conceptualised as a two-level game in which national governments sequentially satisfy the demands and pressures of both international imperatives and of domestic actors [87]. Subsequently, Ikenberry, Lake

---

**84** Ikenberry, G. John, David A. Lake, and Michael Mastanduno. "Introduction: Approaches to Explaining American Foreign Economic Policy." In *The State and American Foreign Policy*, G. John Ikenberry, David A. Lake, and Michael Mastanduno (ed.). Ithaca, N.Y.: Cornell University Press, 1988: 9.

**85** Krasner, Stephen D. *Defending the National Interest. Raw Materials Investments and U.S. Foreign Policy*. Princeton, N.J.: Princeton University Press, 1978.

**86** For an overview, see Skocpol, Theda. "Bringing the State Back In. Strategies of Analysis in Current Research." In *Bringing the State Back In*. Peter Evans, Dietrich Rueschemeyer, and Theda Skocpol (ed.). Cambridge: Cambridge University Press, 1985. For an incisive critique of the statist 'reaction', see Almond 88.

**87** Putnam, Robert D. "Diplomacy and Domestic Politics: The Logic of Two-Level Games." *International Organization* 42, no. 3 (June 1988): 433-434. A methodologically related argument (that of 'nested games', in which games are being played in different arenas, but in which events or strategies in one arena influence the way the game in other arenas is played) and Mastanduno pleaded for the development of what they called a 'realist theory of state action', which would put the state at the centre of the analysis, and would systematically examine how the internal and external strategies of a state are interconnected.

All of these perspectives on the role of the 'state' in the process of interest aggregation can also be useful for the study of post-Soviet polities. The tradition of strong state intervention in many areas of Soviet society has left an institutional legacy that can not be changed overnight. Furthermore, the actual size of state bureaucracies has in many of these states even increased, partially in light of the increased complexity of those societies (because of the increasing differentiation of societal interests)[88]. It can not be denied that those bureaucracies do indeed find themselves in an extremely strategic situation from which they can affect the different processes that are taking place in the post-Soviet societies. Most of these polities remain highly centralised in organisational structure (e.g. the so-called 'power vertical' in Russia and Ukraine), and some episodes such as the Chechen crisis demonstrate that we would be foolish to ignore the different bureaucratic actors with their arcane internecine games. It should also be pointed out that this observation applies to different geographical levels (i.e. including regional administration, but also city administrations). It is therefore also crucially important to continue to systematically investigate the actual interests and behavioural patterns of these bureaucratic actors, to which a start is made in some papers of these volumes, as well as in the elite surveys.

### *6.1.7 The Missing Pieces*

The attentive reader will observe that these volumes essentially ignore the one level of analysis which figures most prominently in the Western comparative political literature: the level of the political parties. This emphasis on political parties in developed democracies is certainly understandable. First of all, that level of analytical aggregation is undeniably empirically important, and plays a prominent role in the media coverage of domestic politics of most countries. But beyond that, the 'party-level' also represents a useful analytical 'cut', because parties typically

---

can be found in Tsebelis, George. *Nested Games. Rational Choice in Comparative Politics*. Berkeley, CA: University of California Press, 1990. The latter does not use any foreign policy eexamples, but mentions that the model is applicable to those areas as well.

**88** In Russia, for instance, it is estimated that the state bureaucracy is now larger than it was during the Soviet and perestroika eras.

represent the aggregated preferences of some key societal actors. The position that these parties occupy within the structure of Western polities (and which, it should be pointed out, developed over many decades) is therefore such that they are in a strategically unique position to play off the underlying political lobbies against each other to further their own interests. This idea is nicely illustrated in the following pyramid in Magee-Brock-Young's model of endogenous policy:

In this three-tiered pyramid, the higher tiers (called 'Stackelberg leaders' in game theory) are in a more favourable position because they know the value of the other players' (called 'Stackelberg followers') strategic variables, and can therefore also incorporate that knowledge (which also includes knowledge of how the 'followers will react to those decisions) in their own decisions[89]. Since there are typically far more lobbies than there are parties, this gives the parties ample opportunity to engage in this type of sophisticated strategic behaviour. Looked at from the perspective of society as a whole, this also means that this intermediate layer of interest mediation, aggregation and even manipulation represents a 'buffer' between

**89** In game theory, it is shown that players with such a sophisticated Stackelberg strategy typically perform better than those with a normal Cournot-Nash strategy (who are either unable or unwilling to make those calculations). See Intriligator, Michael D. *Mathematical Optimization and Economic Theory*. Englewood Cliffs, N.J.: Prentice-Hall, 1971.

the multiple raw material interests within a society and the actual decision-makers[90]. In the post-Soviet cases, however, parties have not yet been able to carve out this strategic niche in the political structure, and therefore the lobbies have so far largely been able to simply circumvent what is from their point of view nothing more than an additional expense anyway[91]. The picture that emerges from the post-Soviet polities, therefore, has so far been one of crude (because it is so direct) but sophisticated (because complex strategic calculations underlie it) direct interaction between societal interests and decision-makers.

## 6.2 Public Choice Literature

Finally, there is also a very rich vein of literature in the so-called 'public choice' field[92] with insights that can be applied to any of the analytical 'slices' of the post-Soviet reality presented so far. Although most of this literature tends to be highly abstract, it does provide the analyst with a number of extremely useful concepts and analytical tools that can be used to process these 'slices'. Here especially, it is virtually impossible to review the many ideas that could be usefully applied to the former Soviet Union[93], and therefore a number of illustrative examples will have to suffice.

### *6.2.1 Theories of collective action*

The rich and constantly growing literature examining so-called collective action problems offers a broad range of valuable insights into many real-life policy issues that policy-makers have to deal with. Let us illustrate this on the basis of an example. Lobbying is typically a matter of collective action: different actors with similar interests bundling their efforts to obtain certain redistributional concessions from the authorities. At the same time, however, once the actual 'public good' the

---

**90** In this sense, one may be able to demonstrate positively (i.e. non-normatively) why democracies actually may have superior patterns of interest aggregation to non-democratic polities.

**91** There is no apparent reason why these internediate political layers would not appear with time in those countries as well, and there are already a number of indications pointing in that direction.

**92** For a good introduction, see Frey, Bruno S. "The Public Chice View of International Political Economy." *International Organization* 38, no. 1 (December 1984): 199-223.

**93** And fortunately, there are a number of excellent overviews of the public choice literature, see especially Mueller, Dennis C. *Public Choice II.* Cambridge: Cambridge lobby is trying to obtain is provided, all of the actors with an interest in that good are likely to benefit from it (i.e. they will typically not be easily excluded from those benefits). This creates a complex set of actors' incentives to let the other members of the interest group carry as much of the lobbying cost themselves, which in turn may make the provision of that public good problematic.

This 'logic of collective action' may help us to explain why certain sectors of the economy form more successful lobbies than others. Why is it, for instance, that the gas industry in Russia seems to be so particularly effective in defending its interests in the country's policy-making process? A purely 'economic' sectoral approach – what Gourevitch would call a production profile explanation – would have some quite convincing explanations as to why the fuel-energy complex dooms so large in Russian politics today: one only has to take a look at the percentage of total export that this sector provides to be convinced of its political importance. And yet, this basic given does not yet fully explain why certain branches within this sector are politically more effective than others, especially why the gas sector, for instance, is politically more powerful than the fuel sector. This is where some concepts from the collective action literature may prove very useful.

Jakov Pappe, in his contribution to this volume, for instance, emphasises the importance of the fact that the gas sector in Russia is embodied in one single firm, Gazprom, which bears responsibility for both gas-extraction, transportation and export. This highly centralised organisational embodiment of these economic interests allow one to predict a very high degree of lobbying efficiency. If one then compares this with the situation in the oil-sector, then one is immediately struck by a number of differences: here, the extraction, distribution and export functions are not centralised in one firm, but dispersed across a number of different firms, with a very strong regional component. This then helps to understand why the oil-sector as a singular interest group is at a relative disadvantage vis-à-vis the gas-sector. This example could be a schoolbook illustration of Olson's free-rider-problem[94]. Although Gazprom has to pay all the costs of lobbying for certain types of legislation, it will also capture all the benefits thereof. In case of the oil-sisters, however, the part of the collective benefits each of the oil companies can realistically expect to receive as a result from the lobbying may be so small that it

---

University Press, 1989; Ordeshook, Peter C. *A Political Theory Primer*. New York: Routledge, 1992.

**94** Olson, Mancur Jr. *The Logic of Collective Action. Public Goods and the Theory of Groups*. Cambridge, MA: Harvard University Press, 1965.

does not justify the initial investment. This is all the more so if one factors the competitive element between these firms into the calculation, who each have an incentive to get as much out of this collective lobbying with as small an investment as possible.

There is a wealth of insights from the collective action literature that may help us to explains some of the post-Soviet cases. Olson has also suggested a number of variables that may make the collective action problems connected with lobbying more tractable: 1) if the lobbies are smaller (cf. the Gazprom example); 2) if the actors are more geographically concentrated (e.g. a geographically concentrated industry, which diminishes the costs of organisation); 3) if the members are more similar; and 4) if the members of the interest group face an external threat. The 'crude' interest battles of post-Soviet societies offer an ideal testing ground for some of these hypotheses, and a number of papers in these volumes offer some important pieces of empirical information about these questions.

### *6.2.2 Rent-seeking*

Another part of the public choice literature takes this mode of analysis a step further and asks what the consequences of this endogenous model of political competition are for society as a whole[95]. This is where the debate returns to the idea of economic efficiency: it is one thing to describe actual policy-making in the post-Soviet states as the politically efficient result of a crude battle between different pressure groups, but this does not solve the question about possible welfare losses that occur in this process. The basic idea is once again a very simple one: in this entire process of rent-seeking[96] by the interest groups, a number of expenditures are involved that are socially wasteful: 1) the actual lobbying expenditures from the interest group; 2) the efforts of the bureaucrats to obtain or react to those expenditures; and 3) the economic distortions that rent-seeking typically create[97]. The actual social costs of

**95** For an overview of the main themes from the rent-seeking literature, see Mueller, Dennis C. *Public Choice II.* Cambridge : Cambridge University Press, 1989: 229-246.

**96** The concept was introduced in Krueger, Anne O. "The Political Economy of the Rent-Seeking Society." *American Economic Review* 64 (1974): 291-303, and refers to the fact that the actual result of this lobbying typically accrue only to the rent-seeker (typically through a transfer of income from another group), while the consumer typically loses in the process (though higher prices or other direct or indirect consequences of the rent-seeking).

**97** Buchanan, James M., Robert D. Tollison, and Gordon Tullock. *Toward a Theory of the Rent-Seeking Society.* College Station, Texas: A&M University Press, 1980: 12-14.

this rent-seeking behaviour are extremely difficult to quantify, but some authors have estimated it may in certain cases amount to 40% of a country's GNP[98].

If it is the case that the situation in most post-Soviet societies is somewhat distinct because of the fairly direct patterns of lobbying in what remains an essentially very weak institutional framework, then these societies might provide interesting case studies to explore some of the unresolved issues in the rent-seeking debate.

## 7 Conclusion

This book is not about political science. It is an attempt to present some new analytical perspectives on the post-Soviet policy space, and to inject the policy debates about that area of the world with some more realism. We increasingly felt that many of the current policy debates in the West on the post-Soviet area misrepresent some of the key developments that are taking place there. As was pointed out in the introduction, our main ambition with these papers is to encourage policy-makers and analysts to think about these post-Soviet states with different categories.

We are somewhat surprised by the fact that many of the scholars (undoubtedly inspired by the new institutionalism) seem to be focusing most of their attention on the institutional aspect of the transformations in those societies: on emerging party-systems, electoral systems, the rule of law, property rights, etc. Although we do not wish to dispute the importance of institutions, it seems to us that there are certain units of analysis that ontologically precede these institutions, and that therefore probably deserve analytical primacy. As Joel Migdal has pointed out: "The major struggles in many societies, especially those with fairly new states, are struggles over who has the right and ability to make the countless rules that guide people's social behaviour"[99]. Those are precisely the type of struggles we are witnessing in the post-

**98** In India, Mohammad and Whalley estimate it at 25-40%; Ross finds for Kenya that it might amount to 38% of GNP. Both cited in Magee, Stephen P., William A. Brock, and Leslie Young. *Black Hole Tariffs and Endogenous Policy Theory. Political Economy in General Equilibrium.* Cambridge: Cambridge University Press, 1989: 217. It has even been shown theoretically that under certain conditions, special interest political activity may absorb the entire economy (which Magee, Brock and Young call the 'black hole effect'). See Magee, Stephen P., William A. Brock, and Leslie Young. *Black Hole Tariffs and Endogenous Policy Theory. Political Economy in General Equilibrium.* Cambridge: Cambridge University Press, 1989: 215-226.

**99** Migdal, Joel S. "Strong States, Weak States: Power and Accommodation." In *Understanding Political Development: An Analytic Study.* Myron Weiner, and Samuel P. Huntington (ed.). Boston: Little, Brown, 1987: 397.

Soviet states, and it seems to us that any analysis of these societies that takes these necessarily unstable institutions as the central level of analysis is bound to be misleading, especially with respect to policy prescriptions. As Robert Bates put it:

> Political institutions in the developing world tend to be more fragile: They are less constraining and more frequently changed. The analyses that have so powerfully illustrated the way institutions aggregate the preferences of individuals into collective outcomes in democratic societies therefore offer little assistance to those attempting to develop a theory of governmental behaviour relevant to developing societies[100].

Ultimately, institutions are made by political actors, and therefore we feel our analytical energy is better spent by focusing it on these actors: who they are, what their interests are, and how they are behaving. We are confident that by systematically introducing some of the most politically salient 'slices' of the current post-Soviet polities, we will be able to demonstrate that most of the current neo-realist categories no longer adequately cover what is actually happening in that part of the world. The main intention of this particular contribution was to show that social scientists have developed a number of concepts, theories and methodologies that, while at first sight maybe totally unrelated, may help us to make sense of the different pieces of information about the post-Soviet space that will be presented in the subsequent chapters of these volumes.

An exhaustive overview of the vast literature on endogenous policy formation was beyond the scope of this brief overview. The main points to be made, however, were that 1) the analysis of particular alignments of economic and political interests with their direct and indirect consequences for the foreign policies of those states (and thus for international relations) is something many of today's foreign policy analysts will have to start paying more attention to; and 2) that there are a number of literatures in social science that can usefully be transposed to the analysis of these post-Soviet cases. When exposed to some of the literature from the new political economy, most foreign policy analysts will probably be awed by the impressive combination of the analytical power of micro-economic reasoning with an increasingly sophisticated grasp of the intricate political dynamics this literature displays. At the same time, they will also be struck by the familiarity they will experience in reading the depiction of the actual political machinations behind these abstract models of economic-political markets. The rapid expansion of pressure groups and of professional lobbyists in virtually all countries of the world, even in

---

**100** Bates, Robert H. "Macropolitical Economy in the Field of Development." In *Perspectives on Positive Political Economy*, James E. Alt, and Kenneth A. Shepsle (ed.). Cambridge: Cambridge University Press, 1990: 46.

the area of foreign policy, is obvious for everyone to see. Everybody knows that statesmen typically take a number of influential businessmen on official foreign visits. The press abounds with divulgations about various scandals in which direct links between the highest policy makers and various branches of industry are exposed. And yet, most foreign policy analysts continue to describe the realm of international relations as a 'pure' one, in which diplomats and civil servants serve as detached guardians of the national interest.

It is high time that we readjust our categorical compasses to the actual realities of today's post-Soviet space. We hope that the empirical and methodological material presented in these volumes will assist in that endeavour.

# 3

# USSR: Deconstruction of the Text
# (At the Occasion of the 77th Anniversary of Soviet Discourse)

Sergei Medvedev

## 1 Introduction

It is not widely known that in 1925 an Extraordinary Large Scale Cartography Commission (CheKOKUM) was created under the auspices of the Council of Peoples' Deputies headed by I.S. Unshlicht, who was the Deputy Chairman of the Revolutionary War Council at that time. The commission was assigned to prepare a special edition of the map of the Soviet Union for the tenth anniversary of the October Revolution. At first, it was suggested to use the one-*verst* scale map of the tsarist General Staff but in the course of their work the cartographers, full of revolutionary zeal, decided to use a larger scale: the first state of workers and peasants deserved to have the most precise map in the world. However, the completion dates were put off because the task appeared to be extremely difficult.

In the 1930s thousands of cartographers were involved in the work of the commission which was supervised by OGPU/NKVD in an atmosphere of top secrecy. In 1932 Sergei Kirov became the head of the commission but in 1934 he was replaced by Ordzhonikidze who in turn was succeeded by Lazar Kaganovich in 1937. Unknown *udarniks* [advanced workers] of the first five-year plan periods, *stakhanovets*-cartographers were constantly enlarging the scale of the map. The work went on even during World War II, when the commission was evacuated into the town of Kamyshlov in the Urals. At the final stage of work all the printing capacities of the country were involved and the map was completed in late 1949 to be presented on Joseph Stalin's seventieth birthday. It was a 1:1 scale map in light-pink. It was unrolled at night on 21 December 1949 by Internal Ministry soldiers. The further story of the map becomes vague and has to be unravelled from numerous and often speculative sources. Thus, Borges[1](following Josiah Royce[2]) suggests that due to certain natural reasons and negligence of the keepers, the map gradually deteriorated and that today only fading fragments of it can be seen in distant parts of the state (in the Sayan mountains and in the Kizil-Kum desert, in particular). Jean Baudrillard[3] believes, on the contrary, that the map, which was made of light, firm plastic has survived but that it was the country that deteriorated and began to decay. The 'gigantic map' exists and underneath it, the remnants of the state keep decaying like the body of a fossilised creature. „It is pieces of reality," writes Baudrillard in his refined style „and not the map, which are scattered here, there and everywhere in the deserts which belong not to the Empire, but to ourselves. This is the desert of our own reality".

According to Baudrillard, a sign (the map) appears, in the end, to be more solid and durable than its referent (the country). Consequently, the map becomes the only reality ('hyper-reality', as he labels it), the world of mysterious lines and symbols which exist completely on their own, which combine and intertwine at random. He calls this whimsical play of the emancipated signs a 'symbolic exchange'.

This is how it was. So some names and dates in the story may be wrong, the whole story of the map and the land, of the sign and its referent, of text and life may be only a fantasy, yet it nevertheless correlates with our reality. There is something sad in it, like a song of a coachman, something endless, like the road in the steppe. „It is what I see that I sing", or, perhaps, „it is what I sing that I see".

One thing in this story is irrefutable: Russia is doomed to text, to the power of signs. Orientation of the national cultural tradition to the word turns the words into something spellbinding. Russia has always been tempted to accept the idea of text, of sign, of illusion. Potemkin villages[4] were examples of a specific Russian text, a system of signs without referents. Another example is 'great Russian literature' which used to perform most of the social and political functions, substituting the institutions which did not exist.

The situation of today has not significantly changed. Soviet (as well as contemporary Russian) culture has been developing under the totalitarian dictatorship of literature. Thus, Mikhail Yampolskii, an analyst of modern Russian

---

**1** Borges, Jorge Luis. *Otras inquisiciones*. Buenos Aires: Emece Editores, 1964, c1960.

**2** Royce, Josiah. *The World and the Individual*. New York: Macmillan, 1901

**3** Baudrillard, Jean. *Simulacres et simulation*. Paris: Galilée, 1981.

**4** False wooden villages constructed along the river banks by Grigoryi Potemkin (1739-91), a Russian marshall and a favourite of Tsarina Catherine II, in order to make her believe, as she travelled in the Ukraine, that the countryside was rich and flourishing – translator's note.

cinema, writes that cinema art is 'literature-centred', non-visual and tends to total verbalisation[5].

In this connection it is possible to talk about a specific 'verbal vision[6]' focused not on *objects* but over them and through them on some *speculative entities* which exist exclusively in speech, in words. This vision does not require corporeality, it does not register objects, but classifies them according to specific verbal structures of the mind. Looking, for instance, at the typical Russian landscape, we do not impartially say 'cloud', 'lakes', or 'silo', but we shift at once to abstract levels and become overwhelmed by feelings of melancholy: 'pale spaces' (Akhmatova), 'native land beloved forever' (Matusovskii), Russia..."Broad are my native lands" (a quote from a popular Soviet song of the 1930s). All of these are not geographical facts but political declarations. Alexandr Tvardovskii, while writing his poem *Distance after Distance* on board a trans-Siberian train, was not referring to the distant landscape which he could see through the window, but to ideological scenery: 'landmark after landmark', 'winds of the century', etc.

'Landmarks' deserve special discussion. The semiotics of the national tradition are implemented by a number of specific symbols which include, among others, 'landmarks', milestones (or frontier posts). Those are symbols of the broad and mighty Russian Empire, symbols of coachmen, high roads, the Vladimirka route, the 'Enthusiasts' highway' running across the country from Moscow to Magadan. Posts that are put vertically are signs of a testament, of the high sanction. Posts that are positioned horizontally turn into striped turnpikes, into symbols of earthly power. It was not creation of the empire that was followed by the map and milestones, it was the empire that was doomed to have milestones, and the map[7].

The Russian Empire was the consequence and a hostage of its geography, but not in the geopolitical sense. Ivan Ilin writes about the three burdens of Russia: the burden of the land, of scattered space; the burden of nature – an ocean of land far

5 „...suppression of the multidimensional soundtrack, acoustics of the film goes together with accentuating of the remarks of characters, singling out of the dialogues in the process of mixing after the film has been shot, i.e., together with accentuating of verbal and literary levels" (M. Yampolskii. 'Kino bez kino' [Cinema without Cinema]. *Iskusstvo kino* 1988, no. 6: 90).

6 Ryklin, Michail. *Terrorologiki* [Terrorologics]. Tartu – Moscow, 1992: 17.

7 The symbol of the mile-stone has survived in the Soviet and post-Soviet times: compare it with poetics of the kilometre posts along the Baikal-Amur railway (BAM) indicating the distance from the central post-office in Moscow, or with recent installing and consecrating (!) of the famous frontier post near the town of Narva-Ivangorod on the border with 'Chukhnya' (a

removed from the open sea, a 'broad mirror-like mountainless surface'; and the burden of the people in the sense of ethnic, national and religious diversity.[8] The boundless, insuperable and heterogeneous nature of this space lent itself not to practical (highly impractical, in fact) but rather to symbolic assimilation. Growth of Russia was not an act of economical, strategic or metaphysical necessity – it was a spatial and symbolic act, a semiotic act.

In this context the crisis of representation has been embedded into the semiotics of the Russian Empire. A taste of cardboard has remained from the Potemkin villages as if from the scenery of V. Nabokov's *Invitation to Execution.* But to what extent are signs like 'Russia' and 'empire' representative?[9] Do they represent a feasible political, economic and ethnic reality at all, or do they simulate it, serving, in fact, as functions of other signs, as words that have to be written down in the blank spaces on the map? 'Russian Empire', 'Russian state'... Was Russia an empire at all, was that crazy conglomeration of space and semiotics at all Russian? Labels automatically stick to each other: great-and-mighty-Russian-language, great-and-mighty-Soviet-Union, and as a result of this enchantment these words become self-supplementary: 'Russian' means 'empire', 'state' means 'Russian', 'Soviet' means 'champagne'[10].

In other words, non-referential semiotics, principles of symbolic exchange ('orthodoxy-autocracy-national character') and of simulation had been typical for Russian semiotic space from the very start. Thus, preconditions for the new linguistic mentality of society were formed, a society that was based not on the rational referentiality, but on the constantly increasing role of symbols and codes.

---

highly derogatory Russian nick-name applied to most of the 'northern neighbours' like Baltic states and Finland – translator`s note).

**8** Ilyin, I.A. *O Rossii. Tri rechi, 1926 –1933* [On Russia. Three speeches, 1926 – 1933]. Sofia, 1934: 12-13.

**9** The principle of representation means that a sign is equivalent to reality and is exchangeable with it as freely convertible sign. Saussure`s classical theory of signification is based on a similar concept: the indivisibility of the signifying and the signified which cannot be separated as two sides of a sheet of paper (See: de Saussure, Ferdinand. *Trudy po yazikoznaniyu* [Works in linguistics]. Moscow, 1977: 145). Saussure distinguishes also between the functional and structural aspects of the language – similarly to money, each sign has its consumer value (i.e., it can be exchanged for some real referent) and the exchange value (i.e., it can be exchanged for other signs). Post-structuralists deny the consumer value of signs, their representativeness, reference, correlation with reality. They only recognize their exchange value. The sign becomes free to be used for the purposes of symbolic exchange, simulation, structural and combinatoric games.

**10** A reference to a well-known brand of Soviet champagne that was called 'Sovetskoe Shampanskoe', or Soviet champage

The resistance of the cultural organism was minimal. Any more or less coherent discourse (especially one that pretended to be integral) had a chance to enjoy success and power, which can be proved by the history of ideological movements in Russia in the late 19th and early 20th centuries.

## 2 The 1920s: Deconstruction of Reality

Language is power. Or, to be more precise, power is inherent in language, though not explicitly. „Power inherent in language is invisible, because the fact that any language classifies and that classification is tyranny escapes our notice[11].„ However, if political will is there, language becomes a discourse of power.

The political role of language in Western society was investigated by Roland Barthes. Thus, by the end of the 17th century abstract language norms (taken from the language of the court-room, religious and secular eloquence, Court etiquette) which were far from being commonly used, were in an authoritarian way proclaimed to be common. This was a purely political act. In the rhetorically complete system of language a figure of the correct language speaker appears which becomes political truth. „Political authoritarianism, the dogmatic power of the mind and the unity of the classic language – these are three manifestations of one and the same historical force“[12]. Thus, local language comes to be used as a means of political domination, becomes a discourse of power.

Similar things happened in revolutionary Russia. The political significance of language grew manifold, generating new dogmas of speech. From a semiotic point of view, the Russian revolution was nothing else but the injection (or imposition) of some esoteric, self-sufficient language into an amorphous, poorly structured space. This space was partially prepared for simulation, having been marked by the landmarks of meaningless signs. In this way, favourable conditions had been created for the discourse of power – the foundation for the supremacy of the Soviet discourse was laid.

The establishment of the discourse of power (Soviet 'newspeak') has been recorded in many fictional books during the decades that followed. In these texts, a painful substitution of language took place along with a search for new magic formulas, for signs that allow the joining of power structures. Words lost their

---

**11** Barthes, R. *Leçon: Leçon inaugurale de la chaire de la sémiologie littéraire au Collège de France prononcée le 7 janvier 1977*. Paris: Editions du Seuil, 1978: 12.

conventional meanings, became marks of social affiliation (virtually, of membership in the party of power). The characters of Remizov (*Stirred up Rus'*), Artem Veselyi, Zoshchenko, Andrei Platonov, Babel, Pilnyak did not give names to things but rather tried to determine their own status in relation to them and to power. In Platonov's *Chevengur*, Chepurnyi, chairman of the Revolutionary Committee, has only a vague, dumb 'revolutionary feeling', while his secretary Prokofii Dvanov knows 'how to formulate' and this knowledge allows him and him alone to get hold of the levers of power.

A general passion for abbreviations also contributes to the loss of the representative function of signs as they are sacrificed in the name of the aims of power. This is not a game but rather a conscious desire to hide reality under clumsy, vague and disharmonious abbreviations like TseKuBu, VUFKU, VKhYTEIN. The more unclear they are, the closer to power they stand. Knowing abbreviations is a sign of literacy in general (and literate people have always been well-respected in Russia) and of political literacy in particular.

It is worth mentioning that 'USSR' as an abbreviation suffered the same 'non-referential' fate. The stupefying magic of abbreviation was increased by the power of alliteration: the mystic triple 'S'.[13] As a result of mechanical repetition no one bothers to remember what meaning lies behind these 'S's: a symbolic exchange is going on, not even between the words 'Soyuz' (Union), 'Soviet' and 'Socialism', but between these three 'S'-s which have completely lost their representative referents.[14]

The victorious march of Soviet power across Russia affected, first of all, the language, which became *newspeak* for the non-Russian speaking nations (including those of Eastern Europe in the 1940s). From a means of communication, language was turned into a political instrument. Knowledge of Russian became a mark of status, a password into the system, even a consumer value (language becomes exchangeable for a certain status, for another abstract systematic sign).

The establishment of the Soviet discourse affected all levels of the language, including 'substandard' levels. Even taboo words started to acquire new status in

---

**12** Barthes, R. *Nulevaya stepen' pis'ma* [Writing Degree Zero]. Moscow: Semiotika, 1983: 335.

**13** Triple in Russian, double in English – translator's note.

**14** Impersonality and interchangeability of these 's'-s is proved by the experiment of the author in the middle of the 1980-s: when asked to decipher the abbreviation CSSR (the Czecho-Slovak Socialist Republic – translator`s note ) most of the people answered: Czechoslovak Soviet Socialist Republic.

Soviet times. In Russian tradition, taboo words are mainly used not in their direct normative meaning but either in metaphoric constructions (e.g., „I was screwed by the Party Committee yesterday“[15]) or as having the emotive function of interjections and intensifiers. In other words, referentiality of taboo words becomes reduced, they tend to lose their semantic value and turn into meaningless signs of Soviet discourse. Symbolic exchange of the ideological discourse is reflected in symbolic exchange of the taboo discourse (e.g., senseless 'three-storied' obscenities[16] resembled ideological juggling in official speeches). We may even speak about the functional status of taboo words as an unwritten, obscene practical language of Soviet power.[17] Moreover, in Soviet times obscenities became passwords into the system along with ideological stereotypes. Rising to the top of the *Komsomol* hierarchy, for instance, demanded drinking and swearing skills. Obscenities became a good form of behaviour in the Party, *Komsomol* and especially in army circles, being perceived as a sign of friendliness, of national character. Obscenities were, perhaps, incorporated into the discourse of power.

Thus, emergence of the USSR text occurred as a suppression of reality (which appeared to be pliable) by the use of signs. Before long the first instances of purely symbolic exchange, of a 'short circuit' in the new text started to appear. It is not such a long way from Lenin's brilliant tautology „it is all-mighty because it is true“[18] and from the semiotic equation of his followers „communism = *soviets* + electricity“ to Mayakovskii's classical symbolic exchange: „When we say Lenin we imply the Party, when we say the Party – we imply Lenin“. Implication becomes the most important art, a state virtue which contributes to the constant expansion of the sacral text and to driving profane (real) texts out of existence.

As a matter of fact, power performs classical 'deconstruction' as it is described by Jacques Derrida. The label itself was suggested by Derrida when he tried to translate Heidegger's 'Destruktion' and Freud's 'Abbau' into French. The content of the notion is close to Husserl's *epoch*, to phenomenological reduction, the procedure of 'bracketing' empirical connections and the whole of the philosophical apparatus

---

**15** Compare the anecdote in which American learners of Russian are looking for the proper position in the sentence for the 'indefinite article' 'blya' ('Blya', a shortened variant of the taboo word 'blyad', literally means 'a whore'. It is somewhat identical to the English 'bloody' of 'fuck' that are used figuratively, as speech gap-fillers by certain people – translator's note).

**16** Obscenities insulting the addressee's mother, grandmother and other relatives – translator's note.

**17** S.Zenkin's review of the quoted book by M.Ryklin in *Novoe Literaturnoe Obozrenie*. Moscow (1994), no. 7: 342.

**18** Marxist teaching – translator's note.

(subject, individual, structure, observation instrument), i.e., all those elements which pretend to precede language as discourse. Deployment of the self-sufficient discourse of power in the USSR, total expansion of the symbolic sphere, was inevitably 'bracketing' all profane codes, making them marginal. As a result of deconstruction everything which was external to the text, all non-discourse preconditions of language (the term was suggested by Deleuze and Guattari)[19] was driven out of life. In retrospect, Soviet power could have written on its banners the maxim of Derrida: „There exists nothing beyond text".

That was because everything became text. The USSR as a form of social, state, economic and cultural organisation turned into a space of total textuality. Here we may speak of a peculiar semiotic determinism. It was not we who grew up from some correct texts, it was these texts through which we have grown, writes Mikhail Ryklin.[20]

Thus, reality becomes thin and gradually decays. Gaps that appear in it are mended with speech, by collective chaining of utterances. Collectivisation of speech occurred at the lower levels of Russian culture much earlier than the collectivisation of agriculture[21]. A close social environment completely determines the structure of parlance from the inside; collective words know no solitude, they are aimed at interlocutors, they are contextual, expropriated from speakers. It is significant, that 'Bakhtin's circle' started an investigation into the problem of collective objects of speech in the 1920s. Special attention was paid to collective chaining of utterances[22] and it was suggested as a thesis that the mind determines the word in an illusory way being, in fact, a function of the collective communicative body. Chains of utterance like „I realise because the other one realises, the third one, the fourth one, etc..." or „I speak because the other one speaks, the third one, the fourth one, etc..." may be endlessly continued without bringing any foundation into the world which has become hyper-realistic. Only an infinitely expanding communicative body possesses self-consciousness, reflection and speech[23], while reality itself dissolves into forms of communication, into expressive chaining of acts of parlance. Thus, in the speech

---

**19** Deleuze, Gilles et Felix Guattari. *Capitalisme et schizophrénie. L'Anti-Œdipe*. Paris: Editions de Minuit, 1980: 98.

**20** Ryklin: 59.

**21** By utterances and not by sentences, by speech acts not by language acts, according to Bakhtin.

**22** Ryklin: 200.

**23** See: Voloshinov, V.N. *Marksizm i filisofiya yazyka* [Marxism and the Philosophy of Language]. Leningrad, 1929: 20-21.

of the post-revolutionary decade a new, collective subject, a new social entity, a new collective body is born (reaching its acme in the period of mature Stalinism). In the traditional understanding, such a collective body may be called subjectless (because, in the end, a collective de-individualised subject is an oxymoron), related to later phenomena of subjectlessness and non-reflectiveness of the late Soviet (*perestroika*) and post-Soviet periods.

## 3 The 1930s-1950s: Elimination of Reality

The formation of the collective body at the turn of the 1920s and 1930s marks the breakthrough in the semiotic history of the USSR. If deconstruction still presupposes the existence of reality and only brackets it (i.e., reality is unwanted but it is admitted, implied), then now reality is simply cancelled, washed out by the wave of Soviet discourse[24]. This change in the semiotic paradigm was marked by the transition from the 'red terror' and the terror of the 1920s to the *great terror* of the 1930s. Post-October terror (not in its narrowly applied *CheKa* sense but as a discourse of violence, a discourse in general terms) remained partially referential and rested on certain principles, had certain limits. However, in the 1930s this terror suffered a disaster of a natural, cosmic terror: no principles, no subjects, no grounds at all. From now on terror needed no explanation, it just naturally arose from the Soviet discourse in the process of symbolic exchange[25].

There is an anecdote: a guard talking to one of the prisoners of the labour camps asks him what he was imprisoned for. The answer is: „For nothing". –"You are lying to me, you swine", replies the guard, – „For nothing they give you ten years here, but you've got 15!" This „for nothing" is a mutual recognition of a reality that does not exist: not only the reality of crime, but reality in general[26]. Another episode: an interrogation at the Lubyanka prison in Moscow. The roles of the interrogator and of the accused are, in principle, identical: one writes, the other signs – both of them are exchanging meaningless symbols. In this atmosphere of clear, genuine semiotics

---

**24** Ryklin: 22.

**25** Speaking about the 'Soviet discourse' we refer rather to the post-structuralist understanding of discourse as 'chaining of structures of meaning which have their own rules of combination and transformation' (Coquet, Jean-Claude. *Sémiotique littéraire: contribution à l'analyse sémantique du discours*. Tours: Mame, 1973: 27-28). More traditional understanding of discourse as 'speech plunged into life' is hardly applicable to the USSR where speech incorporates life, where the opposition of speech and life does not exist and 'the Soviet discourse' turns into a pleonasm: 'Soviet means the best' or 'Soviet means discourse'.

**26** Ryklin: 204-205.

many political frame-ups were born, such as the Shakhtinsk, Leningrad and Promparty trials or the accusations of 'digging a tunnel from Bombay to London', etc.

Proceeding from the idea of 'applied terror' (in the sense of 'unjustified repressions', as if repressions may be 'justified' at all!) we observe similar models that are being reproduced up to the present day in other episodes of Soviet life. Take, for instance, the examination of a patient by a doctor. The Soviet discourse implies that 'to treat a patient' does not necessarily mean to treat him physically, but first of all it means to have correct records and reports. The physical examination of a patient is a result of this need to have reports and not the other way round; many diseases exist without being recorded on paper because according to the local norms of medical rationality they are considered to be non-existent[27]. Here we observe the same kind of terror as in the example with the interrogator (both the interrogator and the doctor are writing): the terror of signs, the terror of text.

The same is true for the barber's activity (the barber cuts the client's hair being guided not by fashion or functionalism but by the norms of social appropriateness – he marks the client's hair with social status symbols, i.e., the haircut becomes the product of semiotic activity), for the dressmaker's activity or for the process of buying ready made clothes. Mandelstamm's 'man of the Moskoshvey era[28] is a character without features, a human sign, a person marked like a fruit-fly in a glass box. Signs make it possible to 'short-circuit' people, or to keep people within the framework of normative views of what people should be like. They make it possible 'to shut people up into speech'[29].

This 'shutting up into speech' means that people themselves (the masses, the collective body) become main objects of representation . Soviet terror, as well as Soviet art, appeal to the people, to the collective body, i.e., to the impossible, to a referent that does not exist, because 'masses' is an abstract notion, impossible to represent. Symbols and images of Soviet terror and art are related not to individuals and even not to clusters (gatherings) of individuals, but to signs with no meaning whatsoever. Such is the case with the sculptures and panels at the VDNKh ('Exhibition of Achievements in the National Economy' in Moscow) or in the stations of the Moscow metro. They reflect imaginary (unthinkable in reality) masses, hypothetical bodies. One of the most triumphant and unreal pictures is a

---

**27** Ibid.: 60.

**28** *Moskoshvei* – abbreviation for 'Moscow Textile Factory – translator's note.

**29** Ibid.: 18.

mosaic at the *Kievskaya* circle line metro station depicting public merry-making. Here one can see Lenin and Bogdan Khmelnitskii, transformed faces of various ages, national costumes, musical instruments, flowers, fruit. The triumphant effect is achieved by completely depersonifying the bodies that have risen above reality by overcoming it. Such are the faces of Soviet people on the photos of the 1930s and 1940s: so retouched that they look absolutely sleek as though they had been transfigured by some infinite feeling buried in them[30] Living – in as far as they appear to be living – people do not differ from the cardboard characters of civil-defence posters and safety requirements. These faces look at us from the 'boards of honour', it is them that the character of „Moscow-Petushki" (poem by Viktor Erofeev) sees in the electric train:

„People looked at me indifferently with round eyes as if not focused on anything... I like it. I like the eyes of my people – so empty and bulging. They are constantly bulging but there is no tension in them. A complete lack of any sense – but what an amount of might! (What spiritual might!). These eyes will not sell you out. They will neither sell, nor buy anything. Whatever may happen to my country, in days of doubt and in the days of gloomy reflection, in days of ordeals and hardships – such eyes will never blink. Everything is heavenly dew to them..."[31].

The problem of faces with lost personality, subjectless collective bodies that correlate only with themselves and exchange meaning among themselves was later on re-interpreted by Grigorii Bruskin in his *Fundamental lexicon* which has become one of the classical pieces of socialist art[32].

The examples offered above are attempts to depict (or rather to comprehend) a collective body. However, the masses (and especially nomadic masses of the 'Soviet people' kind) can, as a matter of principle, not be reduced to a visual image (their stasis), cannot be photographed. A collective body is created and exists only in speech, in the collective chaining of utterances. It is being reproduced in speech acts that serve as cells, codes, matrixes and can be correspondingly characterised, first of all, through speech. So what was the new speech, that established itself in the 1930s and 1950s, like?

First of all, this speech was *anonymous* as a principle, which is reflected in the sacramental impersonal phrase „there is a point of view". This is not the 'death of the author' mentioned by Barthes in connection with Balzac's texts (the death from

---

**30** Ibid.: 42, 85.

**31** Yerofeev, Venedikt. *Moskva-Petushki*. Moscow: Prometei, 1989: 26-27.

**32** Compare with 'Doska pocheta' (The board of honour) by A. Petrov.

excessive strain caused by writing).[33] Here we have something else: the dissolution of the author in the total text of collective social life, the cancellation of the very concept of authorship because such texts presuppose that an individual author cannot be born at all. We do not have a palimpsest here, but a desert ('a desert of reality' according to Borges and Baudrillard); not an erasing of the author from the parchment but a total textuality resulting in text, in a piece of literature, in anonymity and authorship at the same time. „Textuality within the framework of collective identity knows neither temptation of the subject, nor temptation of its erasing"[34] This totally anonymous speech resulted in the specific canon of Soviet literature and art, decisively, however prematurely, proclaimed by Mayakovskii.[35] According to this canon a writer (painter, composer) does not create the text (because the authorship right has been long ago indisputably appropriated by the collective body) but looks for social justifications of the text that has already appeared. Writing skills are confined to the art of stenography. For Mayakovskii a poet is only an 'apprentice' to the masses – 'creators of common language'.

Secondly, this speech is *forced.* It is in this period that something which Barthes called the 'fascist nature of language' became evident. Language is neither reactionary, nor progressive, it is simply fascist, not by prohibiting people to speak but by forcing people to speak"[36]

The authoritarian discourse of power becomes reflected in forced speech acts. Denunciation becomes one of the superior speech practices – it is a concentrated speech-act that has grown into a symbol, into a ritual. In the aesthetics of denunciation we see the triumph of speech 'fascism', subjectlessness and specific Soviet reflection (anti-reflection in practice). Even signed reports remain anonymous – they have been written not by a definite person but by the collective body. The same applies to anonymous letters – the problem is not in the fear of disclosure but in the inability to single out the author's individuality in the flow of speech of which denunciation is one of the forms. And finally, the culmination of subjectless, 'fascist' speech is the act of self-denunciation which is a sacrifice to the collective body and to the text, a sacrifice made in ecstasy. It is a ritual sacrifice, similar to prehistoric tribal and sectarian sacrifices.

---

**33** Barthes, R. *Izbrannye raboty. Semiotika. Poetika* [Selected works. Semiotics. Poetics]. Moscow, 1994: 384-391.

**34** Ryklin: 78.

**35** Perhaps, desire to kill the author in himself became the cause of a personal tragedy for the poet.

**36** Barthes, R. *Leçon*: 14.

The absence of individual authorship and the forced nature of speech inevitably lead to *total authorship*, to the 'creative function' of the collective body, to the 'masses as creators of language'. The text of the USSR (discourse of terror), closed and endogenous, generated itself, was a creator or demiurge acting in the name of symbolic effectiveness (semiurgy). Stalin's terror was a 'quasi-artistic act', pathetic to its very end. While ordinary art only imitates the demiurge pathetically, extreme forms of violence are 'demiurgical' by themselves.[37] Aesthetics drawn out of the USSR through the backdoor (generally speaking, art was impossible in the USSR as a non-discourse form) returned through the bathroom window in the shape of overwhelming, total art.

A totally aesthetic (if aesthetics is understood not as a science of beauty but as something wider) text of the USSR can be interpreted by using Bakhtin's concept of total speech authorship. Bakhtin believed that every speaker is a creator and thus eliminated the borderline between text and speech, aesthetic and non-aesthetic entities[38]. On the other hand, the text of the USSR may be interpreted in the formal terms of that time, within the scope of the OPOYAZ[39] theories as follows: the form of the USSR becomes its only content, the USSR becomes a space of plain form. There exists nothing outside the text and outside the act of art; in the semiotic space of the USSR all acts become aesthetic in principle[40]. Paraphrasing Florenskii's words, the Soviet spectacle becomes a synthesis of arts.

Indeed, it is quite appropriate to compare the developed Soviet discourse of the 1930s and 1950s with a continuous liturgy. The text sounds like an on-going liturgy, as if people constantly serve a mass to righteousness and infallibility. In this sacred atmosphere, where bread and water turn to flesh and blood, signs become absolute values and exist only to perform their divine function of servicing.

This totalitarian liturgy of the Soviet newspeak inherited, in a sense, traditions of the Orthodox divine service in the Church Slavonic language – the language of the church discourse of power. Unlike Latin, which became the language of church after having become the language of culture, the Church Slavonic language was born and

---

**37** Ryklin: 17.

**38** Compare also with the ideas of Eugene Cosserieu who claimed that it is the poetic language (and the Soviet discourse is in principle poetic) that follows the norm.

**39** 'Obshchestvo Izucheniya Russkogo Yazyka' – 'Society for the Study of the Russian Language' – Russian school of literary science in 1910-1920 – translator's note.

**40** Ryklin: 34-35.

started to be used solely as the language of liturgy[41]. Communication is practically impossible in Church Slavonic language (loss of communicative properties by a sign is one of the first indications of simulation), this is the language of truth and revelation, the language of power[42]. In the total Soviet liturgy specific divine service language is also used, language that can hardly be used for communication (total speech intercourse is not yet communication), the language not of referential signs but that of codes (similar to traffic lights), the language of truth which does not admit any interpretations.

Turning form into fetish, the totally aesthetic approach to reality becomes the defining feature of the Soviet existence inherited by modern Russia from the USSR. 'Stalinist liturgy' was a predecessor of the 'all-embracing VDNKh', of 'developed socialism' and contemporary Russian 'society of a spectacle'. Entire textuality (aesthetic, liturgical nature) as the form of society in ecstasy means that there is nothing outside speech, outside the collective body. In the 1930s-1950s the reality which had in the beginning been pushed out or 'bracketed' was now abolished in the authoritarian way. The triumph of the collective body meant emergence of self-sufficient people, self-sufficient terror and self-sufficient text. These years became the period of the establishment of the Socialist canon when real Socialism turned to be radical imminence[43]. Utopia (this word according to one version was derived not from 'utopos' but from 'eutopos' – 'a blessed place') turns into atophy and it becomes possible to label the USSR text as 'atophic' in principle.

## 4 The 1960s-1980s: Simulation of Reality

In this way, signs destroyed reality and evidence for this cannot only be found in the times of the *great terror* but also in the generations that followed, which were unsteady, shaky, 'transparent' (Nabokov's term). In the late 1950s, when it was first attempted to translate ideological discourse into the language of common sense, to

---

**41** Frishman. A. 'Dvuyazychie i binarnost kultury' [Bilinguism and the binary nature of culture]. *Nezavisimaya Gazeta* 29 September 1994: 5.

**42** Boris Uspenskii in his work *Raskol i kulturnyi konflikt* [Schasm and the cultural conflict] shows that in the bilingual culture of Ancient Rus' the Church Slavonic language was perceived as means of expression of the divine Truth, i.e., as means of recording and expressing Revelation but not as means of communication. According to Uspenskiy, the Church Slavonic language was understood by the theological theory of language widely spread in Rus, as a system of symbolic representation of the Orthodox religion (i.e., as an Orthodox icon) and not as one of the possible systems of trading information.

**43** Ryklin: 16, 66.

perform the strategy of bringing it all to a common norm (at least in the periphery), it suddenly became evident that reality did not exist as such. Dim lights were turned on and people saw that they were left alone in the empty, endless space of simulation (they might have thought that perhaps it would be better to turn the light off). Thus, change of simulation paradigms happened in the late 1950s which meant transition from the signs that simulate something (it became clear in the early 1950s that such signs were not adequate for providing legitimacy: compare the 'doctors' trial' that failed) to signs hiding the fact that there exists nothing. The USSR turned from a sign abolishing reality by force into a sign that was shyly hiding the absence of reality. The 1960s and 1980s were the era of classical simulation.[44]

Jean Beaudrillard (in his usual refined manner) calls this change of paradigms the transition from 'the theology of truth and mystery' to 'simulation in which there is no God any more'[45]. By the end of the 1950s the Soviet God had died, in the sense that the sacred (sacral) nature of the discourse of power and of the whole text of the USSR had been eliminated. Its secularisation was still to come, the sphere of the sacred and of the profane still remained separated and secular codes, still stayed outside the text. However, it all resulted in the disappearance of signs of 'indulgence', 'guarantee', 'support'. The terror of signs carried on (this is a principal feature of the Soviet discourse, related only to the terror of the state), however it grew from the total into the relative. Here we find another similarity of the Soviet discourse with the history of the church – when God dies, a 'simulacrum religion' is born.

The idea of form evolves into *etiquette* in the period of developed simulation. Jewish and Chinese traditions created strict rules for all occasions in life. Thus, we read in the *Mishnah* that on Saturday night a tailor must not go out with a needle; in the Book of Rituals it is written that a guest must drink the first glass with a serious look and the second one with a respectful and happy face. Similar coding of words and gestures prevailed in the USSR text which turned into a total semiotic etiquette

**44** It's worth stressing that simulation has little to do with lies, fraud, forgery, 'double standard' and other moral defects of the 'developed socialism' that were mentioned by the critics of the Soviet system. Criteria of ethics cannot apply to simulation at all. One could say that 'human morality' is a non-discourse notion, something that exists outside the Soviet text. However, certain relative Soviet ethics used to exist. The ethics of the text. So it would be more justified to say that in the Soviet discourse ethics is the function of a special totalitarian aesthetics; that all that is 'of the text' is moral.

**45** Baudrillard, Jean. „Simulacra and Simulations." In Baudrillard, Jean, *Selected Writings.* Stanford: Stanford University Press, 1988: 170.

(in this respect the stylistics of the Soviet text may be understood as 'using proper words in proper places').

The new stylistics added the speech figure of *praeteritio* to the practice of imperative enforcement of parlance. Ellipsis started to be used not in its direct function of adding dynamics and compression to speech, but primarily for the purpose of hiding sense, eliminating reference.[46] Without information (guidelines) people act as if they were computers in the 'default' mode, i.e., according to the programme (etiquette). The problem of simulation, of praeteritio, of 'speech vision' fits well into the model of Anderson's „The Emperor's New Clothes".

„As normal" is the key word of this era. It is a symbolic word, a synonym of 'being Soviet'. When asked „How are you ?" Soviet people usually answer: „As normal". The degree of simulation in this answer is much higher than, say, in the West, where people answer „I'm fine". In both cases speakers exchange meaningless signs, however while „I'm fine" only distorts reality, „as normal" destroys the very principle of reality. Even more than that: „as normal" becomes a generally used adjective ('normal flat', 'normal job', 'normal wife', 'normal trick', etc.) which implies minimum information, almost zero power of meaning[47]. 'As normal' is a simulacrum sign hiding the absence of reality, „as normal" is equal to silence[48].

In the logic of the Soviet discourse, praeteritio goes together with exhibiting hyper-reality (or is even compensated by it ). The 1960s and 1980s were the 'era of jubilees', a time of exhibiting. Temples were turned into museums; former icons and items of public worship in the total Soviet liturgy were desacralised and transformed into exhibits at a total exhibition. Simulation went on by exhibiting a reality that did not exist; the Soviet territory 'from Moscow to the very outskirts'[49] become one massive VDNKh, a live model of reality. Or, perhaps, the VDNKh was more real than the country itself; people kept coming to see it searching for a 'gulp of reality' and then returned to their phantom existence.

For instance, in the „Poultry farming" pavilion of the VDNKh, model farms were exhibited surrounded by a pastoral landscape and called something like 'Project of

---

**46** Baudrillard intentionally equals ELLEIPSIS of a sign and ELLEIPSIS of sense.

**47** Vladimir Sorokin's book called *Norma* (The Norm), part two of which tells about the life of a Soviet man as of a sequence of several hundred nouns with the adjective 'normal': from the 'normal birth' to the 'normal death'. (Sorokin, Vladimir. *Norma* [The Norm]. Moscow: Obscuri Viri, 1994: 76-98.

**48** In Czechoslovakia after the events of 1968 this word started to be used as an official ideological label: Hussak's regime was implementing the so-called 'policy of normalization'.

**49** A line from a popular Soviet song – translator's note.

Poultry Farm No. 6 in the Kholmogoryi district of Kostroma *oblast*". In the same stand, the hypothetical products of the farm were shown – rows of tins labelled something like 'Cock-rooster in wine', or 'Duck liver mousse'. Nobody had ever seen such delicacies on sale (not even under the counter), nor delivered by special orders; these were mere 'eidolons of food' consumed by means of words[50]. The same applies to the famous Mikoyan's *Book of Delicious and Healthy Food*[51] which fed two generations of Soviet people with images and words, or to the myths about the Eliseev food stores in Moscow and Leningrad, where „under Stalin there was everything money could buy". However, the most universal example was probably the 'sausage' sign – one of the key symbols in the USSR text. Being practically unavailable to most of the population, sausage became an important value in the Soviet symbolic exchange[52] retaining its meaning to this very day (witness the 'sausage at 2.20 roubles a kilo' nostalgia in the discourse of the political opposition).

The aspiration to exhibit reality in the era of developed simulation resulted in the expansion of public spaces such as cinemas, 'cinema and concert halls' (these were novelties of this period), 'palaces of culture'. The Kremlin Palace of Congresses, *Rossiya* cinema and concert hall, *Oktyabr* and *Novorossiysk* cinemas in Moscow are 'cult buildings' of this era. The entire Soviet space became marked with such exhibition halls – through these, it was constantly ready to focus itself, to reflect itself, to turn into a party meeting, a congregation, a conference, a lecture, a film with the indispensable 'News of the day' makeweight. Simulation of the post-Soviet period continues to make use of this exhibition potential: any village 'palace of culture' may become the place where another CPSU Congress is held, and any Moscow cinema may become a political convention centre. The VDNKh itself (renamed nowadays as VVTs: 'All-Russian Exhibition Centre') continues to exhibit hyper-reality which has only slightly changed its semiotics: now there are trading centres in the pavilions and street markets in the open areas[53].

---

**50** Ryklin: 201. We can talk in this connection of the phenomenon of 'enchantment'. Thus, if you keep repeating the word 'khalva' (paste of nuts, sugar and oil, similar to the nougat – translator's note) it may become sweet in your mouth.

**51** Soviet cook-book of the 1950s – translator's note.

**52** Comp. with the 'Salami song' by Timur Kibirov: '... a symbol//wonderful and unachievable//common for everyone – it's you, oh, Sausage!' (Kibirov, Timur. *Santimenty* [Sentiments]. Belgorod: Risk, 1994: 27).

**53** The principle of exposure also influences external aspects of Soviet discourse, such as foreign policy. Essential feature of the international relation of this period is their phantom, hyper-realistic nature. Gigantic simulacra of the 'cold war', first and second stages of detente, Helsinki process and 'European home' appear. Simulation of international relations of this

Not only products that did not exist but the utopian production itself ('Poultry farm No. 6 exists only as a model) were shown at the exhibitions of developed Socialism. Starting from the first five-year plans, the total subjection of the economy to aesthetic values was leading to the destruction of production as such. The notions of five-year plans and state orders (*goszakazy*) belong not to the sphere of economics but rather to an heroic epos, to the trials and tribulations of a mythical hero. It is always necessary to 'struggle' for the completion of tasks (e.g. 'battling for the harvest'). The notion of the 'production drama' from a local artistic genre becomes an overall description of Soviet economy, i.e. production turns into a real drama, into a play that develops according to the laws of aesthetics. Hiding under the slogan of the norm, Soviet economy was in fact oriented not at average statistic growth, but at super-normative, dramatic, heroic development.

The above mentioned can be traced in the tradition of *subbotniks*[54] that was born in the 1920s and developed in the 1930s along two tracks: as the Stakhanov movement on the one hand, and as the GULag[55] on the other. Needless to say, both forms of labour organisation were far from being economically rational.

First of all, through these forms, labour became 'the cause of dignity, the cause of glory and heroism' (this Stakhanov slogan is an obligatory feature of any labour camp)[56] and production itself becomes a side effect. Simulation in such forms as Stakhanov exceeding the production norms by one hundred times eliminates the economy by turning it into a form of non-discourse. By the end of the Stalin era, production of goods was completely replaced by the production of total intercourse, i.e., by the self-reproduction of the collective body, of total speech. Effectiveness of collective bodies is the effectiveness of internal combustion, which does not result in

---

period becomes especially evident in the concept of the nuclear deterrence. It becomes more or less evident for all parties involded (especially in the 70-s and 80-s) that nuclear war is unrealistic, however politics is being build on admitting such possibility, i.e., on a purely semiotic presupposition. The notion of the 'overkill' (i.e., the ability of each party to multiply destroy the enemy) became the peak of hyper-realisation. Having such nuclear potentials is absurd from the point of view of the common sense, but it is quite justified in terms of symbolic exchange. Missiles have been assigned the role of non-referential signs, nuclear deterrence has become a war of symbols.

**54** Free labour on Saturdays– translator's note

**55** *Glavnoe Upravlenie Lagerei*, i.e., 'Chief Administration of Labour Camps', an abbreviation applied usually to the whole system of labour camps in the USSR – translator's note

**56** One cannot but compare this (in the 'early perestroika' manner) with the obligatory 'Arbeit macht frei' on the gates of the Nazi labour camps.

the product. These bodies are so intensive that they simply do not have enough strength to be productive. They are merely products of themselves.[57]

In the 1960s and 1980s production of speech with a certain selection of designators did not aim to push the real economy outside the text but to hide the fact of its absence. A widely spread system of signs was created for this purpose: institutions of *udarniks* and 'preceptors', 'watches' and 'initiatives'. Such events as 'planning production meetings', 'socialist competition' and 'labour relay-races', party and trade-union committees, DOSAAF and the Red Cross, 'patronage' and 'donorship', *subbotniks* and *voskresniks*[58]. Thus the social function of speech replaces production, leaders and workers reproduce the whole complex of social relations and only in this context do they produce anything (and even here, in most cases – nothing).

In this sense, the Soviet economy (if it ever existed at all) could be described in terms of developed simulation as a popular post-structuralist model of a *potlatch* – a feast of North American Indians and some other tribes marked by the symbolic giving and receiving of lavish gifts. Like members of the tribe who try to excel each other in the lavishness of their gifts in order to demonstrate their wealth, Soviet workers and the state kept giving gifts to each other: pseudo-labour was exchanged for social pseudo-guarantees. Wages, remuneration or equivalent exchange became unimportant. All of this was an exchange of meaningless symbols: labour was senseless and economically irrational in the same way, as, for instance, the state guarantee of the 'right to dwelling' which was not supported by anything real. Labour was neither functional, nor obligatory – it became the subject of social choice. The roles that workers played in the so-called division of labour only marked their status. Professions were signs that had value only within the framework of Soviet text and symbolic exchange, but were in no way related to the needs of production. Quotas of personnel, ratios of the number of workers and engineers were determined by social (status) reasons and not by economic ones. The 'Soviet economy' was reproduced as the sum total of signs, as a ritual, mechanically, habitually. The production process was being born in the heart of repeated symbolic actions. Economic forms of activity became side effects of the semiotic activity.

The 'administrative market'[59] also represented, in its essence, a ritual, a kind of potlatch. Participants of the bureaucratic game reproduced their status, position,

---

**57** Ryklin: 39,78.

**58** Free labour on Sundays – translator's note

**59** See the article by Kordonskii in this volume.

rights, i.e., they were also engaged in purely semiotic activities. In order to clarify, to approve or to change their status they exchanged gifts: streams of goods, resources, privileges. Economic reasons became secondary in this symbolic exchange.

At the same time, the large-scale industrial *potlatch* into which Soviet economy was turned in the 1960s-1980s differed markedly from other known forms of *potlatch* described by Marcel Moss, Georges Bataille and other authors, in that the gifts that were being squandered required immense resources. If resources for this continuous symbolic exchange were unlimited, the logic of the most expensive poverty in the world could have been formed into a system for which semi-decay would have been the norm[60] However, resources of industrial and administrative potlatch were limited. It is quite natural that there were attempts to solve the inevitable crisis of the symbolic exchange economy at the level of symbols. We mean here the *perestroika* of the late 1980s as the final stage of simulation, as an attempt to save the very principle of symbolic exchange by introducing new (market, western and other alien) designators.

According to the terms used by Deleuze and Guattari, *perestroika* was the replacement of decay by 'non-corporeal transformation', replacement of explosion by implosion, of external blow by internal shock. *Perestroika* was another semiotic manoeuvre aimed at avoiding reality. Dexterity, resourcefulness, straightforward exchange are typical features of Gorbachev's discourse both at home and abroad. It is worth remembering fantastic word combinations like 'the process started to go on' or the beloved 'philosophy' ('philosophy of the self-supporting economic basis', 'philosophy of new thinking', etc.). The irresponsibility of the *perestroika* lexicon enchanted people. The system was trying to avoid its death by simulating death. By admitting market signs, allegedly lethal to it, the system was including them into its symbolic exchange and by doing this was turning the market into hyper-reality, thus neutralising it. Turning the market into a spectacle infected the system with its symptoms, making it not suffer but constantly making it ill. The inevitable nature of reforms and mutations (if they really can be considered inevitable) was simulated as inevitable and thus was put off for some indefinite period of time[61]. The Novo-Ogarevo process and the unsuccessful Union Treaty were attempts to avoid the split-up of the country by simulating this split-up.

Infection by western and other alien designators was a form of struggling with them, was an attempt to preserve the Soviet discourse, the very text of the USSR.

---

**60** Ibid.: 90.
**61** Ibid.: 91.

However, this process could not remain without any consequences. It is one thing to pretend to be sick (put on a scarf, go to bed), but quite another to simulate the disease (i.e., to cause its symptoms). Simulants can neither be considered as sick, nor as healthy.

By simulating its own death the USSR of the *perestroika* period entered the 'world of shadows'. The gigantic pink map of one-sixth of the whole world was decaying in sight of everyone. The hyper-reality of the USSR was ready to destroy itself, dissolve, disperse ...

## 5 The 1990s: The Era of Temptation

...however, can hyper-reality ever disappear, can something that does not exist stop existing? 'The break-up of the USSR' is a very conventional label for what really happened, because the subject of this break-up did not exist. There existed a non-referential system of signs, a simulacrum, not only distorting reality but also trying to hide its own absence. When the dilapidated map was lifted up, it became evident that there was nothing underneath it: no empire, no state, not even a desert. Just nothing at all. In other words, at some moment (supposedly in December 1991), or rather at some period (1990-1991) the simulacrum revealed its 'simulative nature'. What was the reaction that followed ?

The reaction was silence. The fact of the 'collapse of the Union' itself was not discouraging, but rather the indifference of the public was. The USSR faded away in two days, at most in three. Even the *Pradva* newspaper could not be closed down as quickly as the USSR itself closed down Similarly, in 1917-1918 in an atmosphere of total frozen indifference, the 'simulative nature' of former tsarist Russia became evident[62].

In December 1991 the USSR was no more real than it was before or after. In December the emptiness was called by its name and nothing changed as a result. The secret of emptiness was disclosed but emptiness did not disappear (can it ever disappear at all?), it stayed with us. This total awareness of the secret, keeping totally silent about it, the invisible presence of emptiness mean that we are now

---

**62** 'Rus' faded away in two days, maximum in three. Even *Novoe Vremya* ('New Times' – the author means, perhaps, the name of the magazine – translator's note) could not have been closed down so quickly, as Rus' faded away. It's amazing that it all went to pieces instantly, all – including details and particulars . There was no Kindgom, no Church, no Army left. But what was left at all? Strangely enough – practically nothing. Only mean people '(Rozanov, Vasiliy. 'Apokalipsis nashego vremeni' [The Apocalypse of out Time], 1918.

entering into a specific area of simulation which was labelled by Baudrillard as 'seduction', into the forbidden zone of temptation.

Temptation is, perhaps, the highest degree of simulation, but is it the final one? Temptation is the secret of Polichinelle: „I know that you know that I know", but the very essence of temptation is in keeping this secret as a secret, or the secret of the Court of Madrid – as a secret. Temptation is the intensity of relations between people who know this secret but who keep silent about it.[63] This is conspiracy of silence.

Conspiracy is the right word. Voluntarily or involuntarily, those who used to curse or worship the USSR (in any case, all those who were 'native speakers' of the Soviet language – the only one that was available), all of us are conspirators. Today, the USSR is a conspiracy, a secret, a spell, a lure, witchcraft. Temptation is stronger than simulation: never was the USSR as strong as it is nowadays. Enchantment by the emptiness and by the lack of sense is stronger than enchantment by signs and imaginary sense:

„Being attracted by emptiness is the source of temptation; we can never be tempted simply by the accumulation of signs or by messages of desire, but only by an esoteric conspiracy of absorbing signs. It is in secrecy that temptation is conceived, in this slow or brutal refinement of sense which predetermines conspiracy of signs. Here rather than from any other physical creature or from desire, temptation is born. But at the same time, this is also what makes up the magic of the rules of game"[64]. The game. Having been implicitly aesthetic for decades, the hyper-reality of the USSR now has become an explicit game. Lotman provides a classical example: a striped gown put over a chair is 'a tiger' for a child in the game. The child is not afraid of the gown, but he or she is also not indifferent to it: s/he is 'more afraid than not'. Nowadays the USSR and all its designators – the Union, socialism, Lenin, equality, soviets, struggle, strike, communism, comrade, revolution, Stalin, Motherland, Bolshevik, Great Patriotic War, and so on – all of them have become objects of the game. These are not overwhelming signs of Stalin's era, nor boring simulations of Brezhnev's times, – they are just chips in the game, 'paper tigers' at best. Their hypothetical victims are not afraid of them, but they are 'more afraid than not'; their supporters do not believe in them, but they 'are more

---

**63** Baudrillard, Jean. „Fragmenty iz knigi *O soblazne*" [Fragment out of the book *On temptation*]. *Inostrannaya Literatura* 1994, no. 1: 63.

**64** Baudrillard, Jean. „Iz knigi *O soblazne*" [From the book *On temptation*]. *Segodnya* 10 September 1994: 13.

believing than not'. Even hatred for these signs, quite characteristic of the late 1980s to the early 1990s has deteriorated into a 'tired, distanced non-admittance'.

This, however, does not mean that the game is safe. Games may be lethal, such as, for instance, a love duel – a fight that is born from emptiness. Yet the danger originates not from the signs, but from the very principle of the game, from 'the intensity of relationship' of those involved in the game – from temptation, from the enchantment by emptiness, from the death wish.

In other words, the Soviet discourse has survived throughout the post-Soviet era (in this connection it is doubtful whether the term 'post-Soviet' is correct at all). To this end it had to go to the next level of aesthetics – to turn into a game; and to go to the next level of simulation – to turn into temptation. The only semiotic event of the 1990s is the change of simulation paradigms within the framework of the Soviet discourse. If the USSR had been a total liturgy in the 1930s-1950s and had in the course of desacralisation turned into a total VDNKh in the 1960s-1980s, then turned into a theatrical show, into a total spectacle as a result of the final secularisation the Soviet discourse. An exhibition, during the attendance of which it was still possible to believe that the exhibits existed or, at least, that they were able to reflect outward reality (when we look at a steam engine in the museum, we believe that thousands of such engines keep running along railways), turned into a spectacle, with no one believing in the reality that is going on. Such is the power of the theatre, the power of the game, the power of temptation[65].

The power of simulation – sometimes it looks as if it cannot be overcome. In front of us, in the depths of the USSR text, in the same space of simulation a new semiotic system is being born, officially called 'Russia'.

## 6 Simulation of Power, Power of Simulation

The birth of new semiotics in Russia and in other post-Soviet formations has expanded the resources of the symbolic exchange. New designators pretending to have national, organic character (nation, territory, religion, Fatherland, historical heritage, historical justice, liberation of personality, return into the civilised world, etc.) are as far from the national soil, from reality, as their Soviet pseudo-international predecessors. In this sense the Soviet discourse preserved itself at the

---

**65** Compare: Guy Debor, a sociologist, writes about 'the society of spectacle' (Debord, Guy. *Comments on the society of the spectacle.* Translated by Malcolm Imrie. London; New York: Verso, 1990.).

expense of introducing post-Soviet (mainly Russian) designators. These new signs retained the former method of hyper-realisation of the world. The war between Soviet and Russian values in 1990-1991 (war of decrees, constitutions, Supreme Councils) was, essentially, a war for survival of everything Soviet. The discourse of power implemented itself through self-denial: by simulating its death it was trying to avoid its real agony, „it was trying to break up the evil circle of non-existence, its *déjà vu* and *déjà mort*“.[66]

In many aspects it was a success which resulted in the overproduction of signs, symbols and myths. Today in Russia the area of non-referential semiotics has greatly expanded. A highly speculative text called 'Russia' exists simultaneously with the play-text of the USSR. In fact, both these texts have intertwined and become interchangeable in many of their components. They both exist within the same Soviet discourse, within the same space of simulation; from the semiotic point of view both the USSR and 'post-Soviet Russia' are two sides of one coin, a binary opposition which provides for the existence of a semiotic field.

The crisis of representation affects all spheres of existence, but it is unevenly distributed across the semiotic space. The more the ideas, forms, institutions become centralised, the higher becomes the degree of abstraction – the greater the extent of simulation. In this sense, politics is the highest level of simulation. Politics is perhaps one of the most centripetal, integrative beginnings. The discourse of power works by the logic of expansion and subordination.

Being implemented in hyper-reality, maximum intentions of politics turn out to be maximum simulation. To support its image (or to simply justify its name) power has to simulate some controlled space which it is possible to calculate, forecast or subdue to the laws of referentiality and causality. This kind of simulacrum has been called Russian politics. The generative model of this hyper-reality is Moscow – the focal point in space, a special semiotic system, a political matrix. The very high density and combination of signs and texts within an area of several square kilometres (mainly within the *Sadovoe* [Garden] orbital motorway) generated a special field of pseudo-events aimed at simulating Russian politics. Designators like empire, statehood, etc., that are being used, are of specific Moscow origin and have their value in Moscow's symbolic exchange. Moscow's 'hangout' represents Russia, which does not exist, in the same manner as VDNKh used to represent the non-existent USSR or Disneyland – the non-existent America.

---

**66** Baudrillard, Jean. „Simulacra and Simulations“. In Baudrillard, Jean, *Selected Writings*. Stanford, Stanford University Press, 1988: 178.

The modelling role of Moscow signs may be confirmed by the story of the two coups. Conceived in Moscow and intelligible only in specific Moscow terms, they were projected to the whole of the USSR in August 1991 and to the whole of Russia in October 1993.

However, is it possible to suggest a final interpretation for these events? Months, years keep passing and the truth behind these events fades away, dissolves in abundant commentaries, so that doubt may arise as to whether this truth ever existed at all. Let us take October 'events' of 1993.[67] With a certain degree of reliability they may be interpreted in the following ways: as an armed revolt of the opposition that failed, as a show inspired by Yeltsin to destroy the opposition; as another war between the elite groups to divide property; as a quarrel between the Moscow mafia that controls production of building materials and several non-Moscow (primarily Chechen) mafia groups which control arms and drugs; as a dispute between the factions of the 'force structures' and so on, and so forth ... . Careful observers may count up to two dozens versions that have appeared during the last months. None of them pretend to be complete but all of them are more or less sensible and interchangeable. The whole corpus of interpretations cannot contribute to the creation of a complete picture because the number of such interpretations remains open and depends on the position of the interpreter.

Even more aleatory and diverse are the interpretations of the political events in February-March 1994: the amnesty of the participants of the 'October events', the dissolution of the commission in charge of investigation of these events, and the 'Treaty on Social Accord'. The answer to the straightforward Leninist question „who benefits from all this?“ is very simple: „all“. All participants of the political game. The polyvalence and compatibility of these events with different political positions is unique: each of the acting political forces has been interpreting them for their own benefit.

All this gives rise to the following thought: interpretation is embedded, pre-programmed in the event; interpretation may even precede the event. Just remember the commotion caused by the notorious 'Version Number One'[68] in the upper echelons of Russian power. Baudrillard calls this phenomenon 'precession of the

---

**67** Here is another bashful euphemism: 'Events'. The word is polysemantic, ambivalent, polyvalent and implies multiple interpretations. It is interesting to note that the communist coup in Czechoslovakia in February 1948 was also called 'unorove udalosti' – 'February events'.

**68** This version, which claimed that there was a new alliance of some politicans preparing a coup, was suggested by a number of newspapers.

model', or rather of models of singular events: „first come models and their orbital rotation creates a magnetic field of events. Facts do not have their own trajectories, they emerge at the point where the models cross. This allows all possible interpretations, even the most controversial ones – and all of them are true in a sense that their truth is interchangeable"[69].

Thus, interrelation of the simulacra models ('executive power', 'representative power', 'ideologies', 'parties', 'mafias', 'force structures', 'elites', 'lobbies', 'interest groups', 'regions') determines the format of the key political events. Russian politics is born in the process of local semiotic exchange at the intersection of different simulacra models in Moscow. All events outside the text that are not described by the existing signs, models and paradigms (of the ideological, power, party, administrative and territorial nature) are considered to be non-existent, and are expelled from 'Russian politics'.

Hence, two conclusions may be made. The first is that it is impossible to give a complete and adequate interpretation of modern Russian politics because politics does not have a meaning of its own. Interpretation as reflection seems to be altogether impossible; what is possible, however, is to speak of interpretation as modelling (as an example we may refer to the above-mentioned 'Version Number One'). In this dim light, in this misty air conventional tools of analysis fail – tools, such as finding binary oppositions ('left-wing' – 'right-wing'; 'democracy' – 'authoritarian rule'; 'nationalism' – 'cosmopolitanism', etc.) and their spectral grading ('political spectrum') or hierarchies (levels of power subordination, levels of territorial subordination and inclusion). Classical methods of verification of hypotheses also fail. Controversial interpretations become true, interchangeable and complementary.

In general, the point is not so much to discuss interpretations but, rather, scenarios of Russian politics; not the ideology of power, but alternative scenarios of power that are implemented consecutively or simultaneously[70]. In this situation, the position of an independent observer becomes impossible, any interpreter becomes a writer of scenarios and is inevitably integrated into the discourse; any reflection

---

**69** Baudrillard. *Op. cit.*: 174-175.

**70** Thus, Chinese writer Tsyi Pang in his novel 'The garden of paths that fork' makes his characters, who face a choice, choose not one but all options. Thus they create various future tenses that multiply and fork. Actors in the Russian political game are doing practically the same by choosing mutually exclusive variants: compare the simultaneous implementation of inflation and deflation policy, simultaneous support of the West and Bosnian Serbs, etc. A becomes participation in simulation, in the game of signs. (If interpretation is understood as mediation, then it is worth remembering McLuhan's 'the medium is the message', i.e., interpretation is the only contents of politics).

In other words, in Russian politics the subject is substituted by a hyper-real object, by a simulacrum. Hence, the second conclusion: just as it is to impossible to have a subject of interpretation, equally so power does not possess subjectiveness. There can be no external position from which the discourse of power can be interpreted, and there can be no position of force. Politics is composed as a game of controversial scenarios; people and positions become functions of signs. This also explains the rapid evolution of many politicians of the last decade: from Gorbachev and Rutskoi to Yeltsin and Konstantinov; three-stage changes of the type 'communist-democrat-supporter of statehood' *à-la*-Stankevich. The traditional Soviet explanation („he hesitated together with the Party") is not applicable here; this is something different: politicians wind up in the wheels of symbolic exchange which keep crushing and rotating their weak bodies.

Power is being inevitably destroyed. From now on simulation becomes its task: first, simulation of the space of power under control (see above) and, secondly, production of the effects of power, signs of their own similarity. This production is governed by the law of demand and supply: similarly to 'Russians by summons' (Gleb Pavlovskii) this power becomes 'power by summons'. Statehood and 'powerhood' are being delivered from the depots in Moscow. Payment is performed 'through the completion of works'. Wholesalers are granted price-reductions. Signs are being demanded both by the masses who need a spectacle and the game of signs[71], and by the other participants of the political show. Social union is being formed around disappearing power – a covenant of those who are afraid of political collapse. Ultimately, the game of power is confined to the obsession of power – a life-and-death obsession: the more power gets dissolved – the stronger this obsession becomes. „And when power finally disappears altogether, we will be completely under its thumb"[72]. New Russian authoritarianism, if it comes, will be the epitome of

---

similar choice by the extreme members of the opposition (which confirms its simulative nature) keeps tension in the semiotic field of Russian politics.

**71** Baudrillard, Jean. *In the shadow of the silent majorities--or the end of the social and other essays.* Translated by Paul Foss, Paul Patton and John Johnston. New York, N.Y.: Semiotext(e), 1983: 10.

**72** See: Baudrillard, Jean. „Simulacra and Simulations". In Baudrillard, Jean, *Selected Writings.* Stanford: Stanford University Press, 1988: 179-180. The author writes further on: 'In the society without power melancholy will rule. This had already generated fascism that gave anarchy, the apotheosis of subjectiveness, a dictatorship of signs but not of individuals.

The crisis of representation (not only the political representation of the electorate but of the masses) has revealed itself today in the unprecedented spread of referendums. Having introduced during the course of several years such well-tested methods of simulation as testing and sociological polls, the Soviet discourse has made them the basic political principle (such methods neutralise the meaning by reducing it to the quanta of information, to binary codes, to the simplistic model of the 'question-answer' type which is a parody of the behaviourist 'stimulus-reaction' model: questions absorb, or presuppose, or invent, or even simulate answers[73]. Power structures of all levels apply to referendums – at the level of the USSR (referendum on the existence of the Soviet Union, March 1991), of Russia (referendums in April and December 1993), of republics and regions (mainly referendums about independence), of smaller scale administrative divisions (city, town, etc.). Under the cover of maximum democracy (plebiscite, *veche*[74]) a referendum in fact reduces representation of the masses to a minimum: it is not the masses that express themselves, but it is rather they who are being investigated; it is not the masses that reflect but it is rather they who are being tested. Reducing the contents to the controlled elements to regulated binary oppositions (compare the famous „yes-yes-no-yes" repeated like an incantation in April 1993 for voters who might not even know the questions), indeed to ultimatums, referendums simulate referents. Or, rather, they conceal the fact of their absence. In general, it is possible to doubt the representative potential of most of the general social signs in contemporary Russia.

The simulative nature of the language of ideology, which continues to follow the rules of symbolic exchange or of the semiotic game, is evident from the triad 'legislative-executive-judicial' which does not greatly differ from 'orthodoxy-autocracy-nationality', 'mind-dignity-conscience'[75] or 'Lenin! Party! Komsomol!'[76].

---

society too strong a dose of reference, society that could not stop crying for the lost power' (Ibid.).

73 Baudrillard, Jean. „Symbolic Exchange and Death", in Baudrillard, Jean. *Selected Writings*. Stanford: Stanford University Press, 1988: 142.

74 'A veche' was a popular assembly in medieval Russian towns – translator's note.

75 This epithet was applied to the Communist Party – translators note.

76 There is little sense in complaining about 'the crisis of ideology', 'ideological vacuum' that overtook the USSR or Russia either in the 1960s or in the periods of Gorbachev and Yeltsin. There was (and there is) no ideology. We talk only about changing simulation

Methods of ideological simulation (e.g., involvement of the Orthodox Church into the Soviet power discourse, as was the case in the 1940s) and exposing ideological symbols (reconstruction of the temple of Christ the Saviour in Moscow) have remained the same.

Economic discourse also has a simulative nature. Introduction of market values at neck-breaking speed and hyper-realisation of the market were attempts to avoid market reforms, to preserve former methods of simulation, i.e. to preserve the socialist industrial *potlatch*. 'Russia's entry into the market' was accomplished at the extreme level of abstraction in the forms which western economies had been developing for centuries (stock markets, banks, capital, securities, currency speculation). It is no coincidence that monetarism was the only market strategy in modern Russian history that was pursued over the course of several weeks in 1992. As George Soros writes in his 'Alchemy of Finances', monetary signs have a strong simulation value even under conditions of a developed market. What can one then say about Russia, where monetary values were introduced into the economic discourse in the absence of any market (including monetary market)?

The attitude of the majority of the population towards the market is entirely of the same nature as their attitude towards the game: people deposit their shares, argue about the future of the dollar, and queue up at night to invest their money at interest rates although most of them will get only a small profit or even lose their money as a result of this activity. Quasi-mythology has been formed on the basis of market symbols, in which cultural heroes (tricksters) act: bankers, businessmen, dealers, brokers, realtors; as well as 'evil forces': racketeers, gangs, authorities, 'brigadiers' with their 'mafia wars', 'pushers' and 'intimidators'. The chronic beast known as the 'mafia' is at the bottom of this world (in the symbolism of the octopus there is also mention of a 'worldly serpent')[77]. Most of the new market terms are 'torn away'

---

paradigms and of partial fragmentation of the hyper-real space – instead of one big simulacrum there have appeared several but of a smaller size.

**77** This mythology has been registered as a parody by modern fictional texts. See 'Pyataya kniga dlya chteniya' (Fifth Russian Reader) by Vladimir Tuchkov which has been stylized like Leo Tolstoy's stories for children: 'The currency exchange is wide and deep, it has no end. The sun rises in the exchange and sets here. Nobody has ever reached the bottom of the exchange. He, who did not visit the exchange, did not pray to the dollar'...; 'There once lived a brother and a sister – Vasya and Katya; they had a stock-share. In spring their share disappeared. The children looked for it everywhere but could not find it. One day they were playing in the street by the bank and so they popped into the bank. There was their share with her beautiful dividends ...'; 'A hungry broker was looking for his catch when suddenly he heard a boy crying bitterly in a 'Khrushchev prefab' ('Khrushcheba' – a cheap, usually five-storied prefabricated block of flats of the kind that used to be massively constructed under Khrushchev – translator's from their meaning: compare it all with numerous 'public enterprises' (often trading nothing but thin air, so-called 'ventilators') like 'small enterprises', 'individual private ventures', 'open joint-stock companies', 'closed joint-stock companies', 'partnerships with limited liability', 'societies with limited liability' that can have their seals and letterhead paper made in two hours. The titles of these firms are empty and often interchangeable, their meaning tends to amount to nought. However, even names of big market structures often tend to hide the meaning, to obscure it (perhaps involuntarily), like the clumsy bureaucratic abbreviations of the early Soviet period. People in the street were puzzled by the name *Menatep* ('Inter-bank Association of Scientific and Technical Progress') that appeared one day in Moscow's streets and on the doors of taxi-cabs, puzzled in the same way as they once were by the word *Komintern*[78].

If the facade of the economic discourse is represented by market signs, its reverse side is represented by the old signs of the symbolic Soviet economy (industrial *potlatch*). This is where such signs like 'non-payments crisis', 'decline of production', 'wage delays', 'threat of massive unemployment', 'miner's strike' come from. They make this symbolic economy legitimate and keep it afloat: from the simulation of objects to the simulation of their crisis. In the economic discourse a number of semiotic oppositions has been formed that are composed of both old and new designators (e.g., 'state order – market forces' is similar to the opposition 'communist – democrat' in political discourse). It is already unimportant that today neither the state order nor market forces are real from the point of view of the economy, they are not referential: binary oppositions eliminate the representativeness of each of their components by substituting it with the game of signs.

The discourse of the media is also a simulation. A special language has been formed in recent years on the TV, radio and in popular publications, language that uplifted and updated local speech levels – those emancipated, liberal, westernised, urban levels, including teenager jargon, 'show-off' and 'gritty' slang. This language is, no doubt, lively, dynamic (sometimes even aggressive), but it is used by several percent of the population who pretend to represent all people and who simulate this

---

note) and an old lady saying to him: – If you don't stop crying, I'll give your voucher to the broker' ... . (Tuchkov, Vladimir. 'Pyataya russkaya kniga dlya chteniya: pouchitelnie istorii, sobrannye bliz metro Tul'skaya' [Fifth Russian Reader: Stories picked up by Tulskaya metro station], *Novoe Literaturnoe Obozrenie,* Moscow, 1994, no. 6: 261-270).

**78** Communist International of Youth' – translator's note.

representation. In light of its conventional, esoteric and non-referential features modern discourse in the media reminds one of the language of the *Pravda* editorials.

The above-mentioned is also true for adverts[79] that have not come a long way from the famous „Fly Aeroflot". The weightlessness and the fortuitous nature of Soviet adverts (like „A Book is the best gift" or „Make your savings by way of bank-transfers") were replaced by the rough simulated nature of modern Russian advertising. Today the majority of the advertised goods are consumed as images, as words (this continues the domestic tradition of feeding people with speech – just remember 'Cock-rooster in wine' from the VDNKh) and in certain cases there are no referents behind texts. Subject one: a close-up of a dog appears on the screen. It is breathing heavily. However, during the next ten seconds of the clip nothing happens. Subject two: there is a board on the screen that reads *Suprimex*. Suddenly a drill appears and makes two holes in the board, then someone blows off sawdust and says *Suprimex*. Both clips give no explanations, both the dog and *Suprimex* turn from signs into abstract codes which function in the massive consciousness as symbols of a new inexplicable (and therefore unconquerable) reality[80]. Are these symbols of the new Russia?

Then let it rather be *MMM*. Incidentally, what does this abbreviation stand for? It is a hidden meaning but it has certain connotations: phonetic – with the sacred alliterations of the 'USSR' type; and graphic – with the battlements of the Kremlin wall.

## 7 Conclusion: As Always, About Post-Modernism

We have not yet discussed post-modernism. We spared and cherished this notion, hardly being able to restrain ourselves from putting it to work. But the time has come for the word to be free.

Actually, we could have started using this word from the very first line. The Soviet discourse was inter-textual from the very start. The USSR appeared to be an experiment of interrelating text and reality, however not a modernist (avant-garde) but a purely post-modernist one. By performing deconstruction, simulation, and later

**79** It becomes more and more difficult to draw a line between adverts and the press. The spread of hidden publicity in the press and on the TV ('jeans') leads to the merging of both mass media streams.

**80** Months and even years passed before it became clear that the dog's name was 'Alisa' and that it was the symbol of a stock-exchange and that 'Suprimex' was the name of a bank. But the context was late, late were also the referents: the act of simulation was completed.

on, temptation, power was engaged in purely semiotic activity which requires description, first of all, in post-structuralist terms. But the USSR as a post-modernist text (including 'post-Soviet' Russia) was not reflected in post-modernist terms. In this sense, post-modernism as reflection, as interpretation is still to come in Russia.

Moreover, perhaps there is a tendency to find a way out of total textuality, out of complete semiotics, out of the evil circle of temptation. By eliminating non-discourse preconditions of language, power performed authoritarian non-reflexive deconstruction. The answer may lie in the form of well thought-out deconstruction perceived as an act of post-modernist reflection. As J.H. Miller wrote, „deconstruction is not dismantlement of the text structure but revelation of what has already been dismantled“[81]. In this sense, deconstruction is understood as the symbolic nature of signs, as recognition of unreality (hyper-reality), meaninglessness of the surrounding forms, notions and institutions. As a road to the other side where, judging by the voices, there live creatures like us.

Is deconstructing deconstruction the way to reconstruct reality? Analysis of ecstatic culture leads to the recreation of a referential culture[82]. Post-modernist deconstruction may be compared with psycho-analytical anamnesis, with „processing of the initially forgotten“ (Lyotard), with an old trauma[83]. In this process, reality, having been pushed out by authoritarian signs (in the Freudian sense as well) returns together with the principles of representation: codes and symbols give place to referential signs. According to Derrida's understanding of deconstruction,[84] it is first of all understood as critical analysis of binary oppositions, aimed rather at breaking or destroying their confrontation, at introducing relativity in their relations, than at changing the places of their components. This is a kind of deconstruction that can be applied to modern Russia, where the power of simulation rests on the construction of binary semiotic models. First of all, the opposition 'USSR-Russia' is an imaginary contradiction, a pseudo-choice, a trick which helps to reproduce the Soviet discourse. More primitive oppositions, derived from 'USSR-

---

**81** Miller, J.H. 'Steven's 'Rock' and criticism as cure: II', *Georgia Review* 30 (1976), no. 2: 341.

**82** Ryklin: 89.

**83** Prefix 'post-' in 'post-modernism' does not mean movement of the type 'come-back', 'flash-back', or 'feed-back', i.e., not the recurrent movement but some 'ana-process', the process of analysis, anamnesis, analogy, anamorphosis which re-process something 'initially forgotten' (Lyotar. 'Zametka o smyslakh 'post''. [Notes on the meanings of 'post'], *Inostrannaya Literatura* 1994, no. 1: 59).

**84** Easthope, Anthony. *British Post-Structuralism since 1968*. London: Routledge, 1988: 187-188.

Russia' (socialism-capitalism[85], totalitarianism – democracy, planned economy – market, etc.) are being substituted by new ones: cosmopolitanism (mondialism) – nationalism (patriotism), separatism – centralism, supporting ideas of the Atlantic Union – supporting Eurasian ideas, presidential rule – parliamentary rule, self-determination – inviolability of borders, etc. It is not by accident that Yurii Lotman in his latest work *Culture and explosion* identifies Russia with a cultural form for which binary structures are typical[86]. A binary way of thinking, imaginary alternatives (but, in fact, the ultimatum nature of the 'either ... or' choice) considerable narrow the semiotic field of contemporary Russia, undermine the very possibility of finding a way-out and an option.

Not option but explosion. According to Yurii Lotman, binary structures are doomed to settle conflicts by way of catastrophes, their extreme components are pre-programmed for mutual destruction, for the demolition 'to the basement'. Transition from the 'old' to the 'new' is perceived in the explosive terms of binarism[87]. Binary symbolic exchange 'USSR-Russia' cannot continue infinitely by substituting material explosion by symbolic implosion. On this course, a real explosion is inevitable. That is why post-modernist deconstruction looks for the way out from the well-known symbolic forms, a way outside binary oppositions, looks rather for a way out into the 'different' than into the 'third'.

Deconstruction in this context is first of all an aesthetic act and it reveals itself in the sphere of politics. According to Derrida, deconstruction embraces not only discourses or designators of representation (i.e., secondary systems of simulation modelling such as art, epistemes, philosophemes, sociologemes) but also the underlying structures, material institutions[88]. „Deconstruction, because it never puts the designated meaning in focus, and because it cannot be separated from social and

---

**85** However, the idea of the 'third way' is not the way out of simulation because in its turn it is a member of the simulation opposition 'originality of Russia' – 'copying experience of somebody else'.

**86** Lotman, Yu. M.. *Kultura i vzryv* [Culture and explosion]. Moscow: Gnozis, 1992: 257-260.

**87** „The process that we witness can be described as switching from the binary into a ternary system. However, one cannot but notice the peculiarity of the moment: this transition is being understood in the binary notions. In practice, two possible ways are being worked out. One of them, which had led Gorbachev to the loss of power, lay in substituting reforms by declarations and plans and leading the country into a dead-end fraught with the most gloomy forecasts. The other one, which expressed itself in various plans like '500 days' or other projects for the fast transformation of the economy, is aimed at 'curing like by like', at curing explosion by explosion" (Lotman. *Op. cit.:* 264-265).

**88** Derrida, Jacques. *L'écriture et la différence*. Paris: Editions du Seuil, 1967: 23-24.

institutional problems, must investigate the codes that were borrowed by it from ethics and politics“[89]. This is even justified in a society where aesthetics have become politics. Within the framework of the Soviet discourse, post-modernist deconstruction inevitably becomes a political instrument.

Post-modernism itself does not have political intentions. Post-modernism is not a method, neither it is a strategy, nor an ideology. In this context it would be most reasonable to define it as a definite situation of culture and as a corresponding mental state of society[90], as a non-authoritarian paradigm with a characteristically playful attitude towards linguistic signs[91]. It is rather the ability to see instability and weakness of the usual forms, to comprehend the paradoxical nature of the sacral. As irony, or even more, as self-irony; as parody – and self-parody. Its answer to the game of symbols of power is its own game with these symbols, a game without rules, a game of meanings, a game with a trick. Perhaps, the answer is even nothing but laughter.

Two languages exist in Russian tradition. One of them is the language of the sacred signs, no matter what these signs are: Church Slavonic or ‘red-tape’ language of Peter the Great, Soviet newspeak or Gorbachev's lexicon. This language is mimetic, treating signs as the Revelation, the language of Truth, Goodness and Beauty. Another language is the language of laughter, the language of buffoons, of cheap popular prints, the language of the *yurodivyi* (i.e., the language of the cracked, of God’s fools – beggars and buffoons that lived around monasteries and were supposed to be ‘the people of God’ in old Russia – translator's note). This paradigm of laughter may become the background for post-modernist deconstruction:

The life of the medieval *yurodivyi* people, just like the life of ancient cynics, was a kind of post-modernism for the corresponding periods of history. „The life of a *yurodivyi*, like the life of a cynic was a constant negation of beauty, denial of the generally accepted ideas of beauty or, more precisely, turning this ideal upside down ...“ writes A.M. Panchenko. „*Yurodivyi* people, like post-modernist writers, sense better than others not only the funny illusory nature of official fetishes and sacral

---

**89** Derrida, Jacques. *Psychè. Inventions de l’autre*. Paris: Galilée, 1987: 74.

**90** Some literary analysts and philosophers talk of special ‘post-modernist sensitivity’ (See: *Terminologiya sovremennogo zarubezhnogo literaturovedeniya (Strany Zapadnoi Evropy i SShA)* [Terminology of contemporary foreign literary criticism (Western European countries and the USA)]. Vol. 1, ‘*New critique*’ , *structuralism, receptional aesthetics, narratology, deconstructionism*. Moskva: INION, 1992: 132).

**91** Frishman, A. ‘Dvuyazychie i binarnost kultury’ [Bilinguism and the binary nature of culture]. *Nezavisimaya Gazeta* 29 September 1994: 5.

formulas learnt by heart which many people perceive as absolute, but also the dramatic instability of the criteria of truth and harmony. And vice-versa: perhaps what was said above means that Russian post-modernism, due to a specifically literary tradition (and the *yurodivy* were a typically Russian feature) may be labelled as a projection of the *yurodivyi* pattern onto today's culture with all the consequences"[92].

The tradition of the Russian *yurodivyi* people and especially of the 'post-modernist' approach to the signs of culture, developed by F. Dostoevskii, was followed in this century by Remizov and Rozanov, and by Venedikt Erofeev[93] today. Both his alter-egos – Venichka from *Moskva-Petushki* and Lev Gurevich from *Valpurgieva noch'* perform classical deconstruction of the Soviet discourse[94]. If the former unveils the tragic unreality of all discourses at the same time, in the latter deconstruction is focused to much greater extent. The author observes three unities of classical drama: the unity of place (a special model of Soviet space – a ward in the mental hospital where power belongs to doctors and nurses), the unity of time (a specific Soviet temporal point: the eve of the May Day holiday) and the unity of action (a specific Soviet action: everybody is drinking – doctors and nurses in their room and patients in their ward ). In this local space and time, Gurevich's poetic buffoonery destroys the Soviet discourse, inverts its signs and speech acts (the words and actions of the patients are opposite to their words and actions at the beginning of the play). It is quite natural that in the struggle with signs the patients die: this is the revenge of the text that has been discrowned. The four apocalyptic killers 'with a touch of something classical' in *Moskva-Petushki* are in the same way impersonal and symbolic as the mental hospital attendant Borya the 'neck wringer' who kills Gurevich.

„The contemporary iconclastic *yurodivyi* theme" (Frishman) is not confined only to the works of Erofeev. Dozens of names in literature[95], painting, music (e.g., the

---

**92** Lipovetskiy, Mark. 'Apofeoz chastits s khaosom' [Apotheosis of particles with chaos]. *Znamya* 1992, no. 8: 217.

**93** Ibid.: 215. In this respect Vail writes that 'Venedikt Erofeev is Vasiliy Rozanov who survived through Hitler and Stalin', *Moskovskiye Novosti* 1994, no. 2.

**94** With all this, Erofeev as a writer can be called neither politician, nor post-modernist. He has never been a dissident and his poem *Moskva-Petushki* is too much unbounded (sometimes even too classical and traditional) for the post-modernist canon. This is rather original text – 'Urtext' – of contemporary Russian literary post-modernism.

**95** In connection with Gurevich we may talk of the Jewish theme as a specific form of Russian *yurodivyi* behaviour. Jewish theme is meant here not in ethnic but in the functional poly-stylistics of Schnitke) can be mentioned. Nor is it limited to art. In the totally aesthetic, textual space of the USSR/Russia deconstruction may occur in any sphere, including the purely political sphere. Vladimir Zhirinovskii is an example of this.[96]

The attractiveness of Zhirinovskii (as well as his functional value in the public mind) lies in his *yurodivyi* nature (or in his ugliness)[97], in his playful attitude to the usual notions, symbols and functions. His element is laughter, parody, the grotesque. Zhirinovskii is first of all funny and only then is he arrogant, uncontrollable, threatening, terrible, a 'Russian Hitler', etc. Working for his jocular image, he constantly (and quite prudently) makes a parody of himself. Yet in laughing at himself, he laughs at the authorities, at the very principle of power, because it was he who won the last parliamentary elections.

Zhirinovskii deconstructs the discourse of power from inside, from the point of view of power. For years he has kept himself afloat through destruction, desacralisation of signs. In 1991 during the presidential elections Yeltsin and Ryzhkov appealed to the 'great shadows', like Russia, democracy, gains of socialism... Zhirinovskii, however, promised cheap vodka and won six million votes. He won through vulgarisation, by diminishing the principles of an election campaign. The same story repeated itself during the parliamentary elections of 1993. All of the candidates were talking about 'Great Russia' with respect and national pride, but the voters did not listen because both sides were observing a certain semiotic etiquette. Simulation has lived, it still lives and wins. Zhirinovskii takes the idea of 'Great Russia' to absurdity, to self-denial – to calls of returning Alaska, or washing feet in the Indian ocean. Losing all sense of proportion, breaking etiquette, he destroys the usual environment in which signs function, the very principle of semiotic exchange. In voting for Zhirinovskii, the voters were not against 'the impoverishment of the masses', not against 'the humiliation of Russia' as domestic commentators used to say. Neither were they for the 'Great Russia ' from Anchorage to 'Churkistan'[98] as some genuinely feared in the West. Choosing the parody of 'Great Russia' suggested by Zhirinovskii, people voted rather against the rhetoric of

---

sense (like Gurevich himself, who works as a 'Tartar' in a shop), as a kind of marginal position in culture, as a form of 'schizophrenic discourse' described by Deleuze and Guattari.

**96** We refer once again to 'The Norm' by Vladimir Sorokin where not only the usual Soviet text undergoes deconstruction but also the 'untouchable' symbols of Russia like 'Russia cannot be comprehended by the mind' (Tyutchev) or 'Oh, Russia, my wife!' (Blok), etc.

**97** In Russian 'yurodstvo' and 'urodstvo', i.e., ugliness makes a pun – translator's note.

**98** The author uses here a highly derogatory nick-name for the republics of the post-Soviet Central Asia – translator's note.

'great-power', against the power of simulation represented simultaneously by Gaidar and by Zyuganov[99].

The main principle of 'our hero's' behaviour is the freedom of the game, the unpredictable nature of gestures. His political acts are similar to the suggestions of Dimitryi A. Prigov to elect the President of Russia from the adult population by casting dice. They may also be compared (in a somewhat more institutionalised way) to the activity of the *Beer Lovers Party* who, during the election campaign, put forward slogans like „More beer – less tears" or „Ask for more beer once the head has subsided". Vladimir Zhirinovskii is the first of the acting politicians to have mastered the post-modernist art of gesture.

The common denominator of all these attempts at deconstruction is the game (the game in literature, in painting, in politics). The game is essentially one of iconoclasts[100], establishing the limits of the discourse, „the ability of the culture not to notice something utmost and superior in its aspirations" (Huizinga)[101]. But is the game a way-out of the stupid infinity of the Soviet discourse?

This may be the case. How do you know? There are no post-modernist ways to salvation. The game (both the language of laughter and being *yurodivyi*) plays, it is spontaneous, elusive, instantaneous. It cannot be 'the way', the system, the recipe for a culture that is sick. The game is always on the brink.

Neither a system nor ideology can be constructed from post-modernism (just try to catch Proteus)[102]. Post-modernism is absolute reversibility; perhaps, 'not to trust its own signs' is its essence. Not to trust a single word (Hamlet's „words, words,

---

**99** Allusions of mental inferiority of Zhirinovskii can be also interpreted in the post-modernist sense: in terms of Deleuze and Guattari he is exactly the kind of a 'schizophrenic personality', 'social pervert', 'marginal individual 'who adresses himself to 'schizophrenic discourse' – a kind of language which doubts the generally accepted logic and causality (like in texts of Lewis Carrol, Antonin Arto, Georges Batailles, Scott Fitzgerald, etc.). (See: Gilles Deleuze et Felix Guattari. *Capitalisme et schizophrénie. L'Anti-Oedipe*. Paris: Editions de Minuit, 1980). In this connection it is necessary to mention again that the 'Jewish theme' (presented as 'a son of a lawyer' / this is how Zhirinovskii answered when asked about the nationality of his father by a journalist – translator's note/ and thus even more evident) is one of the forms of 'schizophrenic discourse'.

**100** Movement of the opponents of icons in the Orthodoxy – translator's note

**101** Huizinga, Johan. *Homo ludens. V teni zavtrashnego dnya* [In the shadow of tomorrow]. Moskva: Progress-Akademiya, 1992: 238.

**102** They keep trying and thus post-modernism finds is supporters and critics in Russia, regular 'battles' are going on which help post-modernism to grow up to the level of a 'socially important' symbol, of a nearly alternative ideology and ... imperceptibly it turns into a simulacrum, slides out of the hands that are trying to get a firm hold of it.

words..."). Not to trust *sobornost'*[103] and spirituality, market and democracy, Russian idea and European home, the opened volume of Borges, an unfinished crumpled newspaper, a text named 'USSR: DECONSTRUCTION OF THE TEXT'. Not to trust this long twilight in November that has slowly turned into night.

**103** I .e., 'synodal' Russia, Russia governed by all-Russian council – translator`s note.

# 4

# In Search of Form[1]

Petr Shchedrovitskii

> At the congress of participants of the Browning movement they passed a resolution: to strengthen the movement.
>
> Joke of experts.

## 1 Introduction

This article presents certain framework notions allowing us to analyse the decay, transformation and probable development of what we used to call the Soviet Union, Soviet society and the 'socialist economy of the Soviet type', both from a retrospective and a prospective point of view. German classical philosophy presented us with a methodologeme of 'development' according to which „the key to simian anatomy lies in human anatomy". This means that the answer to the question of what is decaying and what is transforming will change in accordance with the contours and borders of a new emerging entity (first of all in comprehension, reflection and mode of thinking, but subsequently also in practical activity). During this process our assessments and categorical qualifications of the 'pre-existing condition' will certainly be changing.

This paper is not aimed, of course, at reaching any kind of finite conclusion about the nature and direction sense of world historical processes (the sense of history and its goals), nor is it about where we are coming from and where are we going. The speculations suggested are no more than 'sketches', but categorical ones, not depictions of the concrete actions of the local (mainly central – Moscow) politicised

---

**1** From ancient Greek philosophy onwards the category of 'form' has been interpreted as a means of organisation and at the same time, means of existence for this or that object, process and phenomenon. In Plato's philosophy the activity of 'form' is deliberately emphasised. Aristotle uses in the given context the category of 'form' to a large extent in the sense of 'enthelechy'. As it is known, in the philosophic system of Aristotle this notion expressed the unifies of material, formal, functioning and objective reason.

groups with their slightly 'zombified' social basis, to which both domestic and foreign analysts unfortunately pay so much attention.

The author may be considered to be a follower of German classical philosophy and methodology of historical analysis: he is convinced that history is the arena in which the highest sense, the processes of evolution and development of thought and mental activity (as a logical analogy of the world spirit, universal intelligence, God) are realised and that the specific development of social forces is determined by the socio-cultural morphology of the respective (always concrete) cultural or economic region.

To the representatives of post-modernist trends in philosophy, which in recent times have become so widespread in Russia, the reference to German classics may seem to be an anachronism. However, in our methodological approaches we build not only on Hegel and Marx but also on contemporary philosophic discussions, which advocate a return to the classical methodology of historical research and to the values of the age of enlightenment. At the same time, the article has a clear objectivist character: it sets out a specific concept more than approaches and methodology of socio-cultural analysis.

The author is an optimist both by nature and professional orientation. The latter is explained by the character and ethics of socio-cultural analysis: individuals as well as groups of people represent a system that can turn the expected and the possible into reality. If one keeps saying that a certain bank is not reliable, the customers will start withdrawing their money and bankruptcy of the bank will become inevitable (and the same can also happen to its political 'currency'). The author is confident that processes under way on the territory of the former USSR and Russia are of global cultural and historical meaning: history gives birth in pangs and, as a rule, under quite unsanitary conditions.

The overriding aim of these speculations is to look beyond the decay and to contemplate the formation of the new – first of all to a new historical subject which might be able to take over the mission of mental development and also the risks connected with this development, which the 20$^{th}$ century has so clearly demonstrated to us.

## 2 Russia in the Face of the World Economy

During the 20$^{th}$ century the 'world economy' (hereinafter referred to as 'WE') has grown from an idea conceived by a small group of adherents of political ecumenism, single representatives of multi-national capital and multi-national corporations, researchers and futurologists, into the reality of the political and economic self-determination of the main professional groups in a majority of countries[2].

In terms of philosophy and philosophy of history it should be admitted that the so-called WE is unlikely to be the primordial reality (the fundamental space for self-determination of a contemporary individual and the object of first philosophy). WE itself simply indicates deeper and more fundamental processes of evolution and development of thinking and activity (being simultaneously a phase of this development and a crucial point[3]).

As an arena for manoeuvre for multi-national corporations and a separate form of existence for world reproduction processes – unlike economic and trade specialisation of separate territories and countries – the WE developed after the Second World War. Since then, separate territories and countries ceased to impose rules of a 'big political and economic game', called 'world system of division of labour.'

The reality of the WE provides the ultimate arena for most collective processes and a framework for mass consciousness (dealing with the processes of labour and life maintenance). The WE manifests itself in the following ways: through the established international system of division of labour (co-operation), through the system of regional conflicts and contradictions (competition), the struggle for key resources, the activity of international organisations, new forms of fiscal and cultural colonialism as well as through new outbursts of nationalism and regionalism.

Contemporary regional economic co-operation and inter-regional competition (especially European integration and the challenge to the traditional centres of power coming from the Asia-Pacific region) can be perceived as a transitional stage

---

**2** In this case the author applies methodological concept of 'realisation' which takes into account the phenomenon of reflexivity of social systems and builds on the ideas of 'collective mental activity'. These ideas enable to consider the processes of transition from pure thinking reality to that of activity and mental activity.

**3** At the same time the change of economic activity organisation forms is one of the key processes of world development. It is complemented by two other processes: a) historical transformation (complication) of every existing economic organisation form; b) formation of significantly autonomous and independent economic organisations, both attached to the territory and extraterritorial (resulted from implementation of the 'given economic activity organisation form' within the economy in operation). Between different economic organisations numerous relations and connections of interaction, exchange and co-operation emerge. Between the forms of economic activity organisation the relations and connections of competition, ousting, substitution, reflexive absorption and compensation (super-compensation) may exist.

towards a global economic organisation which would assimilate state-of-the-art management techniques with the ecological and cultural peculiarities of countries.

The process of so-called *perestroika* on the territory of the former USSR and other countries of Eastern Europe should also be seen as an implementation of this trend: paraphrasing K. Marx, one can state that changes in the USSR were brought about by a global contradiction between the level of development of production capacities inherent in the world economy and the level of production relations formed in the Soviet Union. Roughly speaking, *perestroika* was necessitated by the deep backwardness of the production and consumption system in the Soviet Union, as compared to the standards and forms of organisation inherent in the world economy at the end of the $20^{th}$ century. The energy embedded within the contradiction and incongruity between the processes taking place in the world and those taking place in those countries could not reveal itself automatically as a subjectless historical 'necessity'. This process itself and its content had to be comprehended by a certain social group (a 'negative class' implementing a historic opportunity) and adjusted to its own 'class' (group) interests. Such comprehension always takes on converted (frequently even inverted) forms that are stipulated by the specific socio-cultural morphology and configuration of active structures (political forces, interests, positions and statuses). It is this subjectivisation of the sense and logic of historical processes that turns the possibility of development of activity and thinking into the reality of concrete historical events (reality fortunately or unfortunately being cardinally different from that of reflexive and ontological thinking about the historical process).

In this case, the role of the proto-subject of cultural and historical transformation was played by the domestic *nomenklatura* which displayed the characteristics of the 'third class' in the terminology of M. Dzilas and those of a 'technostructure' according to Galbraight (as a social and cultural dimension[4]). It is precisely this

---

**4** Comprehension of 'class' in contemporary sociology is different. During a long time this notion had been subject to incisive criticism first of all because of having political contexts connected with the application of the notion in Marxist tradition. K.Marx, as it is known, used this idea within the framework and reality of technical theory of 'changeovers' and he linked the origin of the given 'big groups' and the distribution as well as redistribution of proprietary relations. Modern concept of neo-classes connects this notion to a large extent not with the distribution of statuses but with the utilisation of various types of knowledge, means and techniques of thinking and activity. To analyse the given phenomenon one should be aware of the 'management buy-out' system, which was implemented in the course of modernisation revolutions in Latin America, as well as schemes of establishing command it partnerships on management in the course of privatisation and sanation of industrial enterprises in the former GDR.

social stratum that 'experienced the taste of privatisation' of the management processes and systems (including the existing state administration) and has seen in the above-mentioned contradictions an opportunity to implement its class interests, i.e. those of concrete members of that class. In sociological parlance, the so-called *perestroika* was a 'revolution' accomplished by the *nomenklatura* in order to consolidate a more up-to-date bureaucracy[5].

The subjectivisation was solidified by the early 1980s and had apparent reasons: most participants in the process did not know anything about the historical content of the process itself and merely implemented their personal and group interests. Representatives of literary journalism, who ingenuously think they are outside this process and can assess it as observers, sometimes appear to be in a similar situation.

It would be inappropriate to think that the course and results of this process (or rather, poly-process) are predetermined. No one can guarantee that the 'class revolution' (the coup of the *nomenklatura*), which is going on in one particular country during one particular historical period, will result in the 'integration' of that country and its resources into the world economy or in the resolution of world economic (socio-cultural) and historical contradictions in a manner appropriate to the situation and compatible with the values of that particular historical period[6].

---

**5** The most important feature of the operation of the 'administrative market' model remained the strict connection between the income levels and privileges of separate representatives of the administrative elite and administrative corporations (industrial and regional ones) and a 'place' in the system. Irrespective of the level of participation in activity and professionalism a member of the corporation had no legal and legitimate (here one should take into account the principle dualism of 'legitimacy' and 'legality') opportunities to 'privatise' either activity or its outcomes. In losing a 'place', a concrete individual lost everything automatically.

**6** The established administrative elite (including local regional, quite a numerous and influential group: according to sociologists at the end of the 1970s – beginning of the *oblast'* 1980s at the level it numbered 50-80 families) was interested in privatising the so-called administrative and command system as well converting it from their *de facto* property to *de jure* property, or 'complementing' the existing proprietary rights to a certain 'completeness'. Analysing this situation one should not omit gigantic capital that had been piling up since the early 1960s within the framework of the black market economy, which was an indispensable compensatory system to maintain production, distribution and circulation. In many territories this capital (as well as the lifestyle and consumption type that formed on its basis) almost coalesced with the official (existing) power ministries and also needed legalisation. Thus, on the basis of generational change, the privatisation of the administrative and command system and legalisation of black market capital became a form of implementation of the technical and socio-political modernisation revolution. This issue and the manner of analysis are unlikely to be adequate at all: the economic component of world development processes (being an ultimate limit of self-determination for most social groups and forces) depends, in turn, on many other processes. However, the existing systemic integrity (may it be just WE alone) is not something

In the contemporary world economy there is no specially prepared place for Russia, no 'gap' that could be filled by its existing economic and social morphology. All market gaps (both actually existing and potential) are already filled, all kinds of immediate participation in the WE through specialisation have already been planned and are being implemented by other countries and multinational corporations for five to seven or more years into the future. That is the deep 'intrigue' of the current socio-cultural, organisational and political situation.

It would be bizarre to consider that representatives of some interested class preconceived and designed this process as a whole; only a naive individual could trust Gorbachev's assurances that the 'authors of *perestroika*' had a plan (with the exception of some local projects for destroying the economic and political foundations of the organisational system and numerous 'plans' of palace revolutions). It is even more far-fetched to attribute such a plan to some outside subjects (the US government, Jews, masons, the world financial oligarchy, etc.). Concrete representatives of these groups and organisations are in the same position as internal subjects are; simply put, they understand little and act chiefly by the method of trial and error on the basis of situational factors. This does not rule out the fact that each of these (and many other) groups may not only have interests but also goals, projects, plans, scenarios (at other levels of the community); that attempts were made (more or less successfully) to implement such projects; that coalitions and networks emerged, that institutes and infrastructures were set up, etc.

In other words, the content of the world historical process is achieved not only through interests but also through professional and collective thinking and activity. A new systemic organisation, being a possible outcome of the artificial-natural

---

static and is prone to transformations as a result of transformations of separate countries and activity areas. The underlying problem is that the post-Soviet region aspires to change the means of its inclusion in the international labour division system, WE and the world community at the moment when this community itself is experiencing a certain crisis: development models, the type of economic organisation and type of political culture are all fluctuating.

In philosophic and methodological terms we talk about multi-level processes of mutual assimilation and accommodation of two systemic and at the same time populative integrities. (On the method of analysing the 'populative system' refer to G. Shchedrovitskii 'Problems of building system theory of a compound 'populative' object' – in the book *Systems Analysis*, Annual edition-1975, Moscow: Nauka publishing house, 1976: 235-267).

In this respect, the real development of historical process can neither be imagined as a straight line nor as an erratic one. It is certainly not always the person that faces great hardships and makes many efforts that consequently wins, just as he/she who wins in concrete situations does not always come out on 'top'.

process of development, is growing and forming as an entity (co-organisation) of many infrastructures which mutually limit one another.

Finding their situational (specific and apparently short-term) representative and agent in the *nomenklatura* and being implemented within the fibres of the existing cultural, social and economic organisation (formed on the territory of the former USSR over the last 100-150 years), the world processes will undoubtedly take on a brand-new form, a surprising and unpredictable one which will be the end product of various mutations and the result of an historically contingent search for socio-cultural development of thought and activity.

## 3 Fracture Lines[7]

As we have emphasised above, the contradiction between the systemic effects and the systemic content of world development on the one hand, and the specific processes under way on the territory of one albeit huge country on the other, does of course significantly overstep the limits of economic and even social processes.

Being, in a certain respect, a typical upheaval in the process of modernisation at the end of the 20th century (alongside the processes occurring after the Second World War on the territory of South-east Asia and Latin America), *perestroika* in the former USSR, we believe, has resonated with other, even deeper and more protracted 'historical hesitations' of economic and socio-cultural organisation (inherent in both the 'post-Soviet space' and throughout the whole world[8]). Russia

---

7 For this notion I am obliged to Johan Galtung, the author of the essay 'Eurotopia: die Zukunft eines Kontinents', Vienna, Promedia, 1993. Galtung singles out the following 'fracture lines' inherent in the second half of the 20th century: between mankind and nature, man and woman, age groups and generations, races, classes, nations, territories, superpowers, etc.

**8** One of the key fallacies (which, fortunately has been much discussed in recent times) is the viewpoint that the processes depicted are the result of particular individuals' actions in the years between 1984 and 1994. This, of course, is wrong. Neither can we agree with the widespread standpoint that the 'coup d'état' of 1917 drastically changed the lines of Russia's development and established a new pathological order which should now be eliminated in order to return to Russia's 'golden age'. The decay processes themselves have a more prolonged history then the events of 1984/94. The latter manifest a sort of active (last critical) phase of these processes, a result of their overlapping, which led to a certain resonance effect. Savigny used to affirm that a state is an organic form of people. Without deliberations on the notion of 'state', one can emphasise that if the search and reconstruction of organic forms of political, cultural and economic activity had been carried out more actively and the market of forms had been more saturated, the process would hardly have taken on such extreme characteristics. In one of his essays on Eastern Europe, G. Soros emphasises that if one shakes a rigid structure, it will fall apart quickly – the more rigid the structure the quicker this will happen and the process itself will strike the imagination of external observers.

has in fact found itself at the intersection of several tectonic fracture lines. This overlap of 'resonances' stimulated the internal structural crisis in the fields of culture, education, management technique, consumption and production of economic goods as well as in the field of capital reproduction and circulation, where the crisis took on an irreversible character as early as the 1970s, and it remains in many respects the main motor of the socio-political developments up to the present day.

Needless to say, the appearance of similar tendencies and fracture lines is currently the object of numerous studies and philosophic speculations, united into a particular cultural genre which one could call 'fin de siècle' (the close of the last century also produced a whole range of this kind). The definition of the most important events and tendencies will of course change every year as the distance separating us from the object of analysis – the 20th century – increases. The history of the 19th century (unlike its chronology) was rewritten several times and, as is appropriate, the status and assessment of particular events, persons and processes often changed. We will single out several historical tendencies and contexts that are important from our point of view, that determine the processes taking place and that set limits to local transformations. These are, above all, the globalisation of economic and political activity; transformations in development models; the appearance of world infrastructures and 'new empires'; processes of regionalisation; changes in the area of education, in the labour market and in the realm of organisation, administration and management; changes in the role of a 'state' and statehood as a particular management technique; and also the appearance of the 'cultural policy' field.

Certain issues merit particular attention.

As we have mentioned above, the 20th century brought a sharp increase in the globalisation (internationalisation, integration processes) of economic and political activity. The entire globe with all its resources became the object of economic transformations and economic planning. The notion 'strategic resources' which became widespread after the Second World War implied the idea of managing the earth as a whole: natural resources are assessed many years in advance; the geopolitical and geo-economic advantages of different countries are clear; strategic alliances of resource holders and their users are established.

Of course, within the framework of these developments a new emphasis was placed on the crucial question of the limits of mankind's influence on the environment, the limits of industrial production and perspectives for using models of economic (and social) development which build on the system of inter-generational loans. Like two hundred years ago, 'Malthusian' economic and political analysis has once again become widespread as a form of ecological criticism. Post-war expansion of advanced industrial countries in the 'Third World' and the widespread implementation of the growth models they stimulated (modernisation, industrialisation, inclusion of developing countries in the international labour division system) posed the question of the consequences of these models and possible alternatives of development. In this context, only rich countries can afford to implement projects of 'stable development' and 'socio-ecological market economy'.

If one looks towards the arena of ideology, the second half of the century brought us the recognition of a multiplicity of possible (especially for the countries of the 'second' and 'third' world) paths of development, but this unfortunately hardly affected the real practice of economy management, world division of labour and political decision-making. The formation of world infrastructures (transport, energy, informational, fiscal, etc.) and the consolidation of systemic dependencies between different territories and areas of activity do not negate but, on the contrary, stimulate competition. The competition between enterprises is supplemented and in some respects even supplanted by the rivalry between countries which often begin to behave as 'territorial corporations'. The most important factors of competitiveness of similar corporations are labour ethics, ideology, religion, culture and level of education. To consolidate their positions, countries have to 'settle' into wider regional structures in economic, political and cultural terms.

The collapse of the former USSR as the last multi-national empire of the 19th century model, which formerly relied on mechanisms of direct compulsion and economic opportunities for 'internal colonisation', is taking place against a background of the formation of new multi-regional cultural and economic empires in Europe, Asia and the Pacific Ocean region, as well as on the American continent. On the threshold of the 21st century, contradictions between superpowers (new empires, secondary regions) and separate countries are deepening. Territories are becoming involved in processes of secondary and tertiary colonisation without having any regional resources in their possession except for the traditional 'state', and therefore incapable of withstanding contemporary techniques for mastering resources. As we have already stated (see note [2]), evolution and replacement of forms of economic organisation do not lead to the entire eradication of the pre-existing ones. Every form of economic organisation which is implemented with a certain amount of natural, anthropological and technical material becomes the nucleus of the formation of appropriate economic structure of life[9].

Contemporary world and regional economies are a product of non-systemic co-organisation of different economic organisations. Regionalisation, integration and globalisation of economic activity restrict autonomy and accentuate the contradictions between different economic organisations as well as between countries oriented towards different forms of economic organisation. In other words, the contradictions between different forms of economic organisation and territories involved in the zone of dominance of this or that economic organisation are deepening. The above-mentioned cluster of contradictions manifest themselves in increasing fragmentation and new integration of territories; the overlap of these processes forms the face of modern regionalism. In this context there is also an increase in contradictions between centres (distinct economic and cultural areas involved in some way or another in global transformation and development), points of growth and sources of development on the one hand and miscellaneous and numerous peripheries on the other.

The 20th century has brought an all-time high level of mass education and training that in turn resulted from more complex requirements in the military sphere as well as in the spheres of industrial production and political techniques[10]. Processes of staff training have overstepped the limits of educational institutions (schools, kindergartens, institutions of higher education) and stopped being the object of state monopoly. The 20th century has brought us the ideals of continuous education, the society-agency (where everyone learns from everybody) and ideals of an evolving cultural environment (from a child's playroom to the organisation of a modern city). At the same time, the growth of educational attainment took place against a background of obvious changes in the relaying of culture. The traditional connection between culture and education (inherited from the 'New age') was disrupted: a wide spectrum of cultureless and 'counter-cultural' pedagogics came into being; the

---

**9** Usually when analysing economic history one singles out such ultimate types as 'consumers' and 'producers', 'natural' and 'goods' economy as well as 'pre-industrial', 'industrial' and 'post-industrial' forms of economic organisation. Let us emphasise that in the latter's case, only the 'middle member', i.e., industrial economy is comprehensively characterised.

**10** importance of transition to compulsory secondary education and then – in the 20th century – almost to universal higher education is not practically assessed and its consequences are not analysed even in pedagogical literature, to say nothing of philosophy, culturology and sociology.

destruction of reproduction mechanisms resulted in sundry ‘cultural mutations’ and an entire layer of cultural norms was ‘washed away’.

However paradoxical it may seem, improvements in educational attainment did not just fail to abolish but even aggravated educational inequality. There have been drastic changes in requirements: systems, techniques and styles of administration, participatory organisation and management: methods, the creation of temporary design teams and groups, and the emergence of mobile corporations have all become increasingly important. In the second half of the century ‘ad hoc’ methods of management have become widely spread[11]. Within the last 20 years there has been an almost universal abandonment of hierarchical organisation models based on the principles of direct subordination and unidirectional decision-making; and a movement in the direction of so-called ‘network forms of organisation’ – heterarchical and multi-central ones. This is evidently due to sweeping changes in the structure and intensity of streams of information, in the distribution and utilisation of knowledge in activity systems, in principles and means of decision-making under conditions of incomplete information and collective action, as well as due to the spread of infrastructural and network approaches in principle.

Under conditions of ‘formational change’ in principles and techniques of management in various areas of activity, the problem of stimulating local (social, socio-cultural and economic) development and its subjects remains unresolved; the role and importance of entrepreneurial thinking and activity become more crucial; and the contradictions between evolving and stationary (functioning or inert) regions of mental activity continue to deepen.

Considerable changes took place in the labour market where the increase in importance of preparatory work (programming, designing, planning, developing scenarios) as compared to executive work and the overall intellectualisation of mental activity resulted in a switch from a strategy of ‘selling’ to one of ‘leasing’ working time[12]. Despite the wide spread of individual instrumental (knowledge-

---

**11** One should emphasise in particular the formation of the administrative area with its own manner of specialisation and internal division of labour and also the development of new technologies such as external administration (particularly used under conditions of sanation), administration under crisis and crisis management (damages, local conflicts, etc.), system programming, management of innovations (including staff – training programmes and promotion courses, programmes for the mastering of new technologies, organisational development).

**12** Apparently the comprehension of this very aspect – the opportunity to lease one’s own qualification and system of personal expertise several times simultaneously – led J. Habermas to say that society based on labour has exhausted itself.

instrumental) systems, the contradictions between social, geographical and even socio-cultural (ethnic, linguistic, national) necessity and opportunity of activity (mental activity) in self-determination and personal growth also continue to deepen.

The increase in levels of freedom, the opportunity to access any data bases and informational networks, the freedom of movement and selection of the area of one's activity within the world do at the same time invariably impose new restrictions, conventions and dependencies of a higher level. Within the framework of the described socio-cultural and epistemological context, on the threshold of the 21st century a new anthropological formation is under way, as well as a new type of human being which can be called a 'mosaic human being', not attached to any specific forms (economic, political, cultural, technological or biological) of his/her existence in the world. There is a swift development of various types of 'anthropo-technicians' (psycho-technician, socio-technician, culture-technician, communications-technician) which ensures such modes of human existence as 'being a source of innovations in mental activity' or 'being a guarantor of the reproduction and development of mental activity systems'.

Within the framework of management techniques, the gap between individualism and collectivism continues to widen in all respects (groupism, communalism, corporatism). This contradiction is intensified due to the existing standards and forms of distributing property rights and economic proceeds from the activity as well as owing to the spread of educational techniques. Mental activity always has a collective or group character but training for this activity remains mostly on an individual basis.

One of the ways this contradiction manifests itself is growing through rivalry between privatisation (individualisation, atomisation) and mobilisation (collectivisation, co-operation) mottoes and programmes.

Great influence on the formation of the 'fracture lines' inherent in the 20th century was exerted by the mass embrace and totalisation of political activity. The experience of world wars and revolutions of the 20th century, the appearance of mass ideological movement (socio-reformist, cultural, national) alongside the development of the mass media resulted in a new dimension of political process. In this context the relations between state and society have changed significantly. The role of state institutions and concepts of state sovereignty in finding solutions nations internal and external problems has decreased. Individual functions of the traditional state were transferred to the supra-state level (the level of coalitions of states and super-regions) as well as to the level of territories (local authorities, communes, etc.). To some extent one may state that 'civic society' and the *Rechtsstaat* gradually 'leave the stage' as leading characters in the European historical process of 15-19$^{th}$ centuries and make space for organised structures of other kind: 'intellectual programmes', corporations (united groups and associations using corporate organisation forms) and 'regions'. Under these conditions, the rivalry between three (at least) concepts of statehood are increasing, namely the concept of law, bureaucracy and specific programmes.

In just one century the leading type of political culture has changed: from leader to party and then on to programme-based culture. Before our very eyes a new sphere is forming, as well as a new mental activity type – cultural policy, which assimilates seemingly different sorts of practices such as education, architecture, space and environmental planning, ecology, advertising, public relations, image-making, consulting, law, design, mass media and screen-based technology.

## 4 Collapse of Systemic Organisation

However specific the above-mentioned tendencies may be, in the early 1980s the systemic organisation of the USSR, formed during the preceding decades, started collapsing under the influence of global tectonic processes, external world economic pressure and internal contradictions. The historical role of the *nomenklatura* was largely about rocking and destroying the old form which preserved 'internal' processes (cultural, social, economic) and obstructed 'positive assimilation' of the new content of world developments. We are talking here about the so-called Soviet Union, the Soviet 'empire' and the 'socialist economy' as well as about other local forms of organisation, which, by means of their specific configuration ensured the operation of the economic complex and the reproduction of its forms of appearance. The key issues were how this process would continue and the cost of restructuring the existing organisational forms. Widespread blame placed on particular political leaders and the existing political 'elite' as a whole were mainly provoked by the manner and cost of achieving this 'change of form'. Generally, in our view, not much depended on specific individuals (whatever offices they held): in their activity, they acted like members of their class. Of course, one could deliberate whether it would have been possible (and how) to take another course. Today, however, this is undoubtedly the field of 'historical fantasies'. The entity was subject to collapse, decay and restructuring largely according to the rules of 'assembly and disassembly' it contained. Having lost its form, its forces and energy burst outwards at the same time, making a new, wider space, which for a certain span of time was moving in a confused way. Particular individuals and groups totally failed to readjust themselves to changing socio-political and economic conditions. At this point, the 'ruling class' (at all levels of administration) had no projects or schemes of design, but rather delusions, hopes and pilot projects which came apart on their own under the pressure of circumstances. Their analysis of the situation obviously failed to keep up with developments (and continues to fail up to the present day).

Being unable to keep transformation processes under control, the *nomenklatura* backed the self-organisation of society[13], counting on the resources of the deeply militarised economy, on society's processes of adjustment and on the gigantic adaptation potential of post-Soviet social structure. It is worth mentioning that such an approach is not the worst ideology to adopt during drastic changes and uncertainty. The change of form resulting from the systemic influence of world processes (including economic ones) on the internal structure of socio-cultural and economic-political organisation, cannot be regarded as a momentary act (abandoning one form and taking on another). This process (or poly-process) has its own 'time' and logic. Being the collapse of the old form and a multi-directional collective search (construction and 'cultivation') for a new one, this poly-process can be presented as a particular model.

This particular model was elaborated within the framework of the Moscow Methodological Study-Group in 1987/88[14] and enables one to analyse and forecast

---

**13** One of the key ideas (in the concept of self-organisation) turned out to be the idea of the 'market'. It is comprehended in respect of neo-liberalism and has successfully joined with original Russian roots.

**14** The Moscow Methodological [up to 1962 'Logical'] Coterie (a free association of philosophers, logicians and representatives of social disciplines) was established in the faculty of philosophy at the Moscow State University in 1951-1952. Up to the present day it exists in Russia and other CIS states as a 'methodological movement' and we view its work as a particular manifestation of historical change in forms, techniques of thinking and distribution of methodological thinking which is beginning to substitute philosophical, scientific and engineering-based thinking. Particular means of organising communication between members of the coterie, ways of posing and solving practical (applied) tasks as well as theoretical notions (theory of thinking 1954-1958, theory of activity 1960-1965, theory of comprehension 1966-1974, etc.) which formed in general in the 1950s and 1960s and complement those practices, were undoubtedly stimulated by the socio-cultural situation in the USSR and in particular by the peculiar position of social sciences and philosophy. To a large extent the coterie formed in opposition to official philosophy and science. However, throughout the whole period of its active operation it aspired to take a constructive stand, to develop new methods of problem-resolution and interprofessional communication.

At the source of the coterie were: G. Shchedrovitskii, A. Zynov'ev, B. Gryshin, M. Mamardashvili. Active participants in the coterie's work were: V. Avksentiev, N. Alekseev, O.

the course of basic transformation processes, although it does not answer the questions concerning the normative content of those processes and their outcomes. We single out at least five levels of analysis of the development and tendencies of collapse/liquidation of the old system form (collapse of the poly-system of social organisation) and of substitution of the underlying processes' content: a) macro-ideology, b) structures of power and political system, c) management, including two-strata institutions (and state administration) and management infrastructures, d) economy, and e) micro-ideology and life-style (scheme 1)[15].

---

Anisimov, A. Buryak, V. Davidov, V. Danilova, V. Dubrovskii, O. Genisaretskii, V. Gorokhov, J. Gromyko, A. Zinchenko, V. Zinchenko, N. Kuznetsova, I. Ladenko, V. Lefevre, P. Malinovskii, V. Nikitin, A. Piskopel, S. Popov, A. Puzyrei, V. Rozin, V. Sadovskii, B. Sazonov, A. Tyukov, V. Shvirev, P. Shchedrovitskii, J. Edin, S. Jakobson and many others.

From the very outset the coterie was aimed at solving interdisciplinary problems that required:

a) on the one hand, disobjectivisation of existing ideas, notions, knowledge and what is most important – means and methods of work belonging to separate scientific and engineering-based (technical) disciplines;

b) on the other hand, synthesis of different objective and disciplinary knowledge in its orientation towards a complex problem situation.

In the 40 years of the existence of the united group of people (although having a staff turnover) that make up the coterie, the following was achieved:

a) formation of a certain lifestyle and tradition, their own world-view and ideology, particular attitude to official ideology, forms of interrelationship and communication, organisation of works, ways of including new members;

b) creation of a peculiar sense field, their own language, co-ordinated network of notions and ideas, and what is most important – a certain set of programmes and problems;

c) initiation of a logical and methodological movement which later broke away to form a methodological, systemic, activity, design and game – related movement (the movement of organisational and activity-related games which served as the crystallisation point for the game movement).

Currently within the framework of the methodological movement, the magazines 'Kentavr' ('Centaur') and 'Voprosy metodologii' ('Methodological issues', since 1991) have been published. A number of institutional structures have been set up, in particular the Moscow Academy of Development and Education (J. Gromyko), Interregional Methodological Association (S. Popov), a network of methodological laboratories (A. Zinchenko, V. Nikitin, N. Andreychenko, V. Volkov) and School of Cultural Policy (P. Shchedrovitskii).

**15** The corner-stone of this scheme is made up of several categorical models, borrowed from political science, theory of economy and sociology. Above all it is an opposition of macro-ideology and micro-ideology (form of self-consciousness vs. lifestyle), an opposition of politics and economy which sets up the structure of 'world life', and an opposition of institutes and infrastructures for the implementation of administrative decisions. The application of the given scheme when analysing processes of decay supposes several simple principles:

a) that processes of fluctuation and transformation (decay) occur in all strata simultaneously;

b) that processes in each stratum have a particular character of development and their own critical points;

1. Crisis of ideology.
2. Crisis of power.
3. Crisis of state administration.
   A. Crisis of institutions.
   B. Crisis of implementation of infrastructures.
4. Crisis of economy.
5. Crisis of life-style.

The role of the 'central elite' in the transformation of any the mentioned strata should not be exaggerated. Up to recent times this role boiled down to revealing the process of collapse in front of public consciousness and thus implicitly legitimising it, as well as stimulating processes of adaptation and self-organisation of different social systems.

At this point, we should introduce the category of 'space' (spatial organisation). Human self-determination always takes place in a particular 'virtual space', circumscribed and defined by culture, knowledge and organisation. Existence of something in the socio-cultural world is, first of all, existence by means of a norm, by a normative description, by means of a rule, knowledge and sign. Sign and semiotic space (space of orientations, values, forms of organisation, rules of behaviour, cultural norms) play a leading role not only in political but also in economic processes (this is the efficiency of economic forms of organisation which build a kind of second economic dimension – a knowledge, sign and semiotic dimension). Over the last decade the 'central *nomenklatura* grouping', preserving its leading role in the 'emission of ideological currency' (both borrowed and of domestic production), maintains and solidifies its own central functions (control, management and influence). The so-called *perestroika* occurred chiefly at the expense of utilising resources of the militarised economy on the one hand, and the mono-focal structure of production and distribution of new norms, knowledge and signs on the other. Let us briefly concentrate on the features of the mentioned levels

---

c) that a change of form (or its disintegration) in the upper stratum occurs earlier (in physical and activity time) than in the lower stratum;

d) that process in the upper stratum (alongside its own form) also brings 'form' to other (lower) processes and those, in turn, submit 'material' to the upper ones (which in particular reflection can be interpreted as the content subject to registration or assimilation);

e) that new systemic form can only be the result of co-organisation and mutual adjustment of the processes at all levels (and therefore cannot be designed or constructed for just one single level [process]). It is also the result of mutual integration of two systemic integrities – world economic integrity and that of a country.

of model representation and characterise those 'symbolic events' which can be regarded as manifestations of crucial points of the processes at every level.

The collapse of the leading ideology began quite a long time ago[16]. The generational change in the *nomenklatura* stratum, the growth of opposition from regional leaders and organisational-management elites in the area of production with a view towards gaining more autonomy, the increase in violent crime and growth of black market capital, the formation of new standards in the orientation towards world technology, the import of world informational networks and their products, the growth of the dissident movement – all these factors undermined the foundations of the outdated 'socialist' ideology. Only a slight push was needed to start the process off; when the 'central elite' recognised its lack of competitiveness, this self-disclosure triggered everything off. The events of August 1991 became a crucial point for ideological transformation. The most important ideological changes were not so much the result of career-oriented actions of those who immediately participated in the events around the White House, but were rather brought about by the pragmatic (and even cynical) inaction of the *nomenklatura* which was already involved in commercialisation and had no new ideological form. Since then the ideological space in which society was immersed has collapsed completely and this destruction has to be regarded as a fact of societal life. The liquidation of the Communist Party shifted the centre of gravity of the processes of collapse onto the power level. The 'power' space implies, in this context, the area of interaction, competition and struggle between the pressure groups which had emerged as early as

---

**16** Ideological changes are frequently characterised as a crisis and even collapse of socialist ideology. This is not exactly true: we are witnessing the collapse of institutional forms of support (reproduction) of socialist ideology under increasing solidification of socialist orientations among groups and strata which represent the 'passive' part of world development and modernisation. From this point of view one may contend that the departure of the Communist Party from the political arena is brought about not by the collapse of the socialist and communist idea but evidences, however, deep privatisation of socialism as a form of self-consciousness of declassed and deprofessionalised population groups. When these ideological trends join the processes of estranging large groups of people from solving problems, which affect their living standard, the phenomenon of 'dispersed fascism' (ideology, having neither its own institutional nor state form of support) becomes obvious. The integral characteristic of the processes under way in the FSU in 1989-1991 and especially after August events in 1991 is, in our view, the increase in uncertainty (in consciousness) in large population groups. It hampers elaboration of stable behaviour plans. This condition is aggravated by appearance and increasing spread of critical condition sources. This condition is connected with unsuccessful attempts to act on the basis of the prototypes available at domestic and world practice. These groups control mass information channels and are responsible for ideology formation. When they see inappropriate means being used to change the situation (crisis) it results in ever increasing growth of uncertainty in other social groups.

1954-1964 in times of collapse of the administrative and command system. The list of these forces includes the traditional economic and political groupings known from comparative analysis: the fuel and energy complex, the military-industrial complex and the agro-industrial complex. Up to the end of the 1980s, these groups generally did not undergo any major changes[17]. Their interaction rested on the quasi-institutional structures of the Communist Party and 'Soviet power' which functioned as places for communication between groups and groupings and, at the same time, as a form of negotiation. This way of structuring power relations and 'defining' zones of influence meant that until recently the key pressure groups remained connected with the economic and territorial structure of the socialist and post-socialist economy.

Throughout 1992-1993 repeated attempts were undertaken, first of all to transform the system of education and the mechanisms of power resource accumulation and, secondly, to form a system of strategic alliances among the main pressure groups. In terms of their implementation, these tasks obviously contradicted each other. In addition to that, the consolidation of fiscal and economic elites on the one hand and of central and regional elites on the other was hindered by an increasing conflict between the government (ruling *nomenklatura*) and 'Soviet power' structures (the other part of the *nomenklatura*, exploiting the opportunities of their representative function, which also contended for full power). Throughout 1992-1993 the power field underwent several stages of transformation which were determined by a number of important events: The Seventh Congress of People's Deputies in December 1992, the referendum of spring 1993 and finally the events of October 1993.

In our view, the period of 'Soviet' power as a means of conciliating interests of the main pressure groups came to an irreversibly end in spring 1993. An active period of transformation of the power system and the subsequent co-ordination of a new institutional structure and of existing informal force relations lasted for more than two years and can generally be regarded as ending at the beginning of 1994[18]. The above-mentioned class revolution took place. In Russia (as well as in other CIS

---

**17** Here one can make a reference to the essay by J. Pappe wherein he analyses the structure of post-Soviet elites. Implying by 'elites' social and economic political groups which have distinct economic and organisational outlook J. Pappe suggests also to use the notions 'damped elite' and 'force grouping'. The first category will include gas, oil, aero-space and bank groups and the second – atomic group, the third – respectively coal and agricultural ones.

**18** Here we differ with many analysts and consider that struggle for power is over. The struggle for operation of power has begun.

states) a new power oligarchy came into being (sometimes called the 'new elite') which entirely 'privatised' the mechanisms of administration and property (re)distribution, as well as internal and external resources. 'Privatisation' implies, in this context, the acquisition by a separate individual or a group (corporation) of the key mechanisms of activity management and control. The consolidation of power groups and power relations (with other social groups) is currently being backed up by a poorly screened set of social-patriotic and imperial ideologies. This is: a) a regulated response to external challenges (including the aspiration of developed countries to preserve the Russian Federation as a 'residual empire' for the autonomous maintenance of stability in the former USSR); b) the result of comprehending the harmfulness of purely nationalistic mottoes to 300-400 year-old multi-national social structures; and c) a reflex effect caused by the existing spatial organisation of economic and political activity in Russia (in particular the importance of 'conquering' Siberia and Far East, not only for Russia itself but also in the overall geopolitical and geo-economic perspective).

Transition to the purposeful transformation of the state management system (at the federal, regional and local levels) is not (and will not be) feasible until the period of the struggle for power has ended. The key issue and probable outcome of the third phase of the collapse (1994/96) would seem to be the search, 'selection' and active creation of a new model of state structure (taking into account that the result will simultaneously be the starting point for a new synthesis of structures of ideology, power, economy and lifestyle). The basic model easily allows us to directly formulate the key tasks that have to be dealt with by the state under construction, as well as the conditions for their implementation. The main task is to turn the rest of the processes (levels, models) inside out via the stratum of state management in a spatial and graphic way. This model illustrates that the state (in what amounts to an introversion of its role) should first and foremost ensure: a) economic restructuring and b) change in social policy principles and mechanisms. This will make up the content of a new economic (industrial, investment, etc.) and social policy. The conditions for implementation of these programmes will be the elaboration of a new ideology and the ongoing consolidation (conciliation) of the main power elites' interests (and also inclusion of other social groups in the process).

## 5 Geopolitical Instability

Between the internal collapse of systemic organisation (and the ensuing attempts to dampen these processes and find an adequate solution for the key internal tensions) and the 'external' (in this case – world) context there are a number of peculiar linkages and dependencies. The collapse of the FSU's political system and the transformation of the economic complex over a sixth of the world's land area certainly affects world processes considerably and sometimes seems to be able to change their direction. At the same time, many efforts made by the governing elite 'within' the country turn out to be entirely futile because of underestimation of or quite simply disregard of the systemic context[19].

It should be emphasised that when analysing socio-cultural processes, the categories 'external-internal' are used, as a rule, as a metaphor; in the context of reflexive systems (systems of activity that are permeated with reflexes) the 'external' condition becomes 'internal' and vice versa. Contemporary geopolitics rests on the presumption that the importance and role of a country in the system of world relations is determined by a number of key factors: territory, type of borders, population, level of economic and technological development, fiscal might, racial homogeneity, optimal integration of all social strata, political stability and finally such a 'virtual factor' as national spirit. After the USSR's collapse, a 'large space' which was fairly stable in geopolitical terms took on a (physically) unstable form, being simultaneously pulled into the zones of influence of other regional force centres. Today the USA, Europe and some countries of Asia and the Pacific Ocean region have pretensions to culturally and economically colonise the FSU territories.

Most analysts agree that if Russia is not able to become in the near perspective (15-20 years) a centre of new (both by form and content) continental consolidation

---

**19** A contemporary state of course cannot be built on the sample of 'sovereign states' of 18th and 19th century.

Contemporary state delegates many functions and authorities to the supra-state level and others – to territorial level (local self-government, states, lands, cantons, regions). One of the key tasks of the statehood as a peculiar management technique is efficient inclusion of national (country) resources in world (regional) economy (WE) and effective usage of the WE's opportunities for development of its own territory and population. N.Bukharin used to contend that the level of country's wealth (hence social policy fulfilled) depends to a large extent on its place in the world system of labour division. Debts and oil as well as perspectives of existing as a large 'eco-colony' can hardly be considered to be the means of country's participation in the WE, although in terms of notion one will have to consider namely this way. The neutral external observer unlike any resident and representative of the given country never cares for the way it participates in world economic co-operation and exchange.

(on Eurasia's mainland) it will turn into (here one is inclined to agree with the concepts of the so-called 'new right') an arena for action on the part of two other continental and world empires (proto-empires). We should emphasise that the USSR's collapse was itself stimulated to a large extent by the increased influence that the external centres of force exerted. A move towards Russia's breakaway from the USSR, outlined in general terms long before the events of 1991, was to a large extent determined by purely pragmatic reasons: stakes in the resource potential of the Russian Federation, comprehension of the deep dependence of the newly formed CIS countries upon Russia in both economic and cultural terms, desire to get rid of the problems piled up in the 'near abroad' at one fell swoop, etc. Today it is clear that the economic and political situation in the majority of CIS countries proved much worse than that in Russia.

At the same time, the problem of frontiers grew acute: the Russian Federation, being by its historical origin the result of territorial expansion and colonisation, does not currently have stable borders. A new cluster of geopolitical and geo-economic tensions are now forming around Russia. These tensions carry the danger of serious and prolonged regional conflicts. For the last ten years both the power elite and the majority of social (professional) groups have continued to interpret the world order (in its real, intended and designed respect) as anything but an idyllic area of mutual assistance and mutual concessions. Despite significant changes in international economic and political rivalry since the world wars, struggle for domination and control over the key resources – materials (raw materials, means of production, finances), intellectual and 'human' resources (air, pure water, territory as such) – remain the essence of these processes. The competition between enterprises is increasingly being subordinated to that between countries and even blocs and strategic alliances of countries. No doubt, in this rivalry the paramount role is played by the resource of 'freedom' (an economic and political organisation which promotes the mobilisation of individual and group will). However, no less important is the opportunity of expansion, control and domination. Nowadays it is possible to conclude that a country which has embarked upon the trail of 'catch-up' development is not free to choose its own place in the WE and the international system of division of labour that is currently under formation.

Of course, for the current situation the most appropriate models for solving contradictions and conflicts between different social groups (classes; e.g. between workers and entrepreneurs) are those that can be borrowed from the history of capitalism.

In this case, one may state that after a certain lapse of time the tremendous change in systems of activity as well as the objective necessity of expanding sales and stimulating increased consumption will result in serious concern on the part of the developed producing countries regarding the emerging discrepancies and differences in living standards across various regions of the world. Subsequently, these countries will adopt special compensatory economic policies. The specific shape of existing competitive relations between countries manifests itself most illustratively in the Yugoslavian conflict and in the strategy of fiscal and cultural neo-colonialism which is on the rise in many countries of Latin America, as well as in the Baltic republics of the FSU. So far, Russia's relations with new CIS countries cannot be called trouble-free because of energy contradictions. Discriminated against in the outside world, Russia behaves like a 'shark' of international competition in its 'near abroad' and 'internal colonies'. In other words, the completed structure of world economic co-operation and political interaction imposes quite stringent conditions of participation on separate countries in world and regional development – both with respect to the character of this participation (place, specific types of specialisation, co-operation) and its mechanism (means of participation). We mentioned above that there was no prearranged place for Russia in the WE and the international division of labour. At the end of the 1960s and the beginning of the 1970s there may have been an opportunity for Russia to assume a place among the 'newly industrialising countries', but it was missed. The right wing cherished the hope that a second industrialisation wave in the countries of Asia and the Pacific Ocean region and Latin America would not take place and that later it would be possible to wriggle into the 'club' of influential countries on the crest of a world raw material (primarily energy) crisis. However these opportunities were utilised in an extremely inefficient way. Today the WE only includes the Russian gas industry and some areas of armaments production. Russia's oil resources have lost their significance as a world resource in the middle-term perspective (although they make up an important sector of the CIS internal economic complex) and most lines of production are not able to enter the world market competitively. And even if it does ever happen that Russian export branches 'move up' to the world market, this does not necessarily signify their full participation in the WE. The primary condition for international competitiveness of a country's resources nowadays is not the absolute capacity of its resources, but rather the relative possibility to use these resources (and their specific combination) in world economic relations and organisational processes. Furthermore, the situation with respect to relations between countries has apparently changed to a considerable extent since K. Schmidt formulated his notion that the a change in the rank-order of a state within a state system was based on the possibility of the use of force. Today one can single out at least three mechanisms whereby countries change their status in world processes: we will call them, respectively, the strategies of 'war', 'struggle' and 'game'. These mechanisms merit more detailed attention.

If one considers that economic activity is primarily consumption and control over the natural resources of a territory and 'bowels' of the earth (this very standpoint was prevalent at the end of the 19th-beginning of the 20th century), then a direct war strategy is the only way to change status and place in the international system of division of labour. Such a viewpoint provoked the two previous world wars, aimed at re-dividing zones of influence and up to the present day it remains a corner stone of many regional conflicts[20].

The countries of Asia and the Pacific Ocean region and Latin America which embarked in the middle of the century on the road to development and modernisation and which have now mastered the industrial model of development, in fact elaborated another mechanism of participation in the WE, which can be called a 'export strategy' and (within the framework of introduced typology) and should be attributed to the area of 'struggle' for markets. The essence of this strategy consisted in using a specific configuration of internal resources and mobilising them (which was akin to 'war-wages' i.e., underpaid labour, stringent control, over-exploitation of the environment) to create competitive products and break into the key markets, to a large extent ousting products of other countries (including those of advanced ones). Confronted with this new strategy, developed countries themselves took into account the experience of the 'young tigers' and in the mid-1970s set up an alternative strategy, aimed at maintaining (and even solidifying) their positions in the international system of labour division and world political system. This strategy was connected with the creation of a world fiscal (currency and banking) space which virtually performed the functions of multi-regional fiscal supervision (hence management) of local (regional) economic and social activity. Consequently, establishment of an international export strategy (as distinct from other managerial

---

**20** In this respect Germany's experience is very interesting. The country lost almost all the wars in which it was involved in 19th and 20th centuries. As early as at that time the limitations of the strategy and its non-constructive nature were comprehended. From war benefited those who observed the belligerents from the sidelines and made profiles at the expense of assistance to one of them or to both sides involved in the conflict.

strategies) does not and cannot lead to a significant change in a country's world ranking.

Thus for a country (the national economy as a whole, particular industries and professional groups and even elite groups of management, as the experience of Asia and Pacific Ocean region and Latin American countries illustrates) there remains only one single effective and realistic way to transform the existing network of dependencies as well as its own 'place' in the systemic context of world organisation, which we will term 'game'. This is first and foremost the competition of programmes, management techniques and solutions to problems (of multi-national and ultimately world character), techniques of thinking (first of all collective, group, interdisciplinary, inter-professional), competition between knowledge systems (the most efficient techniques of knowledge use) and semiotic (sign) machines. An example of such a game can be traced in the history of creating free economic zones in various regions of the world. Nation states evidently attracted multi-national corporations and entrepreneurial projects to their territories, setting up favourable conditions for their activity. Put differently, the only means of a country's inclusion in the WE and the international division of labour is via the establishment of a technique of intellectual activity organisation which would exceed the world average technique through the efficient organisation and utilisation of human (individual and collective, but in any event, primarily intellectual) resources.

The strategy of the 'game' always presumes the formulation of new rules of interaction and interrelation, new principles of management, new fashions, new lifestyles and a new system of semiotic (sign) activity regulation with the aim of reaching a position of leadership in the elaboration and acceleration of these new rules in the world community. Finally, it is always reflexive management: using every opportunity to turn one's weak points into strong ones by means of better intellectual organisation and also using the strength of other players as a resource for the initiation of world processes in directions which suit everyone.

## 6 Origin and Opportunities of Post-Soviet Bureaucracy

The underlying thesis of this section is that the post-Soviet '*nomenklatura*', desiring to become a true bureaucracy (i.e., to master contemporary management techniques) and adopt prototypes of 'power administration' that exist in the modern world's financial oligarchy, is apparently a 'failed class' – to the same extent as Marx's 'notorious' proletariat.

This is caused by at least three reasons:

- the origin and history of the formation of the post-Soviet *nomenklatura* (a peculiar 'genetic code' of the given social group);
- the direction of future development which is determined by the class itself as well as by external conditions and restrictions (a sort of a crisis of both traditional and degenerated types of 'red tape');
- the intricacy of the problems it has to solve.

In ontological terms this thesis is obvious: it is impossible to enter a new space of activity and life without experiencing change. By using the historical opportunity of development and Russia's systemic integration into world processes, the '*nomenklatura*' will annihilate itself as a class and drastically transform its own form of existence. In other words, the current *nomenklatura* (which existed even up to 1985) cannot assimilate the processes under way and therefore will be ousted from the central flow of political and administrative processes.

In previous paragraphs we have generally outlined the 'internal' and 'external' tasks the post-Soviet *nomenklatura* faces. There are three main elements:

- managing processes of systemic collapse;
- overcoming geopolitical and geo-economic instability of the Russian Federation and the entire CIS;
- solving a number of world problems and contradictions – basic lines of fracture inherent in world development on the threshold of the third millennium.

Many 'expert societies' resort to the notion of the 'administrative market' (S. Kordonskii and V. Naishul are those who introduced this term into Russian analytical literature). In this context this market can be called the 'cradle' of the Russian *nomenklatura*. According to this concept, there had been no 'administrative and command system' in the USSR since 1948, i.e., a hierarchic decision-making system, system of administration and subordination. Such a system did indeed exist in the 1930s and 1940s but later experienced a collapse (which possibly became one of the key reasons for the collapse of the entire existing systemic organisation).

In the course of the administrative and command system's collapse relations between different economic and political power groups (industrial and territorial) gradually turn into a system of 'heterarchical tenders': every group which possesses certain resources (material, organisational, socio-political) exerts influence on other groups in order to benefit as much as possible. The privatisation of the administrative and command system becomes a key process. Privatisation implies in this case, as we have mentioned above, the process under which separate fragments of the administrative system, channels of information and decision-making are privatised , i.e., entirely become private or communal property of the administrative staff. The basic unit of administrative tender is a separate administrative favour. People involved in administration exchange these favours[21]. In the area of the administrative market, economic logic is virtually redundant, as is the logic of cost and profitability assessment[22]. The administrative market (like all other markets) operates mainly as a semiotic (sign) machine. Every participant in the administrative market has a system of signs (marks) which define his/her status. A participant's status is determined by the extent to which he can affect the processes of distribution, redistribution and exchange of resources. By the end of the 1960s the structure of places in the administrative market started to differ considerably from that of the administrative and command system[23]. The administrative market reflexively spreads throughout the process of decision-making and administration; the administrative and command system starts existing within this market and in conformity to its regulations. Until the early 1990s the Communist Party played the role of 'lubricant', still holding control over the administrative market; the latter is thus not competitive but oligopolistic. It still facilitates the implementation of a certain number of goals which are established as state priorities: the maintenance of the flow of resources between agriculture, the military-industrial complex and the fuel and energy complex; between donor and recipient regions in the processes of

---

**21** Processes of resources distribution, their redistribution, exchange, processes of supply as well as planning or non-planning become elements of administrative services provided. Delivery of cargoes and goods to the destination, including in state plans the programmes as a 'separate line', solving social conflicts, housing, providing minimal wages and salaries in exchange for minimal output – all these are the administrative services the circulation of which makes up the tissue of administrative market.

**22** Of paramount importance are opportuneness, necessity and maintenance of stability of administrative corporations. Directors of factories aspire to have staff numbers as large as possible, thus getting the opportunities to receive more resources irrespective of whether the workers are engaged in productive labour or not. It is also desirable to have 'labour teams' (a wonderful invention of administrative market) under severe climatic and living conditions, etc.

**23** The administrative market is not an exclusive feature of Soviet and post-Soviet society. Administrative market exists every where. However, the important feature of domestic situation is the fact that administrative market is a form in which all other markets exist and are implemented: markets of goods, services, information, means of production and labour. They and corresponding processes 'live' within the administrative market because of their involvement in it as well as through its mediation.

assimilation; strengthening defence capacity and maintaining friendly relations in other regions of the world.

In the mid-1980s the privatisation of the administrative and command system was augmented by another key process of contemporary market modernisation. The need for modernisation was caused by two groups of reasons: 'external', i.e., those connected with the challenge of the world economy; and 'internal', i.e., those caused by the need to consolidate the achieved degree of privatisation of the administrative and command system by the main elite groups. At the same time, modernisation does not change the social nature of a particular society at any given moment. In the context of modernisation changes, the recalibration of places and rank-orders in the administrative market is well under way. Administrative status has started converting itself into financial and material assets. In spite of the fact that a functionary holds a certain office in the existing administrative and command system, the administrative service he performs may be worth nothing.

This process of rank-ordering is the first condition for modernisation and it is precisely modernisation itself that becomes the basic content of the first period of so-called *perestroika*[24]. We should emphasise that so-called regionalisation or territorial fragmentation of the FSU, nowadays of Russia, should also be considered as one of the trends of administrative and command system privatisation and administrative market modernisation. The year 1992, which officially became the year of 'price liberalisation' and 'launch of economic reform' in Russia was, undoubtedly, the year of drastic modernisation. Owing to Gaidar's actions, all participants in the administrative market understood that instead of a very labour-consuming (re)distribution of hundreds of different resources, one could distribute or control the distribution of just two 'key' resources: finances and legal rights. Later, the post-Soviet *nomenklatura* successfully mastered new control techniques (as Gaidar first demonstrated) and started using so-called 'economic' instruments of administration often in a far more refined way than their 'teacher from the scientific community'. Moreover, having expertise in operating in an administrative market and experience of *perestroika* (intensively mastering new administrative techniques), the post-Soviet *nomenklatura* sees its future in a 'financial' (above all banking) and financial

---

**24** It is worth recollecting a wave of liquidation of administrative structures, followed by 'unexpected' resurgence of these structures under new titles but with the same people. One can mention 'the second wave of turning companies into share-holding companies' whereby the method of 'negative deposit' was actively used. A functionary brings in a commitment 'not to hinder' in form of a share and requires to register this deposit as a share of the authorised capital.

industrial oligarchy. Some experts are of the opinion that this actually was the goal of the whole process of *perestroika* and in particular the reason why formal authorities (government) tolerated corruption, capital formation schemes, etc.

There is a relatively widespread standpoint that a similar social (and socio-cultural) new order – financial and financial industrial oligarchy – has just been established in Russia. In the authors´s opinion this is incorrect. There are at least four groups of reasons that prompt a different point of view. Firstly, in Russia no new stable semiotic space has been established where the problems of legitimising wealth, creating a new system of cultural and social images, legalising and legitimising assets and their holders can be solved. Factually, there is no large body of legitimate capital (hence there is no capital as such: even a huge amount of money is not yet capital) nor of large-scale legitimate personal (not corporate) capital (with the exception of show-business and sports).

Secondly, up to 80% of financial assets originate from state money (in the first, second or third derivative), including rights and privileges (export quotas, special permits, etc.) converted to financial assets. Without state support neither investment nor import/export operations (on a significant geo-economic scale) nor even preservation of these assets is possible.

Thirdly, the scale (mass) of formed financial assets is incommensurable with that of industrial capital and above all with the capital necessary for the implementation of big infrastructural projects, conversion programmes, and project funding in industry.

Fourthly, there is no appropriately staffed specialised fiscal infrastructure that includes non-banking financial institutions, an developed securities market, holdings in operation (it should be especially emphasised that organisational administrative staff [even in the banking sphere] have no financial-semiotic reality; this manifests itself mainly in the fact that banks keep operating as big credit and loan establishments).

It should be added that in the process of shaping itself the current *nomenklatura* is orienting itself towards the models of financial-industrial groups which proved themselves in some countries of Europe (primarily in Germany) and in many the countries of Asia and the Pacific Ocean region. These groups are regarded as subjects of technological modernisation within the country and as potential participants in world economic rivalry if they receive substantial support from the state. This does not mean that we exclude the possibility and prospects of creating a post-Soviet financial-industrial oligarchy or multi-national corporations which can be in operation on the territory of the entire CIS and. We simply emphasise that today a similar subject of transformation and development is absent and that the formation of this subject (if no insurmountable obstacles appear on its way) is likely to take several more years.

However, the question we would like to pose is more deeply directed. What are the demands made of a subject of development today? What does it mean to be an administrative elite in a systemic world?

Today, being an 'elite' implies also to supervise main channels and currents of 'resources'. It implies being able to purposefully include these resources in various national and international processes, thus achieving ultimate utilisation efficiency and augmentation of the resource basis. In order to be able to do this, one should be in possession of up-to-date thinking techniques and be trained to use the existing range of semiotic machines and synergistic capabilities of humanised forms of activity (capabilities of signs, expertise, cultural norms, ideology, those of joint, group and collective mental activity). Unfortunately the existing *nomenklatura* has neither the necessary culture (mainly socio-humane and philosophic), nor the appropriate intellectual and technical grounding; they are unaware of the types of social processes under way and cannot accelerate or direct them properly. In particular, this manifests itself in their inability to work with mass political processes under conditions of inter-professional communication, incomplete information, uncertainty and collective action, under conditions of innovation, crisis, accidents, extreme conditions and calamities. It also manifests itself in incomprehension of contemporary demands for research and design work, lack of skill in use of network forms of organisation, informational techniques, mobile corporations and multi-focal management systems inherent in 'high' forms of activity and thinking. The existing *nomenklatura* are unfortunately not able to operate systems of intelligence and reflection. Roughly speaking, it (in its bulk) is simply illiterate in social and humane terms. 'Economism' (as a particular form of injection of a humane approach) cannot offset the dramatic absence of a complex of socio-humane knowledge and modern anthropological techniques.

Confronted with the problem which was previously outlined, namely to adjust the collapsing and re-emerging systemic integrity of Russia to that of world economic and cultural development of thinking and activity, the *nomenklatura* clearly shies away from it and aspires to replace this task with a number of pseudo-goals: maintenance (stabilisation) of production, elaboration of investment projects, mastering democratic political culture, 'restoration' of empire or its economic and political equivalent, preservation of ideological supervision of the training and development of an individual, etc. But even in implementing the enumerated objectives (seemingly custom-tailored for the *nomenklatura*'s genesis and world-view), the concrete representatives of the new *nomenklatura* interpret these goals and way of their achievement in such a narrow-minded and outdated way that they cannot, in principle, be implemented under the current conditions[25].

Thus, we have arrived at the question of change in the leading subject of transformations and development on the threshold of the 2lst century.

## 7 In Search of Subject

The modernisation revolutions of the 1970s, the 'explosive' economic growth of countries of Asia and the Pacific Ocean region and the change in the world's geo-economic correlation of forces, regional reforms of the early 1980s in advanced industrial countries, *perestroika* and the collapse of the USSR and, finally, the economic slump of the early 1990s again put the issue of the driving forces and subjects of world development on the agenda of philosophic and methodological, theoretical and practical deliberations. A philosophic and methodological view of the subject of development was probably first put into an articulated form by Hegel. He introduced the notion of 'negative class' as the means or form of realising historical opportunity. At the same time, the historical process is regarded and categorised as 'natural-artificial' and analysis leans towards discovering those mechanisms which 'obstruct' or 'stimulate' purely evolutionary movement.

Working within the realm of philosophy (and methodology) of history, Hegel was not interested in concrete sociology and never objectivised his ideas in sociological reality. In other words, he was not concerned with the question as to which concrete social group (stratum or class in the secondary, specifically sociological sense) would take over the function of the negative class. At the same time, French thinkers of utopian orientation made attempts to practically create an ideal social organisation and comprehended their experience in socio-practical terms. With Saint Simon the notion of class gains a realistic tinge. Discussion of the actual social stratum (group, class) which implements historical opportunity and ensures, through its activity, the

**25** In this respect there was a widespread phrase, coined by V. Chernomyrdin: 'we wanted to improve but improved away'. In this respect the article keeps developing the tenor of the other article by this author – 'forms of economic organisation and up-to-date entrepreneurial strategies' (*Kentavr* [Centaur] 1993, no. 2, as well as the collection 'Programming cultural development: regional aspects', 2nd issue, Moscow, 1993).

course of historical development (in particular, in terms of socio-economic transformations), gained a new momentum in the second half of the last century and at the beginning of this century in German and Russian social-democracy. In his teaching K. Marx synthesised a number of different lines of European cultural and intellectual development. Having linked the socio-practical orientation of French utopians and the principle of historical development, borrowed from classical German philosophy, he gave specific sociological and even socio-political content to the idea of 'negative class', affirming that the proletariat is the stratum upon which one could build while carrying out socio-political innovations.

In his analysis of the origin of capitalism Max Weber underlined the role of Protestant communities and also paid attention to the phenomenon of modern bureaucracy. Lev Trotskii regarded the youth as the agent of development which takes over the responsibility for the next 'step' of the movement through generational revolution. Lenin used to state that a similar function could only be performed by a party of a new type, combining the might of a military organisation with the means of mass ideological mobilisation. Half a century later Milovan Dzilas delineated this phenomenon in terms of establishment of a 'third class' – the 'partocracy'. In the mid-1920s K. Mannheim (regarding the matter in specifically sociological terms, unlike Schelling) put forward the thesis that intellectuals, as possessors of knowledge and of the resource of freedom, are the social group which ensures development. Very close in spirit are all interpretations which regard an engineering community or administrative elite as a subject of development.

A similar standpoint became widely spread in Germany and Russia under the influence of scientific and technical progress in the 1880s. The aims of industrialisation, intensive industrial development and expansion of infrastructures spotlight engineer-entrepreneurs as the authors and organisers of large-scale projects. Analogous ideas in the 1960s were developed by Galbraith who considered the technostructure (the engineering-technical and engineering-managerial elite) to be the motivating force of development. Concurrently, within the framework of the first programmes on re-privatising nationalised branches of industry and areas of activity in advanced countries, as well as within the framework of the modernisation of South-eastern Asia and Latin America, the concept of the managers' revolution is becoming widely spread.

Thus the question arises: who, which social and professional group will replace the *nomenklatura*, which dreams of becoming the 'bureaucracy' and financial-industrial oligarchy? Which group will substitute the contemporary bureaucracy, which privatised the state administration and fiscal system as a subject of reproduction and development of activity systems? What resource can be compared, in terms of influence, with the monopoly in the distribution of finances and rights? What are the dynamics of the substitution of the leading subject of development in the world context and under Russia's particular conditions?

A comprehensive answer to this question can hardly be found.

However, two underlying hypothesis can be put forward. Firstly, in the world context the given social group (potential subject of development and reproduction) should possess state-of-the-art techniques of collective thinking and problem resolution, new methods of production and utilisation expertise. 'Expertise' (and all it implies) and not capital will play the role of a key resource for the entire formation of mental activity.

Secondly, in Russia the only group that can take over this mission, is a group that would be able to present and solve world problems (present Russia's problems as world ones) alongside finding solutions to 'domestic' (Russia's own) problems. The only group that can become the subject of socio-cultural and economic development is the group that is prepared to provide the driving force and assume the responsibility for:

- elaborating a new ideology of 'life building', new approaches to solving world problems, new principles and frameworks of thinking and activity organisation;
- creating new epistemological strategies: techniques of synthesis, co-organisation, production and engineer reconstruction of knowledge and knowledge systems as well as setting up new distribution (transmission) channels and new means of knowledge utilisation;
- implementing contemporary principles and schemes of management which would take into account the cultural and educational level of the population, the capabilities of informational technologies and network forms of organisation (professional and inter-professional communities), the fluctuation of the demographic and ecological situation, etc.

We have already emphasised the role and importance of corporate forms of social action and economic and political activity. Today, however, other (in a sense – more mobile and democratic) forms of group and collective organisation become increasingly important. These can be called 'framework groups' (associations), 'intentional associations', 'business networks'. These groups and amalgamations utilise the organisational abilities of corporations, particular corporate (organisational) frameworks to implement their goals, values, principles and forms of life. Associations of multi-national professionals, using modern, flexible techniques of thinking, change the internal structure of corporations (corporate forms of organisation), which can be characterised as neo-corporatism. It is probable that a certain foresight about the tendencies and changes mentioned and the appearance of associations operating both within corporate frameworks and between (over) the corporations led Galbraith to his concept of a 'technostructure' combining state administrative organs, large business and professional (primarily engineering) elites.

However, it would be more exact to talk about anthropo-structures (united by close intentional and conceptual affinities) which combine organisations of different scale and type. It is most likely that those socio-cultural groups that succeed in implementing the development mission will have to form and exist as kindred intentional (conceptual) associations and anthropo-structures. In this respect the situation in Russia can be called tragic but certainly not hopeless. Of course, the ecological situation is catastrophic, technological (first of all infrastructural and production) complexes are outdated in physical and moral terms, equipment is worn out, existing systems of administration and management cannot ensure neither further operation nor development. However, one particular resource (the creation and accumulation of which is an extremely time- and labour-consuming process) has been maintained, the non-availability of which has always been the key problem for most countries in the course of their development. This resource is what is often called 'human resource and human capital': the educational and qualificational as well as cultural potential of Russia's population which still remains extremely high according to overall world standards.

Russia possesses a rich cultural heritage and huge historical experience of cultural (including philosophical and religious) self-determination of the individual and of united groups. Russia is in possession of state-of-the-art educational and staff training techniques (although some of them still have an experimental or laboratory status). Over the last 40 years in Russia extremely effective techniques of thinking and collective problem resolution were developed. To return to the issue of Russia's inclusion in the international system of division of labour (i.e., to the issue of Russia's assimilation with the key problems and contradictions of the WE), one can currently single out several different directions of inclusion:

- elaboration of new techniques of management and problem resolution (at the level of separate enterprises, post-Soviet multi-national corporations, separate territories and regions, temporary design and research groups and mobile corporations), including development and experimental phasing in of new systems of knowledge and semiotic machines;

- individual (and collective) operations and services demanding high qualification and personal initiative;
- creation of non-technologically organised systems (important not only for the military sphere but also for equipping research activity, ecology and designing human-machine systems);
- the fourth direction supposes (despite the limitations of this strategy that were mentioned previously) the establishment of several 'export' industries (this task still can be implemented nowadays in the aircraft and space industry, in the realm of organic synthesis, informatics and systemic programming, in some fields of armaments production, possibly in watch-making and textile industry, and in some branches of shipbuilding and metallurgy).

The directions mentioned are clearly connected with possibilities in specific areas of educational and staff training system, created on the territory in question, as well as with particular aspects in the operation of science, the military-industrial complex and a number of other industrial and service sectors. As an entire spectrum of fields that used to be backed by state subsidies collapses, highly qualified experts enter the labour market: engineers, military people, researchers, representatives of applied (natural and social) sciences, entrepreneurs, cinema and art specialists, managers, experts in the area of information, mass media, programmers, security experts, etc. These people make up the area of supply in the market of qualified services and often even compete with similar experts and professionals in other countries and regions. Concurrently, one can observe an increase in the supply of equipment, machine tools, operating systems, quality assessment systems, research plants, mostly constructed on an individual basis and often not ready for production-type operation. There are already a great number of projects, the intellectual aspect of which is worked out in Russia and the actual realisation of which is exported or designed from the very beginning in the countries of the CIS, Europe, Asia and the Pacific Occan region.

For the internal situation this means that concurrently with post-Soviet *nomenklatura* and financial 'oligarchy', a stratum of free professionals is emerging that is creating a market of reputation and qualification in various areas of activity. We are convinced that on the threshold of the $21^{st}$ century a stratum of 'interlockers', i.e., strategic intermediaries between different types of knowledge and types (spheres) of activity will form. The particular ways of existence and reproduction for this group are framework groups, intentional associations, intellectual corporations and business networks (including inter-professional ones). At the same time, this stratum turns out to be a consumer of a broad spectrum of secondary services (informational, organisational, educational, etc.) that could employ a large number of the population.

In the long-term perspective one can talk about establishment of a number of 'big technologies' on the basis of these networks, corporations and other national resources and with regard to world problems. The term 'small technology' (since the 1890s) implies either combination of science and production (for instance in the chemical industry) or progressive operations (Taylor's 'fixed form of production organisation', a conveyer), whereas 'big' technologies are the result of organisation and technologisation of reproduction processes (contours) of production systems or service systems. The typical example is the 'technology of American engineering' which originated on the conveyer of the Ford motor works where 'T' version automobiles were produced and later through changes in the salary payment system, construction of roads and systems of roadside service, mass advertising, housing technology, design competition – it embraced all systems of reproduction of the common American's lifestyle. Today one can enumerate such world-wide technologies as intensive agriculture, personal computers, the diamond business (including the formation of elite demand and fashion for jewellery), fast food technology (taking in urban infrastructures and contemporary tourism in big cities), world-wide transport, etc. The determining factor in the formation of 'big technologies' is the analysis and design of the social and cultural processes which maintain the reproduction and development of mental activity (as, for example, solvent demand for goods and services). The existence and expansion of 'big technologies' in the contemporary world prove the hypothesis that social and cultural policy covers economic planning and sets up 'zones' (gaps) for new forms of life and activity (consumption). On the threshold of the 21st century alongside the transition to infrastructural (network) forms of organisation, one may talk about the formation of at least four 'big (the biggest) technologies':

- *health technology* (includes ecological design, medical service, recreation, sports, disease prevention, the pharmaceutical industry, system of social and medical insurance, creation of new foodstuffs, ecological agriculture);
- technology of *socio-production systems development* (includes engineering, technological design, entrepreneurship, innovative activity, staff training and

upgrading, organisational consulting, investment activity, communications, construction of industrial entities and withdrawing them from operation, marketing);

- technology of *cultural policy and activity organisation* (includes city and regional planning, demographic planning, family planning, housing, organisation of living conditions and infrastructures (which ensure the quality of life), advertising, cultural industry, screen technologies, political consulting, law, design, mass media);
- technology of *personal growth* (including personal psychological technique, educational techniques of different levels, self-education systems, making personal investment plans, programmes of increased of mobility, employment programme, migration programme, programme for the creation of individual informational and instrumental-epistemic systems).

Currently the key resource of every country is predominantly made up of universally mastered (not only by the elite stratum) technologies of thinking, comprehension, reflection and professional activity. Of course, the pioneer developments in this area were the property of a minority for quite a long time. The only thing that may challenge the process of distribution and intensive mastering of these developments, alongside the utilisation of capabilities of modern educational and staff training infrastructures, mass media and informational technologies, is the system of principles and formal organisation of socio-public systems, considered as a specific area for the application of the synergistic potential of collective mental activity and objectivised manifestation of rationalism.

It is quite justified to consider the establishment of similar technologies and their elements possible on Russia's territory and regard events and tendencies under way through the prism of the restoration of complete forms of thinking and activity organisation, inherent in contemporary world development.

# 5

# The Structure of Economic Space in Post-*Perestroika* Society and the Transformation of the Administrative Market

Simon Kordonskii

> Menshikov also stole, but the country was getting rich
> Lt.- Gen. A. Lebed'

## 1 Introduction

The ideology of economic liberalism as applied to Russia has become inadequate, above all because its moderateness no longer suits the new economic agents, while the followers of socialism are not happy with its radical nature. By putting limits on state-run economic regulation, the reformers clearly repelled those people that are engaged in the privatisation of public property. But at the same time, they also incurred the wrath of all entities living off the state budget, who were thus deprived of their faith in the future as well of their state-guaranteed consumer status. The reasoning of the economists who through circumstance have become civil servants and have started implementing ideas borrowed from the West is logically simple. They assert they have cleared the way for the omnipotent market laws to enter into effect, not merely in words but in deed, too. However, the laws that were released by them from their socialist shackles for some reason seem to result in actions that cannot be explained in terms of canonical theories. The economists, as befits all Soviet social scholars, find a wealth of explanations for this in political, rather than economic, terms. The personified enemies from the government, the Federal assembly and the Presidential Administration, play a far greater role in their explanations than the objective and indestructible laws of the market economy. There is a certain rational kernel in the economists' reasoning, but it has nothing to do with persons in power. They are confronted with a system of interaction called the administrative market, where power and money are reciprocally convertible according to specifically Russian laws.

The Russian territory became the second factor that thwarted the reformers' plans. When their best and brightest came to power, they were quickly confronted with the necessity to subsidise the transport of supplies to the Russian North, the agricultural spring investments and the maintenance of the ex-USSR armed forces throughout the vast Eurasian expanses. This quickly sobered up the most brilliant reform-minded economists-turned-rulers and speeded up their transmutation into bureaucrats. The spatial factor, exogenous from the viewpoint of canonical economic theory, proved to be decisive.

Many, if not all problems of Russia as part of Eurasia stem from the necessity to control a vast and largely untapped geographical space. The present-day Russian territory has been conquered over hundreds of years in the course of which all kinds of marginal groups, from the Cossacks to convicts, colonised areas populated by autochthonous peoples, turning them into the empire's provinces. The system of imperial rule and the relationship between the Centre and the periphery varied from century to century in form only.

The tensions and absurdities in the empire's social structure did not attain a new quality through the establishment of a new social organisation of society (as was the case in Europe). Instead they were eliminated in the course of a directional or situational emigration of the marginal groups. These settled in the new imperial territories and reproduced the empire's social structure, its systems, strata and public institutions. The exiled, deported, the former convicts and even those evading debt repayment (or their first generation descendants) would become governors, district chiefs, justices of the peace, political commissars, chairmen of local soviets and secretaries of regional Communist Party committees; they were granted inheritable or personal nobility rights, Communist Party membership and the right to govern territories as big as European states.

During this geographical and social pioneering no need for any economic modernisation ever arose. The colonised territories became raw-material appendages to the Centre which alienated and distributed among them the resources required to maintain life and social structures. The dual alienating/distributory relationship between the Centre and the periphery also determined the state's territorial and administrative organisation, whereby the power structure at any lower level of administrative control reproduced more or less exactly the same structure of a higher level, and whereby any two adjoining levels of the administrative and territorial hierarchy were in a state of permanent bargaining (especially in Soviet times). This bargaining essentially pertained to the proportions between the industrial, alimentary and raw material goods alienated from a lower level and distributed by a higher one (in favour of lower levels and sectors of the economy). It was bargaining between adjoining levels of the administrative and territorial hierarchy coupled with administrative rivalry between the national economy sectors that constituted the administrative market.

Relations between adjoining levels of the administrative and territorial hierarchy did not require any economic innovations, since the only way to solve problems of alienation and distribution was to enhance one's status level (of a *oblast'*, region, district, city) in the administrative hierarchy, which automatically ensured the right to increase the amount of resources alienated from lower levels and acquired by the level in question. There were periods in the national history when traditional resources exhausted themselves, or when the state became too weak to requisition or distribute anything. There were epochs of social revolutions which always ended in the reproduction of the former relationship between the Centre and the periphery, based on new varieties of resources or a new, more intricate form of coercive alienation and distribution.

In modern times the administrative market came to be based on fuel and raw material resources, free labour of convicts and military construction units as well as on the compulsory labour of educated people. The fall in energy resources production, disappearance of the free labour force (there was nobody to imprison any more, and the convicts' work ceased to be effective) resulted in the system's inefficiency. Another cause of this lay in the natural limit (from the viewpoint of the leading world powers) set to the armed export of social tensions, such as the aggression in Afghanistan. The system no longer provided either the necessary level of alienation of resources by the Centre from the lower echelons or the necessary level of distribution.

*Perestroika* and the reforms of the last decade may be regarded as a search for resources aimed at maintaining the former relationship between the Centre and the periphery. It started with the 'struggle to strengthen work discipline', then the authorities looked for candidates for imprisonment among dissidents, alcoholics, illicit income earners and 'pilferers of socialist property'. Ultimately this all culminated in a search for 'ways to increase national economic efficiency', in *uskorenie* ('acceleration') and in a change of the economy's sectoral organisation. However, no resources were found which resulted in the collapse of the USSR.

Russia, as the successor-state to the USSR not only in terms of foreign economic debts, continued the search for resources. A last minute reserve was found in the market, in capitalism, in money. Tapping this resource became the essence of post-*perestroika* life. However, the market and money, even in their crudest form, proved incompatible with both the social structure, the time-tested Centre-periphery relationship, and with the sectoral organisation of the economy, i.e., with the state.

The 'market reforms' are of great positive significance for Russia, but this has no connection with the achievements cited by the authorities when they are defending themselves against the opposition, conservative economists and citizens of the recently great state. The positive outcome of 'radical economic reform' lies in deepening social stratification, commercialisation of the authorities (i.e., rise of corruption), dynamic social movement (more because an ever greater part of the populace has to 'wheel and deal' in order to survive than because they have such values), and above all in the destruction of Russia's administrative and territorial structure, in the country's regionalisation, i.e., in the transformation of the age-old Centre-periphery relationship. The main achievement of the reformers is precisely that what they are accused of by their socialist and fundamentalist opponents.

The force, used by the high-brow economists and former Communist Party (CPSU) functionaries since turned anti-Communists against the social and administrative-territorial structures (and not against the economy, as they think), started the convertibility of state statuses (and not of the rouble) and made it possible to almost legally determine the price of a governmental post or a desired economic and political decision. In the author's opinion, the all-out corruption and bribery which is gradually destroying the multi-level structure of imperial rule is a much lesser evil than another revolution (i.e., the violent change in the social structure and in property relations). The result of this revolution the advent to power of people who do not know what to do with it, intending to create some new kind of 'bright future'.

The post-*perestroika* economic and social changes were not a direct result of reformist activities. The idealist reformers, motivated by the purely Marxist idea of economic laws dominating over socio-political and administrative realities, created conditions for liberating the social groups that had been formed under real socialism from the fetters of any laws. The ongoing struggle of sectoral and regional groups against the federal authorities and among themselves engenders new rules which the next generation of university-level economists is likely to study in a decade or so, terming them 'the Russian amendments of basic economic laws'.

Before the reforms, the country did not have a social stratum that was vitally interested in economic liberalisation and the formation of a political system other than the administrative market. The 1992 reforms facilitated the formation of this stratum which requires above all a real change in the relationship between power and property as well as in the Centre-periphery relationship. The 'new people' are interested in an accelerated social stratification (which broadens their social basis) and in the formation of power institutions that would be capable of keeping the 'new lumpen' in check, this being the less savoury side of the process of creation of a '*nouveaux riches*' stratum. The commercialisation of power, no matter how unattractive it may look, also speeds up the formation of a 'new people' stratum interested in changing the power-property relationship.

Russia is now facing a multi-level system of interests based on a new social stratification. The rate of social stratification is extremely fast (by sociological standards, measuring time in terms of generations), and people who find themselves in this or that social stratum are very seldom aware of their new position. Still coarser identifications and contrasts exist in the individual awareness of one's social status. Furthermore, the strata themselves have not yet taken a clear-cut economic or institutionalised shape. People who are members of one social group by external indications still belong to social reference groups of the pre-*perestroika* society by force of their internal, personal feelings. The 'new people' are interested in a strong state. This interest is manifested in local actions (in a distorted manner typical of contemporary Russia) such as the establishment of their own security forces and successful attempts to contact specific governmental functionaries, making them into their agents of influence. However, local preferences acquired by individual 'new people' or their groups are neutralising one another, which accelerates the disintegration of the existing state institutions.

The new Russians think it ineffective to get involved in the existing political system or to try to pressure or financially support the existing power institutions. This state with all its institutions – presidency, representative bodies of power, political organisations and repressive facilities – has had its day. Being aware of this, the 'new people' take to active politics.

To the author's mind, one can highlight two diametrically opposed trends in the outlook of people who have already left socialism but are still tied up with by provenance. According to the first of these, the state is regarded as a value per se, and what the state has stolen over seventy years of its history is treated as property of the whole nation. The bearers of this kind of outlook (the new poor) regard the appropriation (privatisation) of state property as theft. The new poor do not consider themselves and others as fully-fledged juridical persons (they do not accept existence outside this state) and therefore protest against the attempts of leaders to distribute state property.

The other trend regards the state as a minimum of power institutions ensuring protection of the property appropriated from the same state. Those who adhere to this viewpoint (the *nouveaux riches*) consider themselves 'super-full-fledged' juridical persons, and therefore they are not happy with the fact that the state treats them as 'second-rate' citizens and prefers to deal with work collectives, industries, enterprises, regional bodies of authorities, etc. The *nouveaux riches* consider that they themselves are the state and intend to build the state around and out of themselves.

Property in this state, as nowhere else, falls under one of Proudhon's definitions. In the USSR and its successor states, all fixed assets have been stolen and each metre of settled space is an unknown grave and someone's stolen life. The state itself used to commit armed robbery of everyone and everything: its own citizens, citizens of other states, the environment, time and space. For their part, the citizens thieved and resold what they had stolen from the state.

The problem of the equitable division of objects stolen cannot be solved in principle; the stolen objects can only be re-stolen, which our populace has been actively doing over the past 30 years. Some people stole more, others less, but all citizens want to legalise their theft. As long as the stolen values retained this label, they could not be an item of routine commercial operations; they could only be consumed or exchanged furtively for similar stolen 'gear'. Real economic dynamics start when stolen things are treated as property. The economic content of the current, initial stage of modernisation consists in the legalised right to possess and trade the property and resources stolen from this state.

The political content of what is going on can be regarded as a response to the legalisation of property rights. Each person in Russia regards what he or she possesses as having been obtained honestly, by right, earned, while everyone else's property was unlawfully obtained, i.e., stolen. Civilians strive to gain legal possession of what they think belongs to them, but they protest against similar actions and endeavours on the part of all others. Accusations of corruption are the main argument in political discussions of today. Most of these accusations are true. There is not a single person in Russia who has never stolen or used a stolen object. Those who assert their honesty („I've never even walked off with a paper-clip", claimed a participant in a discussion during *perestroika*) forget that they live in flats built by convicts, wore clothes made by convicts (the stolen labour and lifetime of tens of millions of people), have used equipment based on stolen technology, etc.

The main demand of the advocates of 'establishing order' is the imprisonment of thieves and corruptionists, more precisely those they point at. Their demands display an unconscious desire to return to a social condition where one could use stolen objects and at the same time believe sincerely in one's own inherent honesty and decency. For those calling for order, objects stolen by the state are more legitimate than things stolen by the citizens of this state.

What is ordinary to representatives of all strata in the new society is, in the author's opinion, the ignorance about their recent history. The memories of post-*perestroika* political and economic personalities of the most recent past (five to ten years) have been purged. They have been replaced by a false memory about what did not and could not happen to their people. Citizens of the state think about what was before the socialist revolution, in the twenties, thirties or sixties, as if it had been yesterday. They do not think at all about what was or could have been in the seventies and eighties and what in fact determines their existence today.

## 2 The Administrative Market as a Socio-Economic System

### 2.1 A Fragment of Recent History

The administrative market formed during the construction of a socialised state with an equitable distribution system is now being degraded in accordance with laws that are basically determined by its own internal structural features. The material core of the administrative market is the fuel and raw material complex on the basis of which a huge (in terms of the number of people and raw materials involved) system has been erected to manufacture the critically needed machines and mechanisms. The system is modernised only in certain, as a rule strategically important, component parts. The rest of material production is in its internal structure of a shop-floor technical rather than technological nature. It is based on skills and intuitive knowledge handed down from generation to generation and circulating in isolated groups among highly educated people (especially in previously secret areas of material culture). Naturally, in case of necessity the educated people manufacture (using the know-how obtained 'operationally' by the state intelligence services) instruments, mechanisms and machines which on the face of it seem impossible to make without advanced technology.

Discussions concerning the technologically advanced system in the USSR and what has remained of it are as justifiable as the hypotheses about the existence in the mythological past of a technologically advanced civilisation which left behind certain artefacts, for example the Egyptian pyramids, columns made of chemically pure iron and incomprehensible mural images. Our far distant archaeologist-descendants are likely to be amazed as they explore the ruined launch silos for Soviet strategic missiles, huge radiation and chemical dumps and the remains of other great five-year-plan projects. They will be guessing as to which unknown civilisation created them and why. We know only too well (although we try to forget) that these were made by convicts and army construction units equipped with spades, pickaxes and wheelbarrows for the majestic and senseless purpose of equitable distribution.

The post-*perestroika* line-up arose from the administrative market relations established in the Brezhnev era. The pre-Revolutionary, Stalinist and Khrushchevite versions of the administrative market vanished as soon as their specific resources were exhausted. Under Brezhnev, power on the administrative market was distributed among the sectoral and territorial hierarchies of management. This distribution was uneven and certain sectoral or territorial groups (e.g. the Dnepropetrovsk group, *sredmash* (medium mechanical engineering) and other so-called mafias) dominated at specific periods of the state's modern history. Unevenness in the distribution of power created conflicts in the system in the form of a leadership struggle between the first persons of one particular CPSU-*nomenklatura* rank. The struggle of the 'mafias' resulted above all in the leaders' personal movement across the hierarchies of sectoral and territorial power.

The territorial and sectoral hierarchies themselves existed due to the fact that the highest management levels of territories and industries alienated things produced at the lower levels (this procedure was known as meeting the state delivery targets) and then distributed what had been stolen according to Brezhnev's criteria of social justice, which meant that each republic, *oblast'*, city, district, industrial sector, enterprise and social reference group of civilians received money and goods from the state according to 'labour' and socio-economic standards.

The struggle of state functionaries against the state-sponsored Robin Hood-like logic gave birth to a certain administrative market relationship whereby virtually every resource of the state (including the armed forces) became the object of bargaining. After the overwhelming majority of resources had become an administrative commodity, the administrative market displayed the state's double nature: it existed on one hand (made decisions, applied sanctions), and did not exist on the other hand, because even the application of sanctions became the object of administrative bargaining. The very existence of the USSR became the object of an administrative trade leading to self-destruction of this bazaar's all-Union level.

The Soviet administrative market could exist in conditions where the administrative statuses of these bargainers were clearly defined. Each hierarchy at each level of its organisation issued its own administrative currency prior to *perestroika*. It was ordinary knowledge that papers with a 'CPSU Central Committee' letterhead were of more value than those with an '*Oblast'* Party Committee' or ' Soviet of People's Deputies' letterhead. Sheets of paper acquired in the course of office fulfil the functions of securities, each type of which had a definite expiration date. It was only the Politburo-signed papers that were fully convertible, even in hard currency, while all other papers could be converted only occasionally. The incomplete convertibility of socialist securities (resolutions) led to a certain indeterminacy in their circulation.

This indeterminacy was compensated by a special kind of relations within the administrative market – relations of mutual exchange, when civil servants of one level exchanged administrative favours at their consumer value. One could 'grease the palm' of a civil servant for a desired decision, but one could also pressurise him from above and get the same result. But in any situation the status of a decision-maker was quite clear. The collapse of the administrative market's highest level – the USSR governmental bodies – eliminated the status-generating source, i.e., the system which would determine seniority and rank of the administrative currency.

The administrative market was naturally struck with panic. All currencies were devaluated and a struggle for seniority ensued between the emitters. This struggle came to be called the 'political life of the *perestroika* epoch'. It was born in those places where the struggling sides concentrated their efforts: where sectors and territories confronted each other and in the traditional conflict-laden parts of this state. The industrial sectors were 'lowered' in the course of their transformation to the level at which they came into a direct contact with regional bodies of authority in the struggle for re-distribution of resources. The regions reached the status of largely self-determined administrative subjects. One can assume that a certain stability will be achieved only when the industries and regions come to terms with each other, i.e., when a certain number of industries in a region will coalesce into an administrative-territorial unit of a state-level rank whose governing bodies will generate statuses.

The zone between sectors and regions is now being filled with human vestiges of the former power system who are coming together, establishing unions of entrepreneurs, banking alliances, political parties and other organisations.

They are aware of the absence of administrative currency generators or their substitutes but do not reflect much on it. The '*nouveaux riches*' are now all trying to issue currencies of their own. However their currencies are not in demand, neither among the other '*nouveaux riches*', nor in what has remained of the state.

Each of today's actors wants the space under him to be organised like an administrative market (so that he alone generates and determines statuses), but at the same time wants the space above and around him to be organised in purely market terms so that all may be administratively equal but different only in the amount of money resources possessed.

The state is a form for matching political and economic relations in a system of power institutions. This matching was complete in the USSR and Russia, where all forms of matching were reduced in force structures. Today these force structures are also disintegrating. This results in the disappearance of the normative space of administrative trade where predictable actions might be possible. The state's tax system and force structures are now reorienting themselves towards administrative trade with new people, i.e., entrepreneurs and financiers. However, they have virtually nothing to offer the buyer since the administrative currency resources have been exhausted. This therefore creates a vital necessity for businesses to establish their own political institutions.

The future Russian state may arise from the 'new people's' political organisations. It is only they who (as a social group) are interested in preserving a single linguistic, cultural and financial space. This space may become a new Russia whose borders will not necessarily coincide with those of the existing federation, the former USSR and Comecon. The ideology for the political unification of the *nouveaux riches* may be extremely liberal – until they have to actually rule the country or what emerges from it. The state arising from the new people's political associations will have, above all, to provide social guarantees to these people themselves.

## 3 Formal Presentation of the Administrative Market Structure

The pre-*perestroika* administrative market was identical with the state. The state would set the hierarchies of statuses and related administrative currencies either explicitly or implicitly, and in its striving to modify itself, it was constrained by the established status ontology. Since the sixties all management decisions without exception have been reduced to changing status hierarchies, increasing or decreasing the amount of administrative currency involved in status determination. The top priority given to mechanical engineering (i.e., raising the prestige of managers) gave way to a similar priority in the agro-industrial complex which, in its turn, gave way to an accelerated development of the military-industrial complex. An indispensable feature of political life were the resolutions of the CPSU Central Committee and the USSR Council of Ministers on specific regions (non-black-earth areas, Siberia, the Far East, republics, *oblasts* and *krais*). To have a 'private' resolution passed for one's region was a quite realisable dream for every first secretary of a republican or regional Party committee.

The diversity of administrative currencies and unearned incomes has already been discussed above. This diversity was not reduced to and did not flow out of the state's administrative-territorial and industrial structure. It came into being of its own accord in the rather contradictory process of building socialism in an isolated country. To classify the sources of this diversity, one must describe the status-setting structure and related sources of administrative currencies. To do so, let us introduce the notions of the levels and forms of activity as well as interaction between them, thus setting a formal technique of description. The structure of this technique (fan matrices) allows one to arrange ideas about multi-aspected properties of natural phenomena in an extremely idealised configuration, thus providing some explanatory and predictive capabilities.

The suggested formal design is an attempt to reconstruct interactions in the Brezhnevite administrative market and its structures that were transformed in the course of reforms. This study tries to consider the structure of the post-*perestroika* economic institutions as a result of the disintegration of the administrative market established in the USSR in the mid-1980s. In so doing, we have chosen the one representation of the administrative market out of the many possible that presents it as a set of formal positions of people (statuses) and interaction between the statuses with respect to administrative bargaining.

The first part of the design attempts to explicate statuses in the administrative bargaining relations in their pre-*perestroika* form. The second part describes the transformation of administrative market relations into post-*perestroika* economic structures associated with the differentiation between the administrative market's political (and administrative) components and its purely economic ones, as well as with the formation of post-*perestroika* administrative market relations. The formal construction presented in this study does not, naturally, claim to be an exhaustive treatment of the problem and is clearly restricted by the initial axiomatics and chosen relations between the statuses which are, in the author's opinion, of interest for analysis of the administrative market's political-economic structure in both its Soviet and then Russian version. The reader is presumed to be aware of the general concept of the administrative market; hence, its structural, functional and organisational features that have been described elsewhere are not being considered.

The further exposition of this paper is based on an a priori statement about the existence of the administrative market, i.e., a political-economic system containing (among many other specific features) not only money of various spheres of circulation but also some different administrative currencies (the term 'administrative currency' was introduced by G. Sapov and popularised by V. Naishul).

State-paid work time was the main source of income for the overwhelming majority of civilians, but the total income, the ways of spending it and the number of consumer benefits an individual could pay for, depended on his position in various socio-economic hierarchies regulated to a large extent, but not entirely, by the Party and *nomenklatura* rules.

The possession of power was another main source of income. The amount of administrative currency possessed by a specific person in authority was a yardstick of his/her power. The very fact that values could be alienated from other civilians or socialist institutions and that this could be followed by their redistribution (no matter whether legitimate or illegitimate, legal or illegal from the viewpoint of the official law) meant that a state citizen possessed administrative currency. This description is admittedly incomplete, because administrative currency refers not only to opportunities but also to some definite forms of realisation. Like roubles, administrative currency was either cash or cashless (the currency of a direct order or of an indirect instruction in the system of co-ordination of interests) and could represent different nominal values (letterhead Party paper was valued higher than that of executive bodies), etc.

Roubles and administrative currencies could be partially converted into each other: roubles could buy a certain, albeit not very elevated status (although, according to some sources, statuses of the Supreme Soviet members and some posts in the executive bodies became the object of purchase and sale in the last years of the USSR's existence). At the same time, certain statuses and related administrative currencies allowed one to make money, i.e., to extract roubles out of status-related power and connections. It is the status' characteristics that determined the kind and amount of administrative currency held by a status-bearer.

The total amount of actual incomes, consisting of employment gains proper and administrative currency-related earnings, ranked civilians in the system of economic and political relations, the latter being inseparable from the former on the administrative market. The sources and amounts of income gained by lower status civilians were officially supposed to be fully 'transparent'; i.e., evident for the higher status bearers. If incomes of the lower status civilians exceeded a certain standard level, they were declared unearned, i.e., contrasting with the a priori determined place of an individual in the administrative market system. At the same time, the amounts of incomes of the higher status civilians were 'opaque' for the lower-status bearers. The lower strata regarded the higher status strata's incomes as unearned because the power hierarchy regulations that were within the reach of the lower strata did not say anything about the sources of incomes, i.e., about converting the administrative currency into roubles and consumer values.

Let us return again to the initial identification. Labour incomes (in the socialist sense of this notion) were fixed by the state and determined by the normative position of an individual in the state hierarchies of management and distribution. Labour incomes also included an administrative currency part to the extent that this part was connected with the individual's state-fixed status within the distribution and power system.

Unearned incomes were not associated with the actual possession of administrative currency, but with a non-standard conversion of that currency into other values, i.e., using one's status related power in other, e.g., economic, activities. By unearned incomes are meant in this study, above all, those gained while converting administrative currency into roubles. Since unearned incomes were derived by people from their position in the power hierarchies, their possession by the lower-strata populace could have been regarded as an indication of an illegal variety of administrative currency and as a vivid manifestation of the fact that the state has some hidden hierarchies of power within which some regulations allow making money without having any state-fixed rights to do so. The very fact that the lower strata were gaining unearned incomes testified, from the higher strata's viewpoint, to violations in the state power system and therefore the state was always combating them.

The former USSR population may be analytically divided into two groups, despite all the arbitrariness of such rigid demarcation. The first group may include that part of the population which lived on their wages, i.e., labour-earned incomes in the socialist sense of the word. These wages also contained additional incomes associated with status and possessing a status-related administrative currency. Legal exchanges of administrative benefits were the essence of life for ordinary people. This part of the population may be said to have lived under real socialism (from each according to status-related abilities, to each according to status-related need, with the creation and maintenance of the status system and the determination of the status-related abilities and needs being performed by the state). This section of the citizens of socialist society is of no interest for further analysis. It is not independent economically, although it now actively participates in economic and political life as a *rentier*. They are 'not spongers but partners', intending to live on the 'dividends' from their Soviet social reference status converted into 'securities', which are floated by representatives of another part of the population.

This (i.e., the other) part of the population has already converted its administrative currency into economic assets proper. It is this part that can be considered economically active and as the medium which gave birth to *perestroika*-related economic relations.

### 3.1 The Pre-*Perestroika* Structure of the Administrative Market

Let us introduce the notions of the levels and forms of activity on the administrative market. By *level of activity* is meant the formal position of a socialist individual within the existing system of power, alienation and distribution (in the economic sense of these notions). The notion of activity level coincides in some cases with that of status in the ordinary sociological sense.

By *form of activity* is meant the activity of an individual belonging to a fixed level of activity and thus possessing a certain well-defined status. The relations between the level and form of activity are in a way comparable to the relations between status and role in the classical status-role theory. A specific logic of this study is that it is discrepancies between the levels and forms of activity that are regarded as key points in the analysis (similarly to dissociation between statuses and roles in the corresponding sociological theory). The formal structure of the relationship between levels and forms of activity is introduced to point out the systematic discrepancy between belonging to an activity level and to a form of activity, and in order to use it as a logical basis for substantive research.

Let us assign the following names to the levels and forms of activity specific for the Soviet version of the administrative market:

- nomenklatura
- civilian

- shadow
- criminal.

By the *nomenklatura* level of activity is meant a set of statuses referred to as *nomenklatura*-related (i.e., a CPSU official sanction was required of obtain them). By the *nomenklatura* form of activity (leadership) is meant a set of roles played by the bearers of various statuses including these that are not related to the *nomenklatura*.

By the *civilian* level of activity is meant a set of statuses not related to the *nomenklatura* but still having a certain degree of socialist officialness. These are teachers, doctors, civil servants in a broad sense, as well as factory workers and peasants. By the civilian form of activity is meant a set of roles of survival under administrative market conditions that are played by the bearers of other, including non-civilian, statuses.

By *shadow* level of activity is meant a set of statuses whose bearers were neither *nomenklatura* nor ordinary civilians (a distinction of which they themselves were aware). These people possessed some non-*nomenklatura* power where boundaries could not be defined a priori. By the shadow form of activity is meant a set of production roles played by the bearers of other, including non-shadow, statuses.

By the *criminal* level of activity is meant a set of statuses determined and controlled by criminal subcultures. People possessing criminal statuses did not belong to the *nomenklatura*, were not ordinary people by definition (e.g., because of their criminal record), did not possess shadow and or poorly defined power. By the criminal form of activity (theft) is meant a set of roles played by the bearers of other statuses, including non-criminal ones.

Now, having introduced the main definitions, let us construct the interaction between them in a matrix.

**Figure 1** *The pre-perestroika structure of economic space*

| forms of activity<br>level of activity | nomenklatura (leadership) | civilian (survival) | shadow (production) | criminal (theft) |
|---|---|---|---|---|
| nomenklatura | **first persons** | civil servants | shadow-nomenklatura | criminalised civil servants |
| civilian | nomenklatura-civilians | **ordinary civilians** | civilians with connections | criminalised civilians |
| shadow | nomenklatura-shadow dealers | private owners | **shop-floor people** | criminalised shadow dealers |
| criminal | nomenklatura-thieves | ordinary thieves | racketeers | **thieves** |

Each cell of the matrix is further referred to as a type. A type is a place name in the formalised representation of the administrative market. The aggregate of types represented in the matrix forms a closed space of notions whose properties are determined through the relationship between types.

One can single out two sets of elements constituting the matrix's inner space. There are diagonal elements (formed by the interaction between the homonymous levels of organisation and forms of activity) and non-diagonal elements formed by the relations between the dissimilar levels and forms of activity. The relations between the homonymous levels and forms of activity are constituted by one diagonal element of the matrix. The relations between the dissimilar levels and forms of activity are constituted by two type elements that are symmetrical to the matrix diagonal, Fig. 1 (e.g., the relations between the *nomenklatura* and civilian levels and forms of activity constitute the types of the *nomenklatura* citizens and civil servants).

Let us look at the matrix space using the lists of types ordered with rows and columns. A set of types related in any way to *nomenklatura* is designated by the row '*nomenklatura* level' and the column '*nomenklatura* form of activity'. The *nomenklatura* as such includes first persons, civil servants, shadow *nomenklatura* and criminalised civil servants. At the same time, belonging to the *nomenklatura* as a role characteristic makes up part of the characteristics of types ordered by the column '*nomenklatura* form of activity'. These are first persons, *nomenklatura* civilians, *nomenklatura* shadow dealers and *nomenklatura* thieves.

The civilian level of activity is designated by the types: *nomenklatura* civilians, ordinary civilians, civilians with connections and criminalised civilians. As a role characteristic, belonging to the civilian level is part of the characteristics of the types: civil servants, ordinary civilians, private owners and ordinary thieves.

The shadow level of activity is designated by the types: *nomenklatura* shadow dealers, private owners, shop-floor people and criminalised shadow dealers. As a role characteristic, the 'shadiness' of an activity form makes up part of the characteristics of these types: shadow *nomenklatura*, civilians with connections, shop-floor people and racketeers.

The criminal level of activity is designated with the types: *nomenklatura* thieves, ordinary thieves, racketeers and thieves. As a role characteristic, criminality characterises the types: criminalised *nomenklatura*, criminalised civilians, criminalised shadow dealers and thieves.

Let us consider those matrix elements in which the names of the levels and forms of activity coincide. These are the diagonal elements in Figure 1 (p. 171): first persons, ordinary civilians, shop-floor people and thieves.

The type 'first persons' is represented by the relationship between the *nomenklatura* level of organisation and the homonymous form of activity (leadership). Definition of this type (like other diagonal elements) includes correspondence of the status and the role played by an individual bearing the status of a first person. 'First persons' is an official term in the administrative language denoting people possessing the highest form of legal administrative currency in a specific organisation, namely the right to sign financial and personnel documents. First persons belonged to the *nomenklatura* and were ranked on the basis of the internal principles of its organisation. The body of first persons was internally dynamic by the logic of each lower-ranked first person striving to raise his position in order to become a higher-rank first person. The institution of *nomenklatura* proper may be treated as a structure with fixed junctions (first person places) and relations between them (graph branches). This structure saw rank mobility of the first persons, i.e., their movement from the junction along the fixed branches.

The type 'ordinary civilians' is determined by the interaction between the civilian level and form of activity (survival) under conditions of real socialism, which was impossible without activity aimed at onward movement across the social reference hierarchies, i.e., without an aspiration to obtain certain benefits that were normatively prescribed to a certain status – an apartment, work, education, medical care and a pension. Ordinary civilians are not homogeneous as a type. Diversity within this type was determined by the aggregate of social reference parameters such as sex, age, education, domicile registration, place of work, ethnicity etc. Each combination of social reference indications corresponded to a well-defined place in the system of distribution, i.e., to status-related opportunities to use the administrative currency. For instance, inhabitants of the metropolitan cities had access to a much more developed system of social opportunities than inhabitants of other settlements, while women and children enjoyed special administrative privileges that were out of reach to men and adults. The ordinary people's inner dynamics were determined by the aspirations of each individual to get the complete set of status-related benefits he/she was formally entitled to, or to change for example his place of residence for a more prestigious one, gain access to a certain 'feeding-trough', etc.

The type 'shop-floor people' is determined by the relationship between the shadow level of organisation and the homonymous form of activity – production of goods and services in short supply. This type's definition comprises economic self-employment, including commercial manufacturing of consumer goods at state-run or co-operative enterprises with the aim to sell them. The shop-floor people did not have any state-sponsored legitimacy, but they had administrative currency of a special shadow kind by strength of their position as producers or distributors of scarce goods. They were not homogeneous, their rank (as a particular social grouping) depended on the particular sector of the national economy where they managed to launch shadow production and on the items they produced. It is only natural that the highest statuses were enjoyed by shop-floor people producing the most critically needed goods at high-status state enterprises. Dynamics among the shop-floor people may be explained by an aspiration to get a higher status in their own relations of shadow production.

The type 'thieves' is defined by the relation between the criminal level and the homonymous form of activity – theft. This type's definition comprises the professional or situational alienation of securities and money from state-run entities and civilians, and the use thereof to satisfy both personal needs and the needs of the criminal subculture as a whole. The thieves also possessed a special kind of administrative currency – authority based on force. The thieves were ranked within the subculture according to types of activity and their internal status. Inner dynamics among the thieves were caused by an aspiration to obtain a higher status in the criminal subculture.

## 3.2 Fragments of the Administrative Market Space and Its Dimensions

### *3.2.1 The* Nomenklatura-*Civilian Dimension*

Let us now consider fragments of Fig. 1 constituted by the pairs of homogeneous levels of organisations and forms of activity. Each fragment comprises two diagonal types and two elements that are symmetrical to that diagonal.

**Figure 2** *The nomenklatura-civilian dimension*

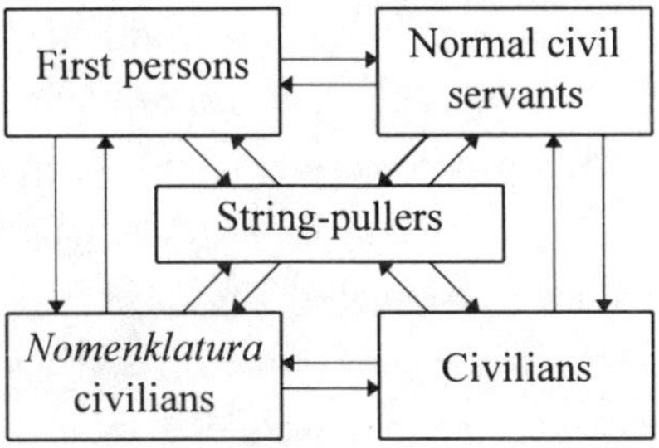


First persons and ordinary civilians were nominally characterised (as types) above. Let us now consider *nomenklatura* civilians and civil servants. The *nomenklatura* civilians (i.e., various people's deputies, artists, specialists, experts, technologists and even cosmonauts) possessed administrative currency due to their position and used it to influence administrative decision-making by the first persons if the decisions could promote their status or enhance its monetary value. They participated in leadership but in a very specific way. The *nomenklatura* civilians' incomes were made up of foreign trips, involvement in state-sponsored development programmes managed by none other than themselves, etc. The *nomenklatura* civilians are known, for example, for their proposals to improve the economy and to find the key links and 'levers' which, if acted upon, might radically change the economic indicators. They were the authors of the ideas of *uskorenie* ('acceleration'), the energy programme, the transformation of mechanical engineering and so on. The market-minded theoreticians can also be classed with *nomenklatura* civilians, for they regarded changes in management principles and renunciation of socialism as nothing more than another state-sponsored programme they could supervise themselves.

The type 'civil servants' comprises specialists in administrative games within the system of statuses fixed by the Party and state bodies. In the course of these games they strove to raise their status and increase the amount of administrative currency allocated by the state for the needs of their status. Civil servants survived in the conditions determined by the first person relations, and hence they totally depended on personal changes in the system of first persons. The system of civil servant statuses derived from the industrial and territorial rank order. Therefore, civil servants' games were aimed at raising the administrative status of specific sectors and territories, because a rise in their status also entailed a rise in the civil servant's status.

First persons, *nomenklatura* civilians and civil servants were in constant structural contact because a rise in the status of territories and industries was, as a rule, connected with specific projects to transform the economy. A typical situation of this kind was an initiative by 'team contract' [*brigadnyi podryad*] put forward by a certain *nomenklatura* individual and supported by civil servants working with the first secretary of the Party regional committee and by other first persons.

To describe the interaction between first persons, *nomenklatura* civilians, civil servants and ordinary civilians (as represented in Fig. 2), it is worth recalling that there was a hierarchy of statuses within each type (hierarchies of first persons, ordinary civil servants, *nomenklatura* and ordinary civilians): people belonging to a specific type strove to move upwards through their hierarchies. The ways of doing so are defined by the formal structure links shown in Fig. 2 with arrows. Thus, an ordinary individual living in a shared flat could try to rise in the hierarchy of other ordinary civilians by attempting to acquire a separate flat, which he could do in different ways. For instance, he could complain to civil servants that his flat did not conform to sanitary norms. The civil servants would intercede with a first person on behalf of this ordinary individual, after which the first person could agree (or not agree) to satisfy those wishes.

There was also another way, when a ordinary individual turned to a *nomenklatura* individual (e.g., a people's deputy), and the latter pleaded with a first person to satisfy the needs of the ordinary individual.

Sometimes the logic and practice of life brought about situations whereby a first person actually paid attention to the unsatisfied needs of an ordinary civilian and instructed civil servants to satisfy his status-related needs.

The network of connections established by the iteration of such relations was an element of the administrative market in the proper sense of this notion. Each change in the position of any types within specific hierarchies was connected with bargaining between the types' representatives united in the Fig. 2 diagram and involved in actions to enhance their ranks. The bargaining ended up in administrative-currency settlements, one of their components being the elevation (or reduction) in rank of a representative of a specific type within the limits set by the type's nominal characteristics.

It must be noted that the network of connections between the types established a functional space at the intersection of direct connections between all those involved in the administrative play. This space is visualised in Fig. 2 as a rectangle. It could be occupied by any bearer of certain typological properties. Owing to the functional features of this place, the desires and needs of all actors could be met by turning to a person occupying this virtual place rather than by using the usual administrative ways. People occupying these spaces came to be called 'string-pullers' [*blatnye*] in everyday parlance, and the method is known as 'pull' [*blat*]. By force of the peculiarities of this kind of relations, the pull in question is called hereinafter 'a civilian-*nomenklatura* pull'. The civilian-nomenklatura 'string-pullers' were pure bearers of the managerial form of activity without, however, a corresponding social status.

The interaction in the tetrad 'first persons-civil servants-*nomenklatura* civilians-ordinary civilians' eventually caused, by means of a certain 'pull', the formation of a relatively closed, latent civilian-*nomenklatura* group, a peculiar hidden dimension of the pre-*perestroika* administrative market which gave rise to one of the characteristics of the economic space in the post-*perestroika* state.

### *3.2.2 The Shadow-Nomenklatura Dimension*

Let us consider the following fragment of Fig. 1 constituted by the relationship between the *nomenklatura* and shadow levels and forms of activity.

**Figure 3** *The Shadow-Nomenklatura Dimension*

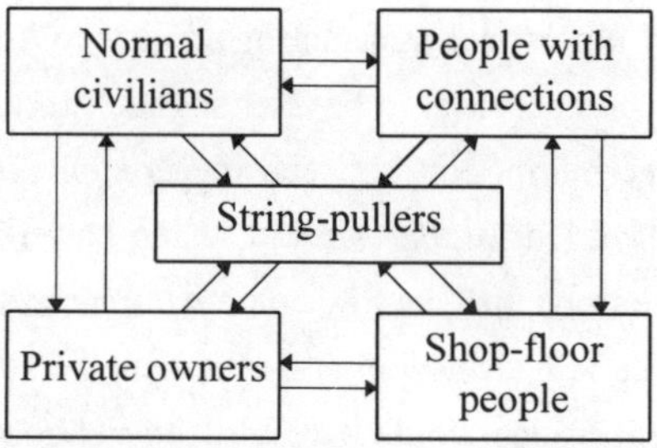


First persons and shop-floor people were discussed above. The shadow-*nomenklatura* was in fact comprised of 'second' persons who, unlike ordinary civil servants, were to be reckoned with in any kind of decision-making. These were people who had been preparing and co-ordinating decisions in the numerous corridors of the management apparatus: assistants, advisers, consultants, speech-writers and other bureaucrats who knew the people, the relationships between them and all the ins and outs in general. It was a kind of amorphous sphere around first persons, outside of which they could not exist. Of course, the shadow-*nomenklatura* functionaries did possess a certain amount of administrative currency which was indirectly converted into the good things of life, but only to the extent the first persons could allow through their medium.

The *nomenklatura* shadow dealers are people possessing a certain governmental or Party status and using it to organise a non-state-sponsored supply of goods and services in popular demand. Virtually every state enterprise had its own 'unaccounted for', concealed production lines turning out items to be bartered in some way or other for different goods and services. Functionaries exercising control over the 'unaccounted for' production and distribution are referred to in this study as *nomenklatura*-shadow dealers.

First persons could develop a need for the unaccounted-for and shadow production and contact the shop-floor people (the actual producers of the unaccounted-for items) in two ways. They could make the *nomenklatura* shadow dealers turn to the shop-floor people, or they could act through their private assistants, i.e., through the shadow *nomenklatura*. The shop-floor people, in their turn, encountered problems which could be solved only by the first persons. In this case, the shop-floor people pleaded with the first person either through the *nomenklatura* shadow dealers or through the shadow *nomenklatura*.

The iteration of these relations brought about a new functional space at the intersection of all links called 'string-pullers' as in the previous case. However, it is a shadow-*nomenklatura* 'pull' rather than a civilian-*nomenklatura* described above. A person occupying this virtual space could mediate to some degree (limited by the extent of his 'pull') in the process of satisfying the needs of all types' representatives without there being any direct contact between them. This was possible thanks to this person's involvement in all links of the shadow-*nomenklatura* structure.

The shadow *nomenklatura* and *nomenklatura* shadow dealers formed a peculiar community, for it was the foremost duty of a personal assistant or adviser to a first person to supply him with necessary goods and services to be exchanged with other first persons. Barter as such is rooted in the interaction between the *nomenklatura* shadow dealers and the shadow *nomenklatura*. During *perestroika*, when barter was institutionalised as a system of economic relations, the shadow *nomenklatura* and the *nomenklatura* shadow dealers, 'diluted' by certain string-pullers, established a single barter space. It was the shadow-*nomenklatura* space would give birth to yet another dimension of the post-*perestroika* economic territory.

### *3.2.3 The Criminal-*Nomenklatura *Dimension*

Let us consider the following fragment of Fig. 1 constituted by the relationship between the *nomenklatura* and criminal levels and forms of activity.

**Figure 4** *Criminal-Nomenklatura Dimension*

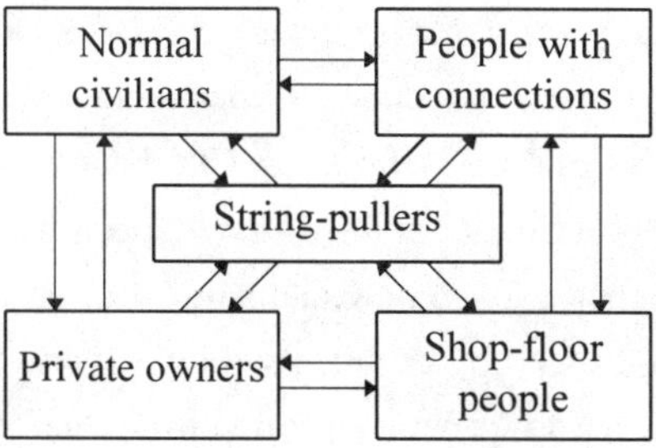


First persons and thieves were characterised above. Criminalised civil servants are those who were professionally in constant contact with the criminal medium (as a rule, at their place of work) and used these contacts to gain 'unearned incomes'. These are officials at the defence, police and security ministries, as well as civil servants who could perform their immediate duties only through unlawful actions made possible only with the help of the above ministries' officials.

An element of the Soviet economic space structure symmetrical to criminalised civil servants is represented by the *nomenklatura* thieves, i.e., representatives of the administrative apparatus who used their position to enrich themselves directly or indirectly by means of public embezzlement.

The logic of Fig. 4 says that if thieves had to enlist the support of first persons to satisfy their needs, they could do so in two ways, as shown by the branches of Fig. 4. Thieves could deal with first persons using the *nomenklatura* thieves as mediators, or they could act through the criminalised *nomenklatura*. In a reverse situation, when thieves had to be called upon to meet the needs of first persons, the latter could also act either through the criminalised *nomenklatura* or through the *nomenklatura* thieves.

The iteration of links in criminal-*nomenklatura* structural relations brought about a virtual functional space at the intersection of links between all parties, a special kind of criminal-*nomenklatura* 'pull'.

The criminalised civil servants and *nomenklatura* thieves complemented each other in the administrative market space. The criminalised civil servants fought sometimes ex-officio with those *nomenklatura* thieves who could not or did not want to 'share' with them, while the latter systematically 'bought' the former or paid them off. It was an ordinary trade on the administrative market, whereby the administrative currency held by criminalised civil servants was converted into the money of the *nomenklatura* thieves and vice versa through the mediation of first persons and thieves. This administrative trade established special interactions between the *nomenklatura* thieves and criminalised civil servants, and formed conditions for a new dimension of the post-*perestroika* economic space, that of the criminal *nomenklatura*.

The existence of this new dimension of the economic space became apparent during the investigation of the Medunov case (first secretary of the Krasnodar Regional Party Committee), particularly through Medunov's connections with the criminalised civil servants at the Ministry of Internal Affairs (the Churbanov case).

During *perestroika*, the potential of the criminal-*nomenklatura* space was used by the state to carry out actions aimed at commercialising the economy. Organisations (such as *ANT*) were set up, headed by criminalised civil servants that had been assigned by the power ministries to generate profits from the sale of military equipment and strategic raw materials. After the USSR's disintegration, such organisations were transformed, took over other elements of the economic space and finally became purely commercial enterprises.

### *3.2.4 The Civilian-Shadow Dimension*

Let us consider the interaction between the civilian and shadow levels and forms of activity.

**Figure 5** *The Civilian-Shadow Dimension*

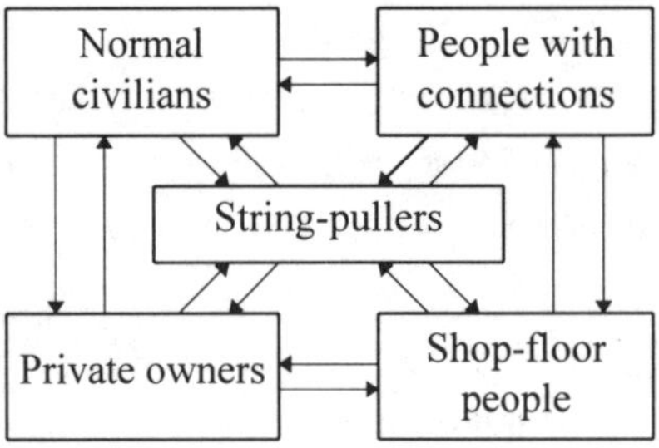


Ordinary civilians and shop-floor people were characterised as types above. People with connections had, by their position, access to all kinds of *nomenklatura*: various relatives and acquaintances of the shop-floor people and other types' representatives who possessed administrative currency, who could and did influence decision-making, including that in the economy, but who above were all mediators in distributing scarce goods.

Private owners (home farmers, maintenance and repair specialists for consumer durables and cars, private-practice doctors and all other institutionalised shadow dealers) represented a peculiar community whose members were engaged in the shadow production of goods and services and thought their business to be quite prestigious and honoured. They resented the absence of an actual status and administrative currency, and they made efforts to acquire these. Since it was people with connections who ensured access to the goods and services produced by private owners, these two types developed rather stable links.

In order to fulfil their aims in this system of relations (to get hold of scarce goods), the ordinary civilians could turn to people with connections or private owners who maintained contacts with the shop-floor people through their own channels. At the same time, to sell and distribute their products, the shop-floor people could use the people with connections or use the services of private owners.

The iteration of relations in this structure gave rise to a special space in the system, the civilian-shadow 'pull'. This space was specific to the field of obtaining scarce goods and it allowed people to circumvent unwanted intermediaries in this process. The 'pull' mediated the interaction between private owners and people with connections, separated structurally in the formal diagram.

*Perestroika* and its aftermath have smoothed over the differences between string-pullers, people with connections and private owners, leading to the creation of a civilian-shadow (by origin) dimension of the new economic space.

### *3.2.5 The Criminal-Civilian Dimension*

Let us consider the relations between the criminal and civilian levels and forms of activity.

**Figure 6** *The Criminal-Civilian Dimension*

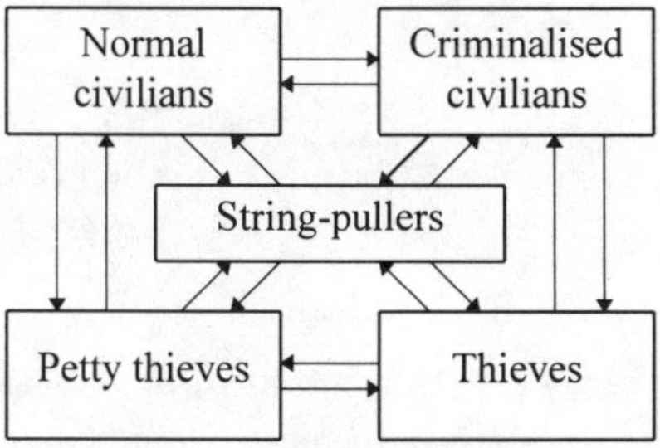


Ordinary civilians and thieves were characterised above.

Petty thieves (pilferers of socialist property) are a commonplace element of the administrative market. Petty theft was a way of life among a sizeable proportion of citizens in a socialist society.

Criminalised civilians are people who for various reasons form part of criminal subcultures, i.e., members of convicts' families, inhabitants of newly settled areas, resettlers, deportees. The relations in this tetrad have been described in Soviet detective novels. This diagram represents interaction in a criminal subculture on the everyday level, where thieves alienate property and money from ordinary civilians using either petty thieves or criminalised civilians, while the ordinary civilians find a common language with thieves using petty thieves and criminalised civilians as mediators.

Iterations of this kind formed a civilian-criminal-'string-pulling' functional place mediating all links in this tetrad.

The existence of this dimension in the economic space (petty thieves and criminalised civilians in their interaction with thieves and ordinary civilians) has not yet been the subject of professional research. One can still conjecture that *perestroika* saw the merger of activities of criminal-civilian string-pullers, petty thieves and criminalised civilians, giving birth to a new unified dimension of the economic space, i.e., the criminal-civilian dimension. This dimension is specific in that it is hierarchised on the principles of criminal subculture, but all actions in it are politically accentuated, the political component being only a means of achieving economic goals. The example of Chechnya as a space organised on criminal-civilian principles is common knowledge. According to various sources of information, the original ethnic conflicts in Armenia and Azerbaidzhan were caused by the division of spheres of influence between the Armenian and Azerbaidzhani criminal-civilian subcultures during their process of institutionalisation, i.e., when string-pullers, petty thieves, thieves and the criminalised civilians were being 'united' in a new single medium of activity.

After the disintegration of the USSR and its hierarchies of authority, some municipalities became impossible to rule outside this space, and, what is more, it is only in municipalities controlled by the criminal-civilian types that it is really possible to predict and manage the behaviour of the strata that were marginalised in the course of economic reform.

### *3.2.6 The Criminal-Shadow Dimension*

Let us now consider relations between the criminal and shadow levels and forms of activity.

**Figure 7** *The Criminal-Shadow Dimension*

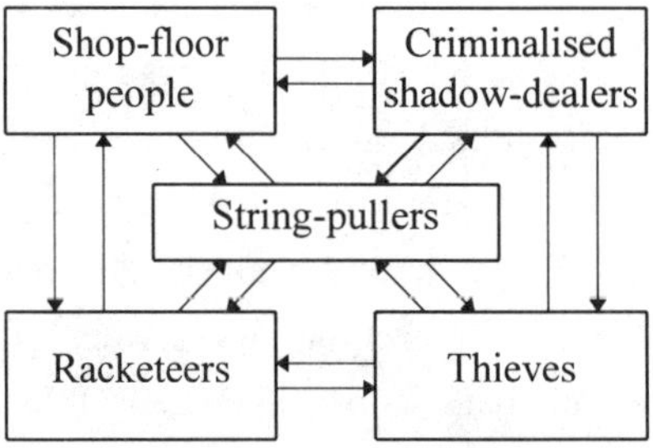


By criminalised shadow dealers are meant social types that gained unearned incomes while organising the satisfaction of illegitimate needs. These are smugglers; drug producers and traffickers; those profiteering from alcohol, motor cars and hard currency; arms dealers, etc. These were highly professional and specialised, if rather localised, types of Soviet business.

By racketeers are meant members of the criminalised subcultures that live off a part of incomes alienated from criminalised shadow dealers. It could be a situational racket (the so-called sport racket – when professional athletes, as bearers of illegitimate needs, provided paid security for criminalised shadow dealers); or a professional racket controlled by a criminal subculture as a whole ('heavies').

This structure was also characterised by its own criminal-shadow pull, whose functions included, among other things, 'show-downs' between members of the criminal-shadow subculture.

*Perestroika* radically expanded the market of illegitimate needs and, accordingly, the prospects for racketeering. A lot of new suppliers and producers appeared, but the racket's abilities with respect to these new businessmen were severely limited because the needs were being legitimised, with the state loosening control over the methods of satisfying them, and thus limiting the racketeers' abilities to control the market. This resulted in the integration of old racketeers (sports-related and professional) and criminalised shadow dealers into a new, criminal-shadow reality (or a new dimension) of the common economic space, for it was only through joint efforts that racketeers and criminalised shadow dealers that could ensure control over the market of illegitimate needs.

Such associations may be exemplified by criminal groupings of the Solntsevo-type in which control over the local markets of illegitimate needs is exercised by the joint efforts of ex-racketeers, former criminalised shadow dealers, ex-thieves and shop-floor people.

Natural administrative market associations could be even more complex than the tetrads shown in Figs. 2 to 7. By complexity is meant here the interaction of types united by three or more levels and forms of activity. For example, it is quite possible to empirically investigate certain structures that are composed of first persons, *nomenklatura* civilians, *nomenklatura* shadow dealers and *nomenklatura* thieves. In everyday language these may be called mafia-type structures. Logically there can be various different forms of mafia-type structures if Fig. 1 diagram is of any indication. It makes sense to analyse them empirically on the basis of the classifications, that were presented above.

## 3.3 The Specifics of Perestroika in Terms of the Administrative Market's Pattern of Interaction

At the outset of *perestroika* the structure of the economic space may be said to have been simple and logical. It was based on the re-distribution of state-owned resources by *nomenklatura*, civilian, shadow and criminal methods. Natural constraints on the use of state-owned resources (in particular, their exhaustion) led to some strains in the economic space structure. At the same time, political liberalisation and the declared economic liberties brought about the legalisation of certain forms and varieties of economic activity which had existed only latently before. We are talking here, above all, about activities that are formally organised as presented in Figs. 2 to 7.

Both the basic types (first persons, civilians, shop-floor people, thieves and others descried in the Fig. 1) and the respective levels and forms of activity were institutionalised in the public awareness before *perestroika*. Legalisation preceded the transformation of the Soviet version of the administrative market into a post-socialist economic space i.e., *perestroika* proper. Transformation dynamics were naturally being determined by the local dimensions described above. The overall structure of the post-socialist economic space was determined in its structure-forming characteristics by those dimensions. Let us recall them, but this time as factors whose relationship determines the structure of the post-socialist economic space. These are *nomenklatura*-civilian, civilian-shadow, criminal-civilian, criminal-shadow, civilian-shadow, and *nomenklatura*-criminal dimensions.

## 4 The Post-*Perestroika* Form of the Administrative Market

The new space of economic activity was created by the interaction between the dimensions of the Soviet administrative market space. By the logic of things it looks as follows: when a new economic space is formed, each of the said dimensions 'bifurcates' into a level of organisation and a form of activity whose relationship develops a structure logically similar to the Fig. 1 matrix, but having more functional spaces.

In essence this means that the above-mentioned dimensions of the Soviet administrative market unfold into a new space with functional spaces filled with new people who were previously (N.B.!) part of the administrative market, mainly as string-pullers and representatives of the types that are symmetrical to the Fig. 1 matrix diagonal. The transformation of dimensions of the Soviet administrative market into organisation levels and activity forms of a new political-economic space, the emergence of new functional spaces and the filling thereof (i.e., the levelling of statuses of the string-pullers and related types, their distribution across the new functional positions in a space formed by the dimensions of a defunct structure) constitute (on the basis of the logic being developed) the political-economic content of *perestroika* and post-*perestroika* economic activity.

At the outset of *perestroika*, the diagonal types (first persons, civilians, shop-floor people and thieves), which had been basic elements of the Soviet administrative market space, found themselves in a situation where their status and administrative currencies came to lose their erstwhile importance. Many representatives of these types became politicised, forming a considerable part of those politicians and statesmen who since the late 1980s had been advocating the revival of the administrative market in its Party-Soviet version. This refers not only to first persons and ordinary civilians but also to the shop-floor people and thieves who no longer had a place in the new economic reality.

At the same time, differences between the status of *nomenklatura* civilians, civil servants and *nomenklatura*-civilian string-pullers, for instance, lost their importance. Representatives of these types (as well as all the others described in the patterns of Figs. 1 to 7) found themselves in s similar situation after the factual elimination of the *nomenklatura* as an institution, and formed a certain unified dimension of space. The new dimensions of their interaction formed the organisation levels and activity forms of the new space.

Two realities may be said to have been formed as a result of the disintegration of the Soviet-style administrative market. One of them is purely political (the former first persons, ordinary civilians, shop-floor people and thieves) and is ideologically orientated towards the restoration of the familiar bargaining structure of in the Soviet administrative space, while the other may be called transitional between the administrative market and the pure market realities.

Let us consider – as a model example – the formation of one fragment of this new space through the interaction between the *nomenklatura*-civilian, civilian-shadow and criminal-shadow dimensions. Each of these dimensions 'bifurcates' into a level of activity and a respective form of activity. The *nomenklatura*-led privatisation (as a form of activity) corresponds to the *nomenklatura*-civilian level of activity, the institutionalisation of private property (stolen in the Soviet administrative market) corresponds to the civilian-shadow level of activity, and professional robbery and gangsterism correspond to the criminal-shadow level of activity. The logic of interaction leading to the formation of a new market space is presented in graph 1 and figure 8, which correspond to a fragment of the matrices in Figs. 1 and 8 and which bind these up in one genetic pattern. Graph 1 and the matrix of Fig. 8 are isomorphic in that they represent two components of one structure.

**Figure 8** *A fragment in the structure of the post-perestroika economic space*

| forms of activity<br>levels of activity | nomenklatura-civilian<br>nomenklatura privatisation | civilian-shadow<br>institutionalisation of private property | criminal-shadow<br>professional theft |
|---|---|---|---|
| nomenklatura-civilian | **new first persons** | new first persons-heads of private companies | criminalised-civil servants of the new authorities |
| civilian-shadow | owners of enterprises created during the nomenklatura privatisation of shadow capital | **owners of enterprises, created during the privatisation of shop-floor capital** | heads of security services of private enterprises |
| criminal-shadow | owners of legal enterprises, designed to meet illegitimate needs | leaders of commercialised criminal organisations | **leaders of groupings** |

In this case, the relations between the homonymous levels and forms of activity (diagonal elements) are identical with the basic elements of the new space. These are new first persons (unlike the first persons of the Soviet administrative market, the new first persons have the right to sign documents on the denationalisation of property), the legalised shop-floor shadow dealers (i.e., people previously active in the shadow interaction of the administrative market who managed to shape their economic activity into an acceptable civilian form), and leaders of Solntsevo-type groupings (at the intersection of criminal-shadow level and form of activity – the result of the interaction between criminalised shadow dealers and racketeers) in which the interests of the producers of illegitimate services and goods are organisationally associated with those of their 'protectors'.

The new elements of this space fragment arise in the interaction between the *nomenklatura*-civilian, civilian-shadow and criminal-shadow dimensions of the old administrative market which became the organisation levels and activity forms of the new space. Thus, the intersection of the criminal-shadow level and the civilian-shadow form of activity is associated with heads of the commercialised criminal organisations, new-generation racketeers undertaking the protection of certain types of businesses (such as the late O. Kvantrishvili, author of the term 'organised sports' [*organizovannaya sportivnost'*], head of the '21st Century' association).

At the same time, the intersection of the civilian-shadow level and the criminal-shadow form of activity is associated with security chiefs at private enterprises geared towards rendering their services to those capable of paying for them. These are, as a rule, former law enforcement personnel, Afghanistan war veterans, and excommandos who have contacts with the armed forces and now continue to conduct a familiar line of business.

The heads of the commercialised criminal organisations and the security chiefs of private enterprises represent types which are symmetrical to the diagonal. They complement each other to some extent but they also compete with each other in carrying out and combating the organised and situational racket.

The *nomenklatura*-led privatisation on the civilian-shadow level of activity is manifested in the formation of the type 'owners of enterprises' set up during the *nomenklatura*-led privatisation of shadow (shop-floor) capital. The institutionalisation of private property on the *nomenklatura*-civilian level is manifested in the formation of the type 'new first persons-heads of private companies and enterprises'. Professional theft on the *nomenklatura*-civilian level causes the formation of the type 'criminalised civil servants of the new authorities'. The *nomenklatura*-led privatisation on the criminal-shadow level engenders the type 'owners of legal enterprises designed to meet illegitimate needs'. These are casinos, brothels, arms and drug traffic 'outlets' etc. Publications in the mass media provide sufficient grounds to personify these types.

The overall (within the relations drawn from the logic of Fig. 1) structure of the post-*perestroika* space of economic activity is presented in Fig. 9 where the six dimensions of the pre-*perestroika* economic space specified above constitute the matrix of Fig. 9. The levels of activity as well as the reduced graphs of their respective dimensions are plotted on the matrix lines, while the columns contain the names of the respective kinds of activity, as in the matrix of Fig. 8.

| level of activity<br>forms of activity | nomenklatura-civilian<br>privatisation | nomenklatura-shadow<br>shadow privatisation | nomenklatura-criminal<br>criminal privatisation | civilian-shadow<br>institutionalisation of personal property | civilian-criminal<br>petty theft | criminal-shadow<br>professional theft |
|---|---|---|---|---|---|---|
| nomenklatura-civilian (first persons–civil servants–nomenklatura civilians–ordinary civilians) | new first persons | former first persons, turned heads of funds, companies and enterprises | functionaries, distributing state credits, licenses and quotas | new first persons - managers of private companies | stealing heads of state enterprises | criminalised civil servants of the new authorities |
| nomenklatura-shadow (first persons–shadow nomenklatura–nomenklatura-shadow-dealers–shop-floor people) | owners of major banks, set up with legal state capital and with shop-floor capital | heads-distributors of action banks and other enterprises set up with semi-legal (including CPSU) state capital and shop-floor capital | heads of economic entities, set up during the denationalisation of the MIC branches and of the power structures with participation of shadow capital | owners of companies and enterprises set up with privatised state capital and shop-floor capital | stealing heads of shadow-privatised enterprises | criminalised heads of commercialised state enterprises and organisations |
| nomenklatura-criminal (first persons–criminalised civil servants–nomenklatura thieves–thieves) | owners of companies set up with participation of legal USSR state capital and of criminal capital | heads-distributor of companies, set up during the shadow privatisation of state capital and criminal capital | heads of companies and other organisations, set up with laundered extra-budgetary means of the USSR | owners of organisations, set up with privatised state capital and criminal capital | stealing heads of criminal-privatised enterprises | heads of private security firms |
| civilian-shadow (ordinary civilians–people with connections–property owners–shop-floor people) | owners of enterprises set up during the nomenklatura privatisation of shop-floor capital | heads-distributors of enterprises and organisations, set up during the shadow-privatisation of shop-floor capital | heads-distributors of companies, FIGs and other pyramid organisations | owners of organisations, set up during the legalisation of shop-floor capital | stealing heads of enterprises, set up during the embezzlement of state capital | heads of security services of private enterprises |
| criminal-civilian (ordinary civilians–criminalised civilians–petty thieves–thieves) | owners of companies and financial institutions, set up during the nomenklatura privatisation of private property | heads-distributors of companies and financial institutions, set up during the shadow privatisation of private property | heads-distributors of economic entities, set up under the nomenklatura-criminal redistribution of private property | owners of companies, set up during the criminal redistribution of private property | stealing heads of private enterprises | heads of private militarised organisation |
| criminal-shadow (shop-floor people–criminalised shadow-dealers–racketeers–thieves) | owners of legal enterprises and organisations aimed at meeting illegitimate needs | heads-distributors of semi-legal enterprises and organisations aimed at meeting illegitimate needs | heads-distributors of illegal enterprises and organisations aimed at meeting illegitimate needs | heads of commercialised criminal organisations | heads of local criminalised organisations-gangs | heads of criminal groupings |

First, let us consider the diagonal elements of Fig. 9 (except for the new first persons, owners of enterprises set up during the legalisation of shop-floor capital, and leaders of groupings) which were identified earlier when describing the matrix of Fig. 8. The diagonal elements of the Fig. 9 matrix (i.e., the types with homonymous levels and forms of activity) are highlighted in bold print, as was done when describing the structure of the Soviet-style administrative market.

The intersection of the *nomenklatura*-shadow form and the corresponding level of activity is identified with the type of an executive head of joint-stock ('collective farm') banks or other enterprises set up by semi-legal (including, Party-owned) capital when merging with shop-floor capital. This type may comprise managers of many big commercial banks, such as *Menatep*.

Criminal privatisation on the *nomenklatura*-criminal level engenders the type consisting of the heads of enterprises and organisations set up to launder state-owned extra-budgetary resources. It is believed that this kind of topological features can be found in A. Tarasov, head of the *Istok* concern, known to have been involved in the governmental fraud with the *Urozhai-90* ['Harvest-90'] checks and export of energy resources and rare raw materials.

Petty theft on the criminal-civilian level engenders the type of larcenous private managers, i.e., people reproducing in the new conditions the appropriative stereotypes of the Soviet administrative market. Further description of the matrix' typological content is presented as an objectivisation of activity forms on different levels of activity.

## 4.1 Nomenklatura-Led Privatisation (The Nomenklatura-Civilian Form of Activity)

The types in the matrix's first column share a common form of activity i.e., *nomenklatura*-led privatisation, but they differ in their level of activity i.e., by the form of denationalised property. New first persons, as has already been mentioned, endorse documents on denationalising the property, thus confirming its official legitimacy. Owners of banks and other entities set up during the *nomenklatura*-led privatisation of legal state-owned and legalised big shop-floor capital are an indispensable element of the post-Soviet elite. By big shop-floor capital we mean those assets of the Soviet shadow industries that are under the direct control of the first persons of the Soviet administrative market.

The *nomenklatura*-led privatisation of criminalised Soviet capital caused the formation of a specific group of new Russians, namely owners of enterprises and organisations which consolidate the *nomenklatura*-privatised (criminal by origin) capital controlled earlier by first persons.

The *nomenklatura*-led privatisation of the small-scale shop-floor capital (i.e., shadow production of 'scarce goods' 'shared' by ordinary civilians and shop-floor people) caused the formation of a group of owners of enterprises set up during the *nomenklatura* led privatisation of small-scale shop-floor capital.

The *nomenklatura*-led privatisation of personally stolen property (i.e., the assets accumulated in the interaction between the ordinary civilians, criminalised civilians, petty thieves and thieves) engendered a specific group of post-Soviet administrative market dealers, namely owners of enterprises set up during the *nomenklatura*-led privatisation of private property.

The *nomenklatura*-led privatisation of criminal assets (amassed through the interaction between shop-floor people, criminalised shadow dealers, racketeers and thieves when organising the satisfaction of illegitimate needs) gave birth to a group of owners of legal enterprises designed to satisfy illegitimate needs: casinos, brothels, night clubs, etc.

### 4.2 Shadow Privatisation (The Nomenklatura-Shadow Form of Activity)

Let us now consider shadow privatisation as a *nomenklatura*-shadow form of activity and its results as types of the second column of matrix 9. Unlike the *nomenklatura* people, the shadow privatisers are not registered as owners of enterprises. They act as disposers of property – presidents, chairpersons or members of boards of directors – heading collective bodies to manage denationalised property.

The shadow privatisation of legal state-owned capital brought about a group of property disposers consisting of former first persons turned first persons of big joint ventures, foundations, joint-stock banks, etc. Thus, N. Ryzhkov, the former head of the USSR Cabinet of Ministers, became chairman of the board of directors at the *Tver'universalbank*, while the former State Planning Committee chief Shcherbakov came to manage the *Interprivatizatsiya* foundation.

The shadow privatisation of state-owned capital carried out with the participation of the shadow (shop-floor) capital brought into play a group of property disposers consisting, in particular, of former *nomenklatura* shadow dealers and their private assistants and advisers who became first persons in commercial banks and other enterprises (such as *Menatep* and *Russian Credit*).

The shadow privatisation of criminalised capital (amassed through the interaction between first persons, thieves, criminalised civil servants and *nomenklatura* thieves) caused the formation of a specific group of property disposers.

A group of disposers of shop-floor capital came into being during the shadow privatisation of personal capitals accumulated through the interaction between ordinary civilians, shop-floor people, people with connections and private owners.

The shadow privatisation of stolen assets (formed through the interaction between ordinary civilians, thieves, petty thieves and criminalised civilians) gave rise to a corresponding group of property disposers.

Finally, the shadow privatisation of the criminal-shadow capitals (formed through the interaction between the shop-floor people, thieves, racketeers and criminalised shadow dealers) created a group of disposers of property used for meeting illegitimate needs.

### 4.3 Criminal Privatisation (The Nomenklatura-Criminal Form of Activity)

Criminal privatisation (i.e., behavioural stereotypes developed in the interaction between first persons, thieves, criminalised civil servants, *nomenklatura* thieves and translated into the post-*perestroika* economic space) on a *nomenklatura*-civilian level formed a group of governmental and political functionaries controlling the distribution of state-sponsored privileges, credits, export-import licences, etc.

The criminal privatisation of *nomenklatura*-shadow assets formed a type consisting of managers of enterprises and organisations which formally belong to the previously top security branches of the national economy and the power structures which were not to be denationalised, but which did de facto become the disposers' property.

The criminal privatisation of *nomenklatura*-criminal assets formed a type consisting of managers of enterprises set up to launder all kinds of extra-budgetary resources of the former USSR (CPSU money, extra-budgetary assets of the defence, police and security ministries, etc.) It also created a type consisting of factory managers overseeing the sale of surplus military equipment. After the USSR's disintegration this type of enterprises and organisations were gradually being commercialised and turned into a notable element of the post-*perestroika* administrative market.

The criminal privatisation of civilian-shadow capital (i.e., assets accumulated through the interaction between ordinary civilians, shop-floor people, people with connections, private owners) brought about a type consisting of managers of joint-stock companies, check investment funds and other pyramid schemes (such as *MMM*). In fact, the activities of *MMM* may be called a perfect example of criminal privatisation on a civilian-shadow level.

The criminal privatisation of criminal-civilian assets (amassed through the interaction between ordinary civilians, criminalised civilians, petty thieves and thieves) formed a type of managers who appropriated and legalised assets which had been stolen previously.

The criminal privatisation of criminal-shadow assets formed a type consisting of managers of illegal enterprises and organisations specialising in satisfying illegitimate needs.

### 4.4 The Institutionalisation of Private Property (The Civilian-Shadow Form of Activity)

The civilian-shadow interactions (between ordinary civilians, people with connections, private owners and shop-floor people) were oriented towards satisfying needs in 'scarce goods'. The corresponding stereotypes of activity are being reproduced in the post-*perestroika* administrative market on all levels of its organisation. The institutionalisation of private property on a *nomenklatura*-civilian level formed a type of new first persons who concurrently own private enterprises and organisations. The property managed by a *nomenklatura*-civilian person as a civil servant became his own, even formally, during the institutionalisation of private property. For example, most private farms were based on parts of collective and state farms whose leading experts became real owners.

The institutionalisation of private property on a *nomenklatura*-shadow level (i.e., assets formed through the interaction between first persons, the shadow *nomenklatura*, *nomenklatura* shadow dealers and shop-floor people) formed a type of owners of companies and enterprises based on the *nomenklatura*-shadow property. In a rather conflictual process of redistribution, the previously amorphous property relations were transformed into the private property of one person, frequently a former first person, sometimes a former shop-floor person.

The institutionalisation of private property on a *nomenklatura*-criminal level formed a type consisting of those who own *nomenklatura*-criminal capital, the private property amassed through interaction between the first persons, criminalised civil servants, *nomenklatura* thieves and thieves, i.e., stolen from the state under Soviet power by groups comprising first persons and professional thieves.

The institutionalisation of private property on a criminal-civilian level (i.e., legalisation of the property stolen from civilians) formed a type consisting of those owning private, most often legal, enterprises based on other people's previously-stolen private property.

The institutionalisation of private property on a criminal-shadow level formed a type consisting of the owners of illegal enterprises specialising in satisfying illegitimate needs and offering special services (such as armed protection and recovery of debts) based on the property amassed through the interaction between shop-floor people, racketeers, thieves and criminalised shadow dealers.

### 4.5 Petty Theft (The Civilian-Criminal Form of Activity)

Petty theft as a form of activity was specific for the interaction between ordinary civilians, criminalised civilians, petty thieves and thieves. The stereotypes of their interaction are being reproduced successfully in the new economic conditions.

As a type, the larcenous managers of state-run enterprises reproduce petty theft on a *nomenklatura*-civilian level. The same stereotypes are being reproduced on a *nomenklatura*-shadow level by petty-theft minded managers of joint-stock companies, banks and funds. Petty thieves as managers of enterprises and organisations based on all forms of assets (*nomenklatura*-criminal, civilian-shadow, criminal-civilian and criminal-shadow) in their new post-*perestroika* reincarnation are an obligatory feature of space. Petty thieves also comprise the leaders of local criminal organisations, especially gangs specialising in robbing passers-by of their property and money.

### 4.6 Professional Theft (The Criminal-Shadow Form of Activity)

Professional theft as a form of activity was formed through the interaction between shop-floor people, criminalised shadow dealers, thieves and racketeers, and is being translated into the new economic space. Professional theft is particularly personified on a *nomenklatura*-civilian level in the existing type consisting of civil servants who are organisers of wide-spread state-sponsored rackets.

On a civilian-shadow level, professional theft exists as a type consisting of criminalised managers of commercialised state-run enterprises and organisations.

On a *nomenklatura*-criminal level, professional theft takes the shape of a type consisting of those who run private security agencies as a legalised form of racket.

On a civilian-shadow level, professional thieves act under the guise of security chiefs at private enterprises. Their functions include, among other things, the repayment of debts.

On a civilian-criminal level, professional theft is manifested in the existing type consisting of the chiefs of private para-military organisations satisfying those needs of other agents of the administrative market which can be met only through armed force.

## 4.7 Dimensions of the Post-Perestroika Economic Space

Let us consider now, as was done in the first part of this study, the Fig. 9 fragments constituted by the level of activity and the form of activity.

Let us take the pair *nomenklatura*-civilian and *nomenklatura*-shadow levels and their respective forms of activity.

**Figure 10** *Nomenklatura-civilian and nomenklatura-shadow*

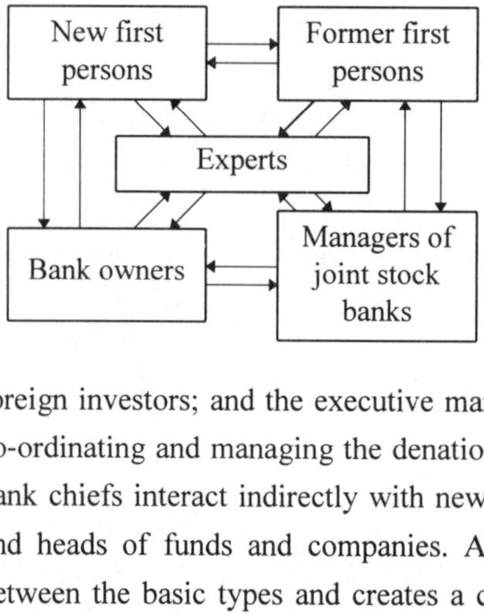


The types presented in this fragment of the diagram are engaged in denationalising and commercialising property. In this process, the owners of big banks set up with state-owned capital represent the interests of national capital; the former first persons, now chiefs of foundations, companies and enterprises, are more associated with foreign investors; and the executive managers of joint-stock banks are in charge of co-ordinating and managing the denationalised property. In their games, joint-stock bank chiefs interact indirectly with new first persons, mainly through bank owners and heads of funds and companies. All this develops a network of connections between the basic types and creates a corresponding functional space (shown as a rectangle at the intersection of links) filled by new people who, at this stage of the administrative market's destruction, carry out the functions of experts, mediators, negotiators, writers of documents and draft resolutions. Unlike the string-pullers who held similar functional places in the Soviet-style administrative market, experts are a structure that is still incomplete organisationally but with a high potential, if the destruction of the administrative market is to give way to natural market relations.

Let us consider the following dimension constituted by the interaction between the *nomenklatura*-civilian and *nomenklatura*-criminal levels of organisation and forms of activity.

**Figure 11** *Nomenklatura-civilian and nomenklatura-criminal*

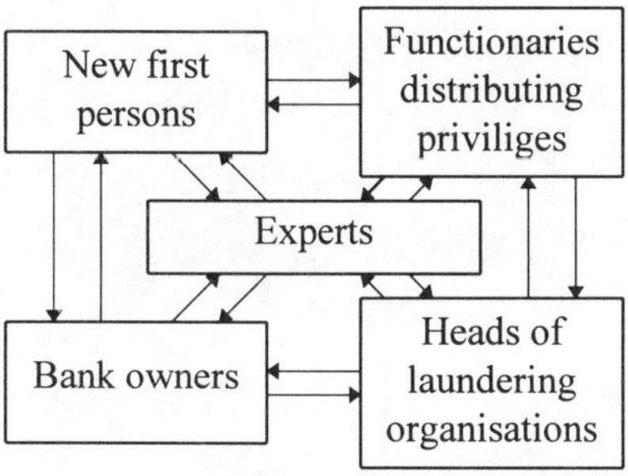


The interactions in this structure are based, as in the former case, on the denationalisation of property. The difference lies in the fact that whereas the owners and disposers of resources obtained during the *nomenklatura*-led and shadow privatisation typically strive to gain control over state-run enterprises, the owners and managers of enterprises with shop-floor and personal capital are more concerned about legalising and aggrandising the assets already accrued in the *perestroika* period. As in the previous case, the intersection of links in this structure becomes a virtual place occupied by mediators, experts and document writers.

Of the whole variety of tetrads, let us consider one more which is in a way polarised by those displayed in the previous figures.

Fig. 12 represents the relations between the *nomenklatura*-civilian and criminal-shadow levels and forms of activity.

**Figure 12** *The nomenklatura-civilian and criminal-shadow level*

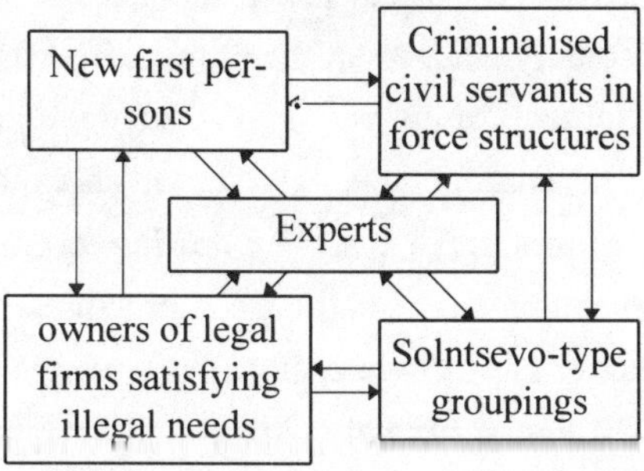


In this pattern, interaction (administrative bargaining) is mainly based on the privatisation of state property. The objects of the bargaining are criminal legal sanctions on the one hand, and licences, soft credits, rights to lease out state property, etc. on the other.

The real-life interactions between post-*perestroika* administrative market agents are, of course, not only based on the tetrad patterns shown in Figs. 10 to 12. The space of matrix 9 may be said to describe the spectrum of probable interactions between the administrative market agents, while the tetrads present the smallest possible fragments of the post-*perestroika* administrative bargaining. This fragmentary description is aimed at presenting possible paths for the further disintegration of the administrative market, as was done while describing the structure of the Soviet administrative-market space.

Those fragments described and those not described can become dimensions of the post-*perestroika* administrative-market economic space, the latter being far richer in purely economic capabilities and free of political expediency. At the moment the future agents of this hypothetical economic space act as mediators in the interaction between the types filling the second-generation economic space. These are second-generation 'string-pullers', mediators, authors of laws and resolutions, consultants and experts who use their status-related inclusion in the 'big sell-off' of state property as the basis for their own future business.

## 4.8 Hierarchism of the Administrative Market

The new first persons, as has already been stressed, possess the highest administrative currency, i.e., the right to sign documents on the denationalisation of property. The second hierarchic level is made up of the owners of banks set up by legal state-owned and shop-floor capitals, the executive heads of joint-stock banks and other enterprises and organisations set up by semi-legal capital, and the former first persons who became heads of foundations, companies and enterprises, i.e., those types that have some *nomenklatura*-shadow components in their activity pattern.

The next hierarchic level is constituted by the types who have some *nomenklatura*-criminal components in their activity pattern: owners of enterprises and organisations set up during the *nomenklatura*-led privatisation with the participation of criminalised state-owned capital, managers of the criminalised state-owned capital, heads of enterprises and organisations set up to launder extra-budgetary state resources, functionaries distributing state credits, licenses and export-import privileges, and managers of enterprises set up during criminal privatisation of the military-industrial complex branches and the force structures.

Still lower in the new administrative market hierarchy are those types where the activity pattern contains some civilian-shadow, criminal-civilian and criminal-shadow components.

However, this is not the only possible hierarchy in the administrative market space. A different hierarchy is possible in which the highest administrative currency is possessed by the leaders of groupings. The next level is made up of types with some criminal-civilian components of activity: leaders of local gangs, larcenous heads of private enterprises and heads of private para-military organisations.

The next level in this variant of hierarchy is constituted by types with civilian-shadow components: security chiefs of private enterprises and organisations, larcenous heads of enterprises set up with stolen shop-floor capital, legalised shop-floor people, etc.

Let us apply the term 'denationalisation' to activities under the first conception of hierarchy, and the term 'privatisation' to activities under the latter conception of hierarchy. Each specific business operation comprises, quite naturally, elements of both privatisation and denationalisation, i.e., legal and criminal components. This is demonstrated by diagrams 10 to 12. The important point here is what kind of business contacts the representative of a type prefers (e.g., some new first persons prefer to deal with the old first persons and bankers who formed their capital during the *nomenklatura*-led privatisation, while other new first persons prefer business dealings with leaders of groupings). Although criminality is not necessarily typical of the new first persons (representatives of this type have in fact become managers of the property previously held by the vanished state but not yet appropriated by the new state), the Solntsevo-type people (as an opposite type) do not typically participate in denationalisation and are active only in privatisation. Between these two polarised types there are various ways of behaviour which combine criminal and legal components in different mixtures.

In the course of denationalisation and privatisation, the contradictory norms of the two hierarchic representations of the administrative market begin to apply: the facilities and functions already privatised by the criminal types start being included in the denationalisation process during which the said facilities and functions could move under the control of the administrative market legalised elements. Property should acquire a proprietor who can be identified by name. However, property privatised by the criminalised types cannot be named, it can only exist anonymously, as property controlled by the 'Solntsevo', 'Dolgie Prudy' and other 'mobs'. Attempts to legalise the criminalised property may, quite naturally, provoke conflicts that are most frequently resolved by force.

## 5 Likely Directions in the Evolution of the Post-*Perestroika* Administrative Market

The post-*perestroika* administrative market is specific in that it is not identical with the state, as was the case before. The post-*perestroika* state and administrative market exist in different social spaces. The state and the branches of its power are dominated by first persons, ordinary civilians, shop-floor people and thieves thrown out of economic activity by force of circumstances but preserving a fraction of the administrative currency and mentality of the Soviet administrative market. The types seem to have been distributed among the branches of power. The federal and regional level administrations are dominated by former first persons and the executive structures of power by former shop-floor people and thieves, while it is former ordinary civilians turned parliamentarians of all levels who are concentrated in the representative bodies of authority. At the same time, the first persons exist outside the *nomenklatura* and strive to restore or reproduce this archaic institution. The shop-floor people have lost control of production (due to absence of shortages) and try to resuscitate the planning institution (as a state-sponsored form of shortages). The thieves have remained without respective executive hierarchies because of the commercialisation of criminal business and, in order to restore their authority, are getting involved in show-downs having co-opted the state-run armed structures for this purpose. Ordinary civilians, whose best representatives work in Parliament, have been deprived of the well-accustomed system of favours and privileges and try to restore it in the new conditions – at least for the parliamentarians as a first step and for all citizens in the foreseeable future. The interaction in the tetrad 'former first persons-former ordinary civilians-former shop-floor people-former thieves' make up the visible content of political life, but this visibility unfolds itself in an executive void. Not a single governmental decision aimed at 'streamlining' the reality has borne any expected results so far. The state, represented by the old administrative market agents, tries to establish control over the post-*perestroika* market, while the new administrative market strives to become a state *per se*.

The further diversification of the economic space is likely to be determined by the way the state develops and treats today's administrative market. If the state gets strengthened as a whole and if its institutions preserve a degree of continuity *vis-à-vis* socialism, the role of the administrative currency will remain as it is or will even increase and the number of its varieties will rise. In the final analysis, the aspiration to preserve the state and to revalue the administrative currency will lead to the 'Latin-Americanisation' of power and the diktat of political and administrative ambitions over economic interests and moral values. However, Latin-Americanisation is not the only or even the most probable way of Russia's development.

If the present-day state is to weaken, its functions will be gradually alienated by the new administrative market which is bound to transform, as time goes by, into a new state entity. In that future state, power will go to the new first persons, managers of joint-stock banks, leaders of groupings and other diagonal types from matrix 9, while the economic space will be determined by the interaction between as yet undefined experts, who have not yet amassed the necessary capital (analogous to string-pullers in the Soviet-style administrative market), and the superdiagonal and subdiagonal types.

Today, the state's relationship with the superdiagonal and subdiagonal types differs substantially. The subdiagonal types regard the administrative currency (distributed by the state of the former first persons, ordinary civilians, shop-floor people and thieves) as a means rather than an end of activity, while for the superdiagonal types the relationship between purely economic and the administrative values is just the reverse (as one businessman said, there are people making politics out of money and people making money out of politics).

Statuses enabling the superdiagonal types to take part in economic life derive from the state and may disappear with it. Therefore these types come out as natural allies of the state in its interaction with the subdiagonal types, the owners and disposers of assets. Representatives of the superdiagonal types reflect upon the situation in their own way and, relying on the state and using methods within their reach, strive to preserve the structures where the administrative currency prevails over money as such, while to possess this currency means to control the activity of potentially market-oriented agents.

Representatives of the subdiagonal types are interested not so much in the revaluation of the administrative currency as in creating conditions under which their personal wealth will not depend on the whims of the authorities, the state or any institutions that lay claim to state-like power functions. Representatives of these types are in favour of denationalisation of the economy and formation of a market space proper, as well as the formation of certain as yet unclear initial political conditions to perform operations with the denationalised and privatised property.

The new owners' interests are not represented, in fact, in the political structure and are lobbied for by the mediating superdiagonal types which have, as a rule, their own political and economic interests. It is felt that the activity of the superdiagonal types who are converting the administrative currency into purely economic assets (and vice versa) may be of a political, or equivalent nature in the post-*perestroika* state structure. This activity is largely of a lobbyist nature, but it assumes a distinct political colouring in a power system where the economy has not yet been differentiated from politics. We already have some stereotypes of this kind of mediating activity when the superdiagonal types act as mediators in and organisers of political functions. The latest example is the election of O. Boiko (who can be viewed as typologically belonging to the owners of banks set up with legal state-owned and shadow capital) as leader of the party *Russia's Democratic Choice*, which may be construed as recognition by this party's leaders (functionaries involved in the distribution of state credits, privileges and other administrative benefits) of their mediating role between business and politics.

The politicisation of Russian business is now taking various shapes, including attempts to control the information market. Especially active here are the representatives of the criminalised types already who already control local publications and the gutter press and who are striving to gain control over local TV channels. This is connected with the fact that, in the absence of a political medium, the informational space replaces the political one. The mass media may be said to be an instrument of forming the political environment and the most powerful legal instrument of lobbying.

Apart from politicisation, i.e., becoming mediators between business and politics, representatives of the superdiagonal types have logical opportunities to convert their statuses and preserve a certain position in the market economy as such.

One of their opportunities – lobbying – consists in investing the administrative currency held by a superdiagonal type in a business organised by a type that is symmetrical to the diagonal. In this process, the superdiagonal types (having a criminal and a shadow component) are being legalised and commercialised in this case.

The third opportunity for the superdiagonal types to evolve (after politicisation and lobbying) is transnationalisation or emigration in one form or another (by emigration is meant conversion of the administrative currency into an internationally accepted status), or engagement in the activities of interstate (transnational) economic institutions. Thus, some representatives of this type e.g., the former first persons, have in fact emigrated and become heads of international foundations and joint ventures. The illegal exporters of strategic raw materials and weapons, and the leaders of criminalised structures are getting involved in the activities of multinational criminalised institutions specialising in trafficking strategic raw materials, arms and drugs as well as other varieties of illegitimate business.

Going only by the logic of the administrative market, one can highlight two stages in the development of economic relations proper and their alienation from the political ones. The first stage witnesses the disintegration of the Soviet-style administrative market (Fig. 1) and formation of the post-*perestroika* administrative market. This results in the advent of a group of politicised former actors (having formed as a new post-*perestroika* state) and groups of new actors that are opposed to the state and in whose activity purely economic and political components are discernible to some extent (Fig. 9)

Actors of the post-*perestroika* economic space, formed mainly as a result of denationalising property, try to privatise the state as well but are themselves 'nationalised' in this case. The new administrative market strives to replace the state in those economic and political niches that were left after the collapse of the world socialist community and the USSR.

The second stage of the administrative market transformation may be associated with the disintegration of both the state (in its present shape) and the interaction system shown in the Fig. 9 diagram. This may result in the formation of a new state (or states) and a new multilevel structure which is no longer an administrative market but is filled with types that are genetically linked with mediators in the post-*perestroika*-style administrative market. The future new persons are currently to be found at the connecting junctions between the various agents of today's administrative market. They are gradually switching over to independent business, generally free from state control, i.e., purely private business. The activities of these people, if they manage to survive, will be free of those political elements that are specific to the administrative market. Even today, they are mostly guided by purely market-oriented criteria of efficiency and personal success.

It may be supposed that the final stage in the decay of the social basis of the administrative market will be represented by a social structure formed through the interaction between groups of the administrative market agents (ordered in the matrix of Fig. 9 ), a group of rentiers (former state budget-paid people), a group of the owners of natural economic units, and groups of the politicised 'former people' controlling the new state.

## 6 In Lieu of Conclusion

The evolution of the administrative market's material base has already caused almost the whole sphere of semi-commercial production of goods, machines and mechanisms to drop out of the material and monetary flows. What remains of the administrative market material base is the fuel and raw material complex, while the educated people who can and do utilise the stolen technologies are being ousted to the financial market currently under creation, where they successfully master the newest (borrowed) techniques of gaining 'dividends' out of commodity symbols (money, shares, bills of exchange, etc.) and invent techniques of their own.

Some denationalised enterprises in the manufacturing industry are gradually being made part of the global technological chains, with the national economy branches within which they were registered decaying in administrative terms. The agrarian and mechanical engineering 'commodity producers' from the stagnating branches, having no economic prospects, merge into politicised structures striving to restore the administrative market in its pre-*perestroika* version.

If today's trends remain intact, Russia will, in the foreseeable future, turn into a unique poly-state entity with a developed fuel and raw material complex used (by multinational corporations in particular) as a lever of pressure on the third-world exporters, with efficient and aggressive financial institutions laying claim to a sizeable part of the world financial market, and with primitive but fast-developing agriculture. High-tech processing and mechanical engineering industries will be developing on a limited scale. Most huge factories and agricultural units – symbols of the 'catch up with and overtake' epoch – will vanish from the economic map but will remain on the political one.

The country's main wealth – raw materials and educated people with great experience of work in the administrative market – may (in the best outcome) convert into financial empires where money will make money with only minimal environmental pollution. As they say, money can buy everything the country needs, including socio-political stability. However, this can only happen if the enriched educated people manage to co-ordinate their political actions and provide initial conditions for self-reproduction. Otherwise the CIS space will very soon turn into a raw material appendage to the world economy and a global dumping ground on which the hierarchised groups of poverty-stricken socialist citizens will be dividing the dregs of the developed civilisations. However, an intermediate variant is most likely, where the developed financial centres will be surrounded by depressed regions-dumping places, controlled by the miniaturised semblances of the Soviet state with a post-*perestroika*-style developed administrative market, which of course will not promote general social stability in the Eurasian space.

The world financial market is very likely to face serious upheavals caused by the 'new Russians' with their free capital, intellect, education and upbringing in the subcultures formed by the necessity to survive under socialism and during privatisation of the state and its property. Even now, when 5-10% of state property has been converted into the 'new Russian' money, many world markets have experienced the cheek of the former physicists and engineers turned bankers and stock-exchange profiteers, and try to restrict their activities by creating the myth of the 'Russian mafia'. One can only imagine what will happen in the near future when the main part of the former USSR state capital gets cashed in, and the socialist rentiers (i.e., the former state budget-paid people who started speculating with privatisation vouchers and then turned to other securities), having gained experience dealing with 'MMM' and similar organisations, launch operations with the securities of foreign institutionalised and private investors. The world of transnational electronic networks and mutual payments now in the making is the most favourable environment for our tradition-free profiteers to prosper.

The following features are characteristic for today's condition of the administrative market:

- the post-*perestroika* business space does not have referents in the state and society political set-up, and hangs in a political vacuum and thus is vulnerable to political arbitrariness and chance;
- the geographic space controlled by the post-*perestroika* administrative market is much narrower than Russia's or the CIS' social space. The administrative market has established itself in a new form in the metropolitan cities and administrative centres, while the social periphery is still dominated by its pre-*perestroika* form, deformed due to the collapse of the *nomenklatura* institution and disappearance of the respective norms;
- the existing post-communist ideologemes implemented in politics are nothing but splinters of socialist mythologemes without any socio-structural or economic groundwork.

It is only the state that consolidates geographic space, while the administrative-market consolidates business and politics. Moreover, it is this administrative market, this politics and this geography that in fact make up the state. At the same time, the state regards itself as a self-contained entity and tries to force the Russian businessmen, politicians and regional leaders to accept its own rules of the game based on apparatchik-related principles and values inherited, to a large degree, from the USSR. The state does not strive to modernise itself, does not create opportunities for self-development of social stratification, for the legalisation of business, for the formation of a natural ideology (as a basis of politics). It restrains the evolution of the Soviet geographic space into a normal space of human activity.

The state is perceived and understood as a constraint by all agents and actors: business people, politicians and regional authorities. Their natural activity is aimed at minimising state interference in their affairs, which takes the shape of an all-against-all struggle: administrative market agents against the new elements of the social structure and politicians, politicians against new business, against changes in the typology of state-sponsored space and for the restoration of the customary relations of the Soviet-style administrative market.

The problem lies in the fact that neither the administrative market nor the new social strata can exist outside this state. No new ideology can be developed, no geographic territories will be inhabited outside it. The Russian state is a value in itself and one must live and try to do one's business within it, regardless of the fact that even if one is of sound mind and lucid memory it is impossible either to live or undertake anything within it.

# 6

# The Russian National Economic Elite in the Political Arena

Vladimir Chervyakov

## 1 The Specifics and Particularities of the Formation of Political Interests in Russian Business

The specific interests of industry and business in the process of liberalizing the economic system of post-communist Russia exert an increasing influence on state decision making, including that of a strategic nature. They also affect both the orientation and quality of these decisions. The specificity and corporate nature of those interests (as well as the need to have access to persons who are formulating and making the most important state decisions) makes the need to increase inter-business ties and search for an appropriate organizational form imperative. It is all the more imperative that the state continue to dominate in both the production sector and in private enterprise.

In 1991-1994, business associations emerged within the system of economic interests representation. These were built out of concrete economic units and influential groups and corporations in Russian business. This means that business circles in Russia have stepped into the political and governmental arenas. This also signifies that groups of economic elites – irrespective of whether their goals are sectoral or group-oriented in nature – have become largely corporatized.

In any case, public associations of industrialists and entrepreuners have been acknowledged by the business elite not only as entities that can defend free enterprise but also as a group that can represent political interests.

However it is impossible to comprehend the role, significance and specificity of these formations as a symptom and algorithmic mechanism of the transformation of the present (post-soviet) economic environment by means of rational choice models alone. What is needed is an understanding of the specificity of current Russian business that illuminates the instinctive pragmatism of its political interests of and its distinctive structural corporate formations. The foundations of the latter are the traditional 'presence' of the commercial-industrial estate affiliated with the state institutions of 19th century imperial Russia, as well as the 'clan and sectoral representation' of the industrial establishment that was linked with the high-level party organs and governmental departments of the USSR.

Such an approach is motivated by the fact that the coexistence of business in the state sector of the economy and in private enterprise (with the former having a decisive influence) led to a rather specific impact on the ideology and practice of present-day Russian business-in-the-making as a whole. In reality, state sector business has become dominant, which means that the activities of state administrative organs are aimed at earning commercial profit through the use of budgetary funds. Therefore, in reality, the state – in the form of government economic bodies – is trying to control state property by means of the latter's actual alienation from the status of national property.

The point of this phenomenon – which gives a qualitative description of the present Russian business environment – is this: governmental (in this case, administrative-management) economic organs are themselves trying to become property owners with the right to hold or transfer property (or more likely sell it for profit) with various forms of ownership (mixed and private) to entrepreneurial entities. This system formalizes their role as one of governmental economic agents authorized to command and manage both budgetary resources and the powers delegated to them.

A comparison of western political institutions with those of Russia provides a specifically different interpretation of such European terms as 'feudalism', 'capitalism' and 'socialism.' (This was actively practised by historians of the Russian state school – Sergei Solovev, Vladimir Klyuchevskii, and their 19th century followers who showed how the rather unique geographical, climatic, natural, demographic and historic conditions of Russia produced qualitative differences in political institutions analogous in name to European institutions.) A vivid example is such a basic notion as private property which, only with the recently-initiated privatization in Russia, has begun to assume the meaning of its European root (which is derived from the Latin term *privare*, which means 'take away' or 'deprive').

In Europe, the basis for a market-oriented development of society was the rapid growth of the circulation sphere [*sfera obrashcheniya*] and promotion of the merchant to the forefront of economic activity, who was willing to finance the centralization of executive power (demanding a parliament at the same time). This occurred during the period of absolutism preceding democracy, and the merchant acted to guarantee the stability of the monetary and trading systems. Thomas Paine, one of the founding fathers of American representative democracy, called on merchants to be 'persons empowered to act as a trusted holder of the public purse for the benefit of the entire nation'.

In Russia, on the other hand, government strengthened the position of the producer, turning the service class nobleman (a person bound by obligations of military service) into a landlord, and turning the merchant into a buyer and industrialist, while tieing the peasant to the land and the factory. The state acted as a main customer of agricultural and industrial output, this being driven to a large extent by the empire's increasing military power. It was through the Treasury acting as the main buyer (*kazna* stands for the State Treasury in Russian and the adjective *kazennyi* implies state property and resources) that the state, in fact, directly controlled production without any necessity whatsoever of worrying about the circulation sphere. The latter was restricted – voluntarily or involuntarily – by the state, and was permitted to develop mainly at the expense of the traditional exchange between agricultural and cattle-breeding regions, as well as imports of luxuries for the landed gentry and consumer goods for middle-level officials.

It is this historically-based lagging of the circulation sphere behind that of production that explains the following paradox of Russian statehood: every difficult step taken toward liberalization and democratization resulted only in the strengthening of executive power. In the final analysis, the Russian producer-industrialist, merchant, landlord and well-to-do peasant – were all invariably drawn to executive power, which they considered to be a Treasury [kazna]. They tried to grab as much as they could from it, while as far as possible, giving nothing in return. Today, Russian producers, businessmen and financiers relate to the Treasury in much the same way: they by various means have received preferential credits from the state and in most cases simply did not repay them. Rather, after turning them over several times, they reimbursed their initial capital, having invested it in valuables and luxuries or having squandered it on recreation or carousing.

Meanwhile, answers to the current mysteries of Russian business should be sought by methodically examining the particularities of the traditional functioning of the Russian economy – which will function as a particular cultural and historic code of the conflicts occurring in Russian business today.

## 2 The Particularities of the Functioning of the Russian Economy (The Traditional Pattern)

The liberal market economy of the West recognized the necessity of regulating the national economy only after the 'Great Depression' of 1930s and the appearance of Keynesian economics. In Russia, however, for centuries the state was not only an active player in economic activity but also played a special role in the domestic economy. Apparently, the circumstances that brought about this kind of state participation in economic activity: a) rather long borders which required fortification; b) the largely flat terrain, absence of natural obstacles, and vulnerability of the state administrative and economic centre to an aggressor from practically any direction; and c) a vastly underpopulated and economically underdeveloped territory.

These circumstances (apart from the fact that until the 18th century Russia had to wage two wars annually on the average) necessitated maximum concentration of all available material, financial and human resources by state authorities (Fig.1). It is no wonder that during the last six centuries Russia has been traditionally distinguished by:

- high taxation levels imposed on the population and the major sectors of economic activity, which were without parallel in Europe;
- unprecedented state expenditures on financing industrial production and capital construction for strategic and related purposes.

The latter presents a topic of special interest for further investigation. In order to asses the extent of state investment in the domestic economy, one should remember, for example, that the overwhelming majority of industrial enterpises constructed during the reign of Peter the Great was built with government funds. Even during the period when the most favourable market conditions existed in tsarist Russia, e.g., in 1913, the state (or Treasury) functioned as a customer, financier and purchaser of nearly 60% of total industrial output. This tendency of the state to become a major investor in domestic production and main consumer of its output became fully developed in the period after October 1917. This was when 'state orders' increased to 100% and exclusively state financing of production and consumption of finished goods made it possible to renounce money in its usual sense and to move to fund distribution, i.e. distribution in kind.[1]

**Figure 1** *The state and the economy before Peter the Great's reforms*

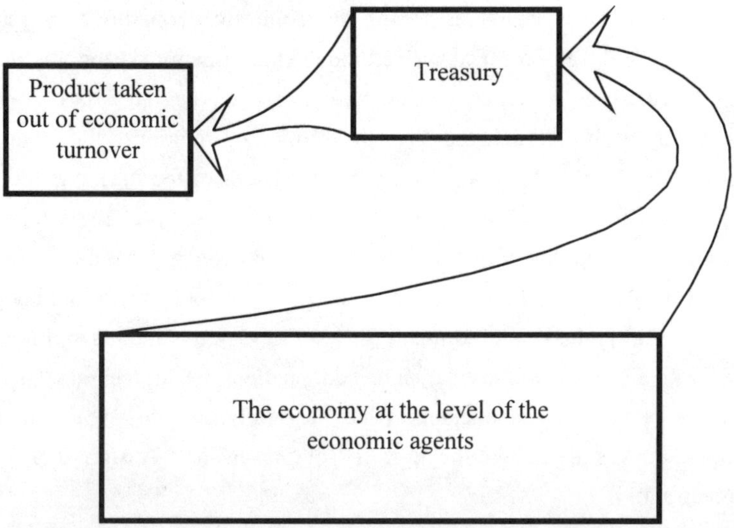


In light of the above, we can state that the Russian state traditionally used administrative measures to withdraw a large portion of the surplus product of the national economy. On the other hand, however, most of the product withdrawn from the economy – at least since Peter the Great's reforms – was immediately invested by the central authorities in industrial production (mainly military) and construction for strategic purposes. Thus, for centuries, the Russian state was not only an economic actor but also a strategic investor in the domestic economy, determining how resources were redistributed. In this context, the economic functions of the Russian state can be defined as follows.

- The maximum possible mobilisation of the national economic resources of the public Treasury through state fiscal organs (i.e. maximum withdrawal of surplus product from the economy).

---

**1** Thus, by the mid-17th century the western border of the Kingdom of Muscovy was protected by a threefold belt of fortresses stretching for over a thousand kilometres; these fortresses were located a one-day's march apart (25-30 km).

- Reinvestment of the withdrawn surplus product into that economic sector that met the state's needs for military power and the opening up of new lands.

As has already been mentioned, this type of economy was formed by the centuries-long mobilisational economic regime and the state's aspirations to concentrate maximal national resources in its hands. Apart from the mobilisational regime which was characteristic of the domestic economy during the last few centuries, the development of such a unique kind of national economy was caused by the particularities of national development as a whole. These are connected with, above all, with the delayed growth of market relations, the concentration of considerable land and human resources in the hands of the state, and the preservation of the latter's role as a leading actor in the economy. All these features inherent in the historic development of Russia's society and economy should not be attributed – in full measure – to the preservation of the basic foundations of feudalism which Western Europe had endured much earlier. They, in the authors' opinion, have more to do with a national culture which had adopted many features of an Oriental style of national economic management (thus, as early as the 14th century a larger population was living on the territory of present-day Austria than in the entire Russian state).

In placing the formation of the unique model of national economic management primarily in the context of national culture, the authors would like to stress their non-judgmental use of the terms employed here before proceeding with a consideration of the national type of the economy. First of all, it should be noted that national culture as such cannot be good or bad since it is the result of a given people coping with a defined natural-economic space under specific historical conditions. In the authors' opinion, one should speak of whether or not the goals and methods of state policy (including economic policy), legal and economic standards, and official values were appropriate for the national culture in question.

In particular, the model of economic management under consideration was not just characterised by shortcomings, which are evident to any more or less objective observer. Apart from the fact that this model allowed the nation, personified in the state, to carry out great mobilisation and concentration of resources during the critical periods of national history, it also enriched the world of economic practice with the experience of an effective state policy aimed at establishing an economic regime with unprecedented profitability of investment in domestic industry. Again, the latter was a consequence of the state's role as a strategic investor in the domestic economy: when investing government funds, the state had to worry about conducting a policy that would provide for maximum profitability on a national scale.

Traditionally, the state policy of raising the profitability of investments on a national scale consisted of three major elements.

*The first* was traditionally the policy of reducing base costs in the economy. The base costs of industrial production – which was traditionally the main economic object of concern for the Russian state – are determined by the cost and price levels of: a) energy resources; b) transportation; c) foodstuffs (the latter became a major criterion of determining the size of labour payments). With the preservation of rather stable consumer prices on the domestic and world markets, reduction of the price of energy by one rouble, for instance, increases the profits on the sale of finished goods by 10-15 roubles. Transportation, energy resources and labour cost are indispensable cost components at all stages of the production process. The more stages are involved in the processing of raw materials and the higher the technological level of a specific product, the more effect a reduction of base prices in the economy will have. This is because every processing stage incurs transportation, energy, and labour costs.

At various stages of Russian national history, the reduction of base prices in the economy was achieved by different means. These included state subsidies and investments in appropriate sectors of the economy, maintaining low prices on production for industrial consumption, lowering the level of popular consumption, and accordingly, reducing labour costs etc.

In fact, the reduction of base costs as a means of increasing economic profitability is not an exclusively Russian invention at all. Practically all economically-developed countries try to pursue similar policies by means of military and political, economic and technological control over the major raw material producing regions of the world, by keeping the level of popular consumption in 'third world' countries low, etc. But Russia, by virtue of its economic self-sufficiency and relative independence from the international division of labour, manages to implement this policy within the framework of a single national economy and national territory[2].

But implementation of the policy of reducing base costs in the economy – apart from the unprecedented profitability of national-scale investments – also entailed inevitable political costs. As an economic autarky and miniature model of the world

**2** Economically speaking, the Bolsheviks did not introduce any principal innovations into the economy. For the most part, their authoritative regime carried the objectively-existing tendencies (toward autarky) to its logical conclusion.

market, Russia had to politically regulate – as a single government – a whole complex of problems concerning the unequal distribution of resources between its raw material, industrial, commercial and financial regions. These are problems that, on the world market, were solved by the severest military and political pressure by developed countries on colonies and less-developed nations – bringing about confrontation between the North and the South. In Russia, those problems were solved by administrative redistribution of economic resources by directive, as well as direct state subsidisation of raw material producing regions (Fig. 4).

The contradiction described above explains the destructive role played by the industrial and commercial regions of the USSR during the last stage of its existence. Regions which accumulated the main part of the surplus profit on their territories (brought about by their effective subsidisation of raw material producing regions), sought to get rid of the necessity of subsidising these regions. However, when that goal was achieved as a result of disintegration of the state, they found themselves under the strict *diktat* of those previously subsidised territories.

Traditionally, the *second element of state policy* aimed at increasing the profitability of investment in the national economy was the stimulation of industrial demand and priority investments in industrial production. This policy manifested itself in the considerable discrepancy between the taxation level of economic entities in the production sphere and the much higher taxes on personal income taxes and trade transactions. Such a disproportionate tax scheme was aimed at pursuing three major goals.

First, it was directed at stimulating the allocation of profits and surplus product (the latter is only in the case of a socialist economy) on developing real production rather than on consumption. The problem of an overextended budget and budget deficit is as old in Russia as budgetary subsidies. This policy was above all aimed at maximising the investment of resources by producers themselves, the 'self-unwinding' [samoraskrutka] of the domestic economy. It is another matter all together that Russia's constant participation in the competition for world leadership resulted in the continual withdrawal of a rather considerable part of GNP from economic turnover. This made the investment of resources by economic actors themselves extremely insignificant when compared with government financing.

Moreover, this policy guaranteed extremely low production costs in the technological cycle from extraction of raw materials to the final product. This was most vividly expressed during the socialist period when practically all national production occurred within an economic system in which prices were close to costs.

Second, and most important, this practice allowed for the withdrawal of the extra profits that had been formed in the economy as a result of centralised governmental policies, in addition to surplus product. The profitability of 'macro-sectors' in the economy was a result of reducing base costs: practically the entire production process (extraction, processing, manufacturing of finished goods) took place in a system in which prices were relatively understated because of their corresponding cost levels. The main added profits were made at a stage that was close to the consumer market, i.e., when selling prices were set by enterprises producing final goods and in trade. The reason for this is that consumer goods – except for those whose prices were state-controlled – were sold according to market demand rather than level of profitability. It was here that draconian Russian taxation rates, traditionally among the highest in the world, came into effect.

This system turned out to be even simpler during the socialist period of Russian history. Regardless of the amount of roubles in circulation and the theoretical and actual presence of buyers and sellers (i.e., certain preconditions of commodity exchange and market), every economic agent operated within in a rigid in-kind distribution system. In this system, buyer and seller were not connected directly, but rather by means of an abstract government 'warehouse' whose entrance gate was called the State Planning Committee and whose exit gate was called the State Supply Committee. The whole building was crowned with a roof called the State Pricing Committee. All the production activities of an economic actor were controlled by the State Planning Committee, which sent down relevant production plans. Supplies were regulated by the State Supply Committee, and all questions of settlements and pricing were decided by the State Pricing Committee. Thus, all actors in the socialist economy dealt, in fact, not with one another but with a certain kind of 'government warehouse' which provided 'in-kind reserves' and received manufactured products. (Note that the term 'socialist economy' is not absolutely correct as it implies a market economy. The existence of public production is better characterised by the term 'narodnoe khozyaistvo' (national economy) which may also include production in kind.)

In such a system of a natural economy, value added was created by final product enterprises nor by retail trade organisations. Any jump in price that might ensure the appearance of goods in the shops sold at a 'real' or inflated price was made by state wholesale trading enterprises. Localising added product in a system which comprised only a few wholesalers permitted its easy withdrawal to the state budget with minimum losses. State centralised pricing allowed prices for 'basic necessities' to be lowered administratively and the reimbursement of such cuts with incommensurably high prices for everything else.

The third goal of this policy consisted in ensuring the stabilisation of the state financial system and preventing the accumulation of a surplus monetary mass in the population. This policy can be observed throughout a rather extended period of Russian history, since the state budget deficit is an inevitable concomitant of a financial system that undertakes concentrated state investment activity.

All state investment presupposes a certain period in which the following expenses are recouped: those related to scientific research on future production, capital construction and the provision of future production facilities with fixed assets, labour payments to those performing the above-mentioned activities, etc. Money invested in new production inevitably has inflationary tendencies until the moment that expenses are recouped, since it is brought into circulation without being backed by a corresponding amount of goods and services, i.e., it is worthless money.

The state, taking on the role of an investor, has to limit emissions in light of the consideration that the amount of budgetary allocations to the social sphere (which is always exclusively a sphere of expenditures), expenses for maintaining the state machinery including the armed forces and police, foreign aid, and domestic investment should somehow correspond to the actual volume of goods and services on the consumer market. Ignoring this rule always leads to higher inflation, destabilisation of the national financial system, and economic crisis.

As a result of the above-mentioned circumstances the state-investor naturally tries to lower the duration of capital construction and money held by the population as much as possible. The latter was usually achieved in Russia by means of a high personal income tax as well as by such methods as the practically obligatory distribution of government bond issues (during Stalin's regime), a state monopoly on trade in the most profitable commodities, and high indirect taxation of consumer goods. The current policy of the Russian Ministry of Finance illustrates that such financial tactics on the part of the state are inevitable, as the Ministry has to resort to traditional measures of reducing popular consumption.

The *third element of the state policy* aimed at increasing the profitability of investment in the national economy traditionally was to maintain a considerable discrepancy between price levels on the world and domestic markets. This was, relatively speaking, called the 'price prism' policy. The main preconditions for conducting such a policy were those described above. The main goal was to increase the profitability of state export operations. Generally speaking, the essence of the policy was rather simple – a ton of grain (which was Russia's major export until the 1970s and whose cost of production was approximately $30 in about 1910 or so) was sold on the world market at the world price (which was about $200 at that time). In this way, exports were fantastically profitable, by world standards.

The major instruments of implementing this policy were:

- in the pre-*Revolutionary period* – the existence of a state export monopoly on certain commodity groups and the use of a 'special exporters' and 'special importers' regime;
- in the *socialist period* – the existence of a state monopoly on foreign trade.

We shall now elaborate on the institution of 'special exporters' and 'special importers,' which implements the policy discussed above in a market economy. The objective conditions required for this policy were traditionally: a) high customs duties on foreign trade transactions, and b) the granting – by a special decision of the state authorities – of substantial priviliges to concrete economic actors trading in specified commodities. The result of these policies was the exclusion of the majority of enterprises from foreign trade in view of their inability to profitably compete with 'special exporters' and 'special importers'. This concentrated foreign trade transactions in a small number of entities, which allowed the state to effectively control and regulate their activities. In fact, introducing the institution of the privileged (special) trading organisation meant the sealing off of the government's economic borders with economic methods.

It should be noted that in 'post-socialist' Russia the main contours of the institution of the privileged foreign trade organisation were spontaneously and rather quickly revived as the most effective mechanism of regulation foreign economic activity.

## 3 The Term 'Economic Interests' and the Limits of its Applicability to Russia

Before taking up this issue, the authors consider it necessary to clarify the limits of applying the term 'economic interests' to the Russian economy at various stages of its functioning. The economy and economic relations are terms which emerged in the framework of a market economy, which is based on the dominance of the real free exchange of products of the productive and intellectual activity of its subjects in production relationships. (This, strictly speaking, is what is usually called 'the economy'). In this essay, the authors have purposefully emphasised the domination of exchange in the relations of production. The economic development of mankind has occurred within the framework of exchange and distribution, and the interaction of each with one another. Even in societies with developed exchange relations they play an extremely important role. Distribution relations dominate, and are practically inevitable, in the following spheres: in particular, in the family, in the state apparatus (the payment of salaries), in settlements between technological subdivisions within enterprises, and in the implementation of public social and private charitable programmes. The opposition and interaction between distribution and exchange on the theoretical level reflects the opposition between on the one hand, communist and socialist ideas which focus on distribution and redistribution relations in society, and on the other, liberal conceptions of the economy which focus on the further development of exchange.

The 'economy' as a market system for economic organisation stands in opposition to systems based on the dominance of relations of distribution and redistribution, which are more correctly characterised by the term 'khozyaistvo' (a production organism which does not necessarily imply the existence of relations of exchange).

The public interests that are connected with and accompany production activities differ based on whether exchange or distribution relations are the dominant form of economic activity in society. The difference in the ways in which economic actors receive their share of the social product determines the difference between interests in systems based on the priority of exchange relations (hereafter referred to as economic ['ekonomicheskie'] interests), and those based on the dominance of distribution relations (hereafter referred to as 'khozyaistvennye' interests).

Distribution relations – which serve as a means of determining one's share of the social product – as a rule, derive from two bases: demand and real availability.

## 4 The Fundamental Principles of the State Investment Mechanism

Implementation of state investment policy was traditionally carried out on the following bases. The first of them, which served as an instrument for 'releasing' state funds into the economy, was the creation of sectors of priority financing and of stable reliable demand. World practice demonstrates that state investment in the economy was nearly always 'selective.' Mass 'infusions' of investment were targeted to one or two sectors which were, at the time, of priority significance for the state. Nearly always, favourites for state investment were sectors related to the national defence, i.e. the military industrial complex (MIC).

**Figure 2** *State and economy after Peter the Great's reforms*

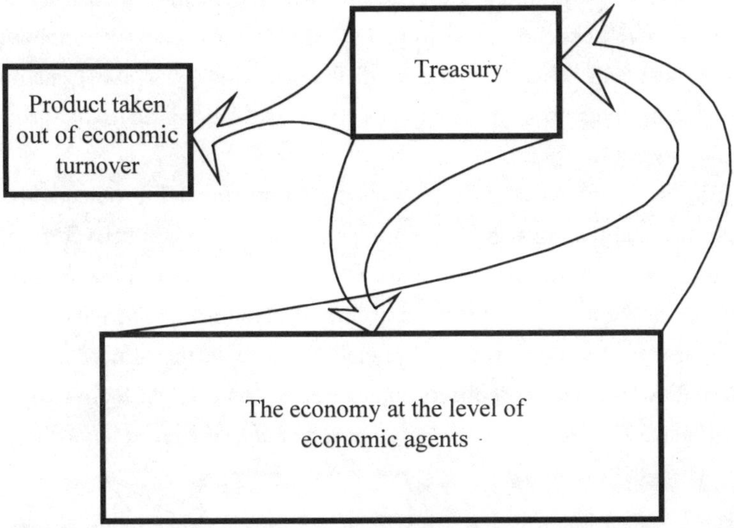


In most developed market economies, there is a variety of sources of investment and reliable demand, with the state budget and state orders playing a considerable, but not necessarily dominant, role. An extremely special situation is the case when the state, due to historic circumstances, has to literally 'maintain' the economy, i.e., when preferential credits and other types of budgetary financing are determinative for the economy. Examples of such situation in the developed countries are government regulation of the economy and budgetary subsidies in the countries most seriously affected by the 'Great Depression' of the 1930s (Nazi Germany, fascist Italy, and Spain), as well as the military mobilisation of the economies of the US, Great Britain and several other countries during World War II.

In these crisis situations, state financing is mainly targeted to priority sector enterprises, in this case enterprises in the MIC. Through the proper orders these enterprises, in their turn, then act as investors in the remaining sectors which can be used to fulfil military orders. In this case, the economy becomes highly militarised, and its structure quickly acquires the form of a pyramid with several defence enterprises comprising the industrial peak and state procurement agencies forming the agricultural top.

At different stages of Russian history several sectors were given priority in state financing. They include transportation (large-scale railroad construction in the late 19th and early 20th centuries under K. Yu. Witte), the MIC (under Witte's successors, and during the entire socialist period), the agro-industrial complex (AIC) (since N.S. Khrushchev came to power), the fuel and energy complex (FEC) (since late 1960s) and several others. In different periods, the above-mentioned sectors were major investors in the numerous enterprises belonging to the 'processing' stage of the production cycle.

The above-indicated priority sectors of state financing objectively served as a niche for establishing stable elite groups whose power was derived from their access to considerable budgetary resources and their significant influence over who would execute the various state-financed programmes. Objectively, sectoral ministries and their elite groupings served as a branch of the state investment mechanism, which directed investment to producers and exercised control over their activities (Fig. 3).

**Figure 3** *Division of labour between regional and sectoral elites*

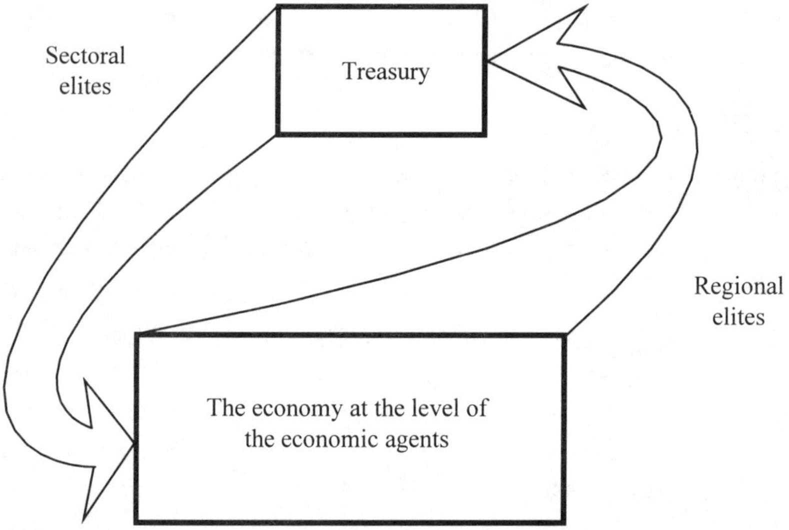


The second basis of the state investment mechanism (which was an instrument of withdrawing the surplus profit from the economy formed as a result of government policy) was the territorial principle of forming the state budget. It also entailed the consolidation of the fiscal, police and military functions of the regional authorities. Practically throughout all of Russian history, the above-mentioned functions were the principally the prerogative of territorial structures. The present configuration of the administrative and territorial units of the Russian Federation is, in particular , also determined by their control and political functions. Thus, according to the official version, the most recent serious 'redrawing' of regions was brought about by the need to 'optimise the number of party organisations', i.e. to raise the efficiency of territorial control and administration.

Therefore, in the most general sense, the state investment mechanism was a part of overall state economic management, which corresponded sufficiently precisely with the structure of the national economy (Fig. 2).

The Russian economy was traditionally built according to the principle of economic autarky, i.e. an isolated and economically self-sufficient economic system. As national production in Russia was in fact a self-sufficient economic system, its structure traditionally encompassed the complete cycle of capital turnover and all technological stages of manufacturing: a) extraction of raw materials; b) the processing and semi-finished goods stage; c) manufacturing of finished products, and d) the sale of finished products to the consumer. Generally speaking, the Russian economic zone was some sort of a miniature of the world market, it being an economic region only partially integrated into the international division of labour because of its economic self-sufficiency.

This economic self-sufficiency and unified industrial which ensured a complete production cycle within a single national territory, was reflected in the territorial and economic division of labour between Russia's regions. We should note at once that the boundaries of Russia's economic regions never coincided with administrative or territorial borders. The latter were units for the administrative replenishing of state coffers were traditionally 'drawn' mostly for fiscal, police, military and political reasons.

This, too, was the basis for the phenomenon of the Russian rouble at that time, causing it to differ from money in the traditional market sense. The essence of this phenomenon was the fact that roubles could purchase only what had been planned by the State Planning Committee and had been included in the plan of a specific enterprise. As a result, the rouble functioned exclusively as a unit of account in appropriating resources in kind.

Meanwhile the Russian economic regions, uniting in most cases similar territories, at different times were constructed according to different principles. Thus, in the Russian Empire the determinative criteria were: a) sufficiency in ensuring intra-regional commodity and money turnover; and b) specialisation in Russia's internal division of labour. In the socialist period of Russian history, the problem of regional markets became irrelevant with an economy trading in kind. Thus the USSR Council of Ministers decided where the 'productive forces' would be located and divided the country into territorial-economic regions (TER). Those regions geographically coincided with the traditional regions of the pre-Revolutionary period. However, the internal division of labour in the USSR was a critical factor in determining their shape.

**Figure 4** *Sectors of prioritised state financing*

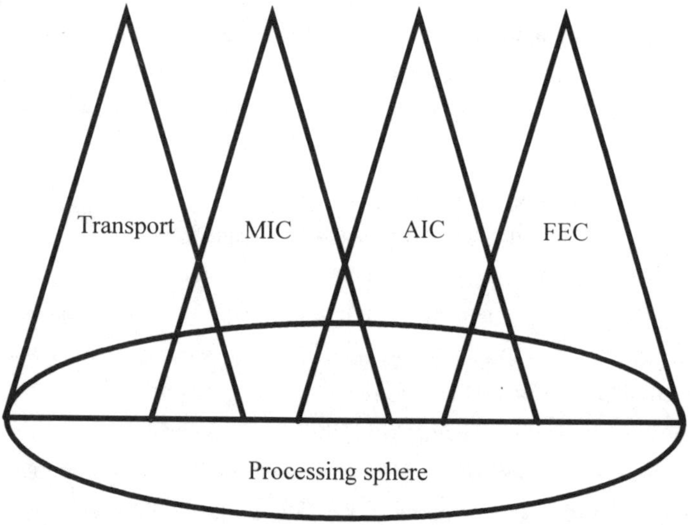


In the Russian Federation, after the disintegration of the USSR and liquidation of its economic bodies, government figures no longer used the terminology of economic districting (instead using primarily financial terminology). Nevertheless, economic districting has survived and has even found political expression in the form of eight inter-regional associations, now existing as public organisations which unite regional heads of administration.

As far as the internal division of labour is concerned, the specialisation of the territorial-economic regions was as follows: raw materials extraction and processing were concentrated in the East and the North of the country; the South specialised in agriculture; the central regions of the country (near the Volga River and the Urals) concentrated primarily on industrial processing and the manufacturing of semi-finished goods; and the west and central regions specialised in manufacturing finished products. There were also two primarily trading regions – the Baltic area (mainly transit trade and transportation) and Moscow (which in addition served as the financial centre of the entire economic space).

In light of the policy discussed above, the interrelations between the TERs and the central budget were as follows:

- in the *East, North and South*, emphasis was placed on reducing the base costs of production. This entailed budget subsidies to the resource extracting and processing sectors as well as to agricultural production;
- in the *central part of the country*, priority was placed on stimulation of industrial demand. This region, which came close to actually turning a profit, required from the central budget outlays primarily directed toward modernising production. It covered its current needs by orders from leading (in budgetary terms) sectors;
- in *West and Central Russia* and in the trading regions (where a major part of surplus profit was made) became the main objects of state fiscal policy and also major sources of central budget revenues.

The administrative and economic centre of the state repeated the budgetary cycle by withdrawing surplus profit from the regions in the last group and using a considerable part of these resources to subsidise the regions in the first group (Fig. 5).

**Figure 5** *Economic-productive cycle of the Russian economy*

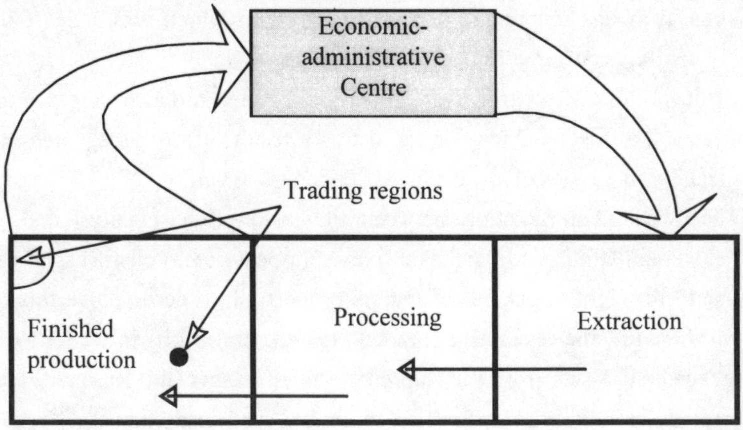


This cultural and historical description of how the Russian economy functioned should help one understand the particularities of property relations in Russia, including those of the Soviet period. It is a key issue in comprehending the political interests of Russian business today.

## 5 The Specificity of Property Relations and Economic Distribution Processes and their Determination of Political Interests of Russian Business

Back in the days of the CPSU and USSR-RSFSR, the soviets of peoples' deputies at various levels were considered to be the official and legal owner of property, whereas the direct proprietor was 'the whole Soviet people', on whose constitutional authority the soviets exercised the rights of possession. The government acted, relatively speaking, as a 'non-commercial (financed by the budget in principle, and social in nature) capital management firm' which alienated a portion of national resources (in accordance with items in the budget) to its own benefit in order to maintain the state machinery, i.e., 'the employees of that firm'.

The Russian campaign of 'universal privatisation-decollectivisation' is an historic action that has to date been only partially comprehended. It has no parallels in world practice (it may only be an irony of history, as usually has been the case in Russia). It is creating the legal basis for turning state enterprises from property (as a result of a voluntary relinquishment of one's share in national property in exchange for a voucher) into assets, i.e. the sum total of real estate subject to allotment. In other words, it means renouncing the old mechanism which was at least functioning, if only barely, according to macro-economic laws.

But the loss of control over property only means that it passes into other hands since, unlike assets which can be lost as a result of mismanagement, property (and especially money) will always have a concrete owner.

The basic contradiction between the soviet (Khasbulatov) and governmental (Yeltsin and Chubais) branches of power in post-communist Russia was exactly the issue of the right to dispose of federal property. In order to solve this problem to its own benefit, the executive branch spared no effort in order to remove the management assets from the Supreme Soviet's aegis (the Russian Federal Property Fund) and transfer it to authorities within its own jurisdiction.

As a result of adopting the new constitution in December 1993, which liquidated the system of soviets and formalised one of a presidential republic, the right to possess federal property passed into the hands of executive branch (especially as the new constitution provides that the president is also the chief executive). Therefore, the Cabinet received the constitutional right to dispose of national property. As a result, it also was endowed with the legal right to carry out privatisation of national (de facto, state-owned) property by transforming entities into joint stock companies (a 29% block of shares, the 'golden share', etc.). At the same time, it became common to authorise governmental administrative bodies to conduct commercial activities 'by rights of being both owner and manager'. What is more, as both the Federal Property Fund (the owner) and the State Property Committee (with the formal right of disposal) wound up in the executive branch.

Naturally, in reality this took the form of mass bribery by interested persons and business concerns in order to obtain positive expert decisions and memoranda addressed to 'decision makers' which would give them the right to virtually own or dispose of profitable resources, orders, contracts and enterprises. In other words, it resulted in wide-spread corruption of the state machinery. To the same extent, economic Regulations which allow one to earn very high profits can also be bought or 'lobbied' for.

At one time, as a result of the division of the circulation of goods and money, money became a commanding and dominant kind of property that gave rise to the principle of the separation of powers – the foundation of representative democracy. It is this phenomenon that made it possible to radically transform the very nature of European states from guardians of landed estates and class privileges into guardians of an order of private property owners which is governed by the laws of civil society. Accordingly, under parliamentarism, the main political struggle was one of changing tax policy for the benefit of one or another class of owners whose very means of earning profits depended on their position in the commodity exchange system.

In the history of parliamentarism, the great struggle between capital and landed property (known as the primitive accumulation period) expressed itself as a constant struggle between the legislative and the executive powers. This phenomenon was very accurately noted at one time by Charles Montesquieu, one of the founders of the principle of the separation of powers and parliamentary (or representative) democracy. He pointed out the principally two-party basis of parliamentary politics as being a situation in which 'a majority of the people' usually 'prefers one of these powers,' and prophetically predicted that a 'mutual hatred between both parties will never cease'.

Therefore, a topical issue related to the 'reality of business' in Russia and the interest representation system connected with it is that of mutual competition in the production, circulation and banking spheres.

But in situations in which parliamentarism exists only formally and in which the government is involved in business on a large-scale (though not very effectively), the differences in forms of property are not as important as the differences in the spheres of economic activity in which government bureaucrats and actual business persons (dispersed among concrete groups) are equally active.

The ideology itself – as well as the actual practice of domestic business circles – are totally linked with governmental organs (both federal and regional) that actually control the ownership and disposal of national property and resources. Accordingly, this is reflected in the forms of representation and organisation taken by Russian business interests (with state and private businesspersons finding themselves in almost equal conditions). Therefore, both state- and private-sector business are more frequently turning out to be allies in the struggle to carry out some type of governmental economic policy (for example, measures that are in the interests of certain economic groups and that are more or less beneficial – more often in a declarative sense than in reality – for the entire national economy).

In reality, the centre's effectual loss of control over national economic life has led to the following phenomena: disillusionment with the veche-like activities of the legislative branch in 1993-1994 and with the powerless laws adopted by them (a disillusionment which is entirely justified), and the criminalisation of business and political activities. The recurring attempts by the Russian state establishment and the supporters of European-style liberalisation to endow the president with maximum powers in the new constitution is nothing other than the last hope of restoring vanishing control by political means. Most likely, the results of these efforts will demonstrate perfectly to what extent this control has already passed to local authorities (or more precisely, to the real property owners behind them – local economic groups and traders in raw materials and semi-finished goods 'for consumption off the premises.')

Accordingly, both the structure of social interests in national production and the particularities of their evolution in the post-socialist period are major factors in the genetics of the economic and political interests of current Russian business. In a basic sense, they are connected with the Treasury (state budget) as a source for obtaining money for circulation in the sphere of economic management and, mostly importantly, to control state property as a well-spring for business activity.

In particular, it is important to take into account the fact that in such an undivided kingdom of distribution relations as the family, goods are, as a rule, apportioned to children (in a 'civilised' society) according to their needs. The distribution of goods, when they are limited both with regard to their quantity and the terms for restocking supplies (e.g. in a sieged fortress or peasant barter economy), determines the minimal individual share by what is physiologically and vitally necessary. The maximum share is assumed to be the entire amount of available resources divided by the number of consumers and the number of days until stocks are renewed. One's actual individual share in this case – which fluctuates between the minimum and the maximum values – depends upon the position of a given subject in the hierarchy of the distribution system, which is in turn determined by his/her social status.

Thus, the goal of an economic system based on distribution relations is to increase the pool of in-kind resources intended for future distribution. Social interests in a distribution system are determined by the striving of individuals for a higher place in the social hierarchy with a correspondingly higher standard of consumption. Within the framework of such a system, economic interests – which derive from social aspirations in concrete economic conditions:

- correspond to major resource distribution channels;
- are determined by the desire of individuals to increase their share of distributed resources, since that determines their influence level in the social hierarchy.

Systems based on exchange relations make the same assumptions as those based on distribution relations when determining the share of the social product due an individual. However, what is meant by the term 'requirement' is not vital physiological needs but individual consumer wants. The assessment of available resources proceeds not from the total number of consumers, but from the number of claimants on an object that will satisfy individual wants. Thus, exchange relations aim at an individualised consumption whose quality and scope are determined by individual wants and exchange resources (i.e., the amount of resources that can be exchanged for an object of individual want. At present, in most cases money serves as an exchange resource.).

A global comparison of exchange and distribution relations and the reasons for the domination of one or the other form in social relations in different historic periods reveals the following essential generalisations:

1. Distribution relations are mostly directed toward public consumption and the survival of humankind as such; exchange relations are oriented at individual consumption in conditions when on a societal scale, there are surplus consumer resources in comparison to their vital minimum. The nature of distribution relations illustrates the fact that governmental social programmes as well as more or less extensive private charity programmes are carried out purely by means of distribution among consumers. The only kind of exchange in charitable activities is street begging, a kind of an auction of human suffering and humiliation.

2. Exchange relations are possible and take place exclusively in those spheres of human activity where allotting a share of the social product to an individual can be connected with an actual expenditure of labour. In particular, pure market relations in the family are practically impossible since they would immediately lead to the physical death of children and elders.
3. Distribution relations become predominant in a society mostly in the following cases.
   a) In cases of a critical shortage of resources when their allotment through exchange could result in the physical death of part of the society or other negative consequences. In particular, the introduction of 'War Communism' (a non-market distribution of resources) in Russia in 1917 was caused by the collapse of domestic production. At this time the leading governmental figure, V.I. Lenin, personally wrote allocation directives, e.g. allotting a car of nails to a specific consumer. Developed countries also had nation-wide distribution systems during World War II, when the majority of the countries involved had to implement a rationing system for the distribution of goods;
   b) In cases of excess resources when exchange becomes senseless. In particular, in the history of socialist Russia, there was a short period when bread and sauerkraut were free in all public catering facilities.

The goal of an economic system based on the domination of exchange relations is to increase the amount of exchange resources as the basis for raising individual consumption standards. The extent to which that goal has been reached is expressed by the economic term 'profit' (the difference between the costs of producing a good and the total gains after its exchange or sale). Profit is an indicator of increased exchange resources as a result of concrete production activity.

The economic interests characteristic of a market-oriented system differ considerably from those of distribution system – both in motivation and complexity of structure. Due to the nature of capital – which is comprised of material and monetary assets combined with labour – two polar social groups are inherent in any system of production relations when exchange relations are dominant:

- the group which functions in the national production process primarily as a holder of material and monetary resources, i.e. the economic elite;
- the group which functions primarily as a holder of labour.

There are plenty of marginal social groups in between them, united in the term 'middle class', the main characteristic of which is that its members are labourholders and that they participate in property relations based on material and monetary assets through individual share-holding (through securities).

As a matter of fact, this social polarity inherent in an economic system dominated by exchange relations brings about a constant balancing between relations of exchange and distribution in a capitalist society. This is due to the never-ending confrontation between individual and public consumption. The social group of owners of the major material and monetary resources of national production – guided by its fundamental economic interests – has to concentrate on establishing favourable conditions for deriving maximum profit from production. Those types of conditions can, in the most general sense, include the reduction of production costs (including labour costs) as well as the expansion of the seller's market.

The social group of primarily labourholders – guided by its fundamental economic interests – has to concentrate on increasing individual consumption standards. The major factors which help to realise these interests include: a) lowering labour reproduction costs (through lower taxes and relatively lower prices on consumer goods); and b) the 'fair' distribution of profits made in specific and national production (through increasing the value of labour on the labour market and broadening state social programmes for the redistribution of national income).

The economic interests of marginal social groups vacillate between these two major interest groups, and combine elements of both groups depending upon their position in the public system of production and distribution.

The balance between these economic interests that exists in normal contemporary capitalist societies can be observed in the fluctuations in their political systems between the domination of conservative elements in state politics (i.e., those oriented to increasing the return on national-scale production) and social-democratic tendencies (i.e., those oriented primarily to redistribution of national income or profit to the medium and lower societal strata).

In light of the above, we can draw some fundamental conclusions about what constitutes the principal differences between 'khozyaistvennye' interests (i.e., those in systems based on distribution relations) and 'economic' interests (i.e., those in systems based on exchange relations); an understanding of these differences will be essential later.

1. The general and most essential difference between 'khozyaistvennye' interests and economic interests (the market form of 'khozyaistvennye' interests) is the *conditionality of individual consumption standards and social influence*. In a 'khozyaistvo,' social influence is determined by one's position in the social

hierarchy of distribution, whereas in an 'economy,' it is are determined by the quantity of exchange resources. In turn, the latter directly or indirectly depends on the efficiency of both individual labour and public production. Therefore, in production systems based on distribution, the standard and the quality of consumption are not objectively linked with efficiency of individual and public labour. Thus, non-economic (compulsory and ideological) factors prevail as labour incentives.

2. 'Khozyaistvennye' interests and economic interests also differ as to the principal methods of raising individual consumption standards. Methods characteristic of the economic interests paradigm are: a) raising the efficiency (profit rate) of economic activities, and b) redistributing derived profits to increase individual consumption standards. Methods characteristic of the 'khozyaistvennye' interests model include: a) lowering the amount of labour expended per unit of consumed material wealth (if wages cannot be increased through the intensification of labour, they are raised by reducing the actual amount of time devoted to the production process), and b) striving to elevate one's status in the distribution hierarchy.
3. 'Khozyaistvennye' interests and economic interests differ significantly when the overall nation is taken into account. On a nation-wide scale, 'khozyaistvennye' interests can be described as allocating the maximum possible quantity of resources for future distribution and consumption. Economic interests consist of establishing favourable conditions for making maximum profit rates on economic activity.
4. The above-mentioned differences between 'khozyaistvennye' interests and economic interests leads to a cardinal difference between the two in the fundamental political conditions necessary to realise these interests on a national scale. An economic system based on distribution relations and characterised by a minimal link between labour efficiency and consumption standards requires a political system with enough political and ideological resources to create social reserves sufficient for the functioning of society. An economic system based on exchange relations requires a political system capable of ensuring the co-ordination of economic interests while incurring minimum costs in the national production process.
5. A system based primarily on distribution relations does not require a plurality of political interests since it has one source of individual consumption – public reserves – and one form of individual income – one's salary (a fixed 'ration' that

is determined by one's position in the public distribution hierarchy). Whereas economic interests are determined by different positions in the public system of production and exchange, 'khozyaistvennye' interests stem from differences in the public system of distribution and consumption. 'Khozyaistvennye' interests express the interests of major consumers of public resources in the national distribution system; they are not related to issues of property, the efficiency of production, and other economic categories.

Having just concluded a preliminary consideration of the difference between economic and 'khozyaistvennye' interests, we deem it appropriate to briefly assess whether Russian society is at all familiar with economic interests as a significant social factor.

The development of economic interests directly depends on the development of market relations in general. If there are no doubts as to the primarily natural character of the Russian economy in the pre-reform (1861) and socialist periods, then the late 19th - early 20th centuries are considered by a number of researchers to be an important historical period for the development of economic interests and domestic market relations. In this context, the authors would not characterise the domestic economy on the eve of the 1917 Revolution as being a market economy (i.e., although it is the only period in Russian history which could be suspected of having market relations prevail in economic activity).

It is well known that the development of a market on a national scale is accompanied by changes in both the social fabric of society and the structure of public production. In particular, some of the commonly accepted obligatory changes are a decline in small peasant land ownership; an overall decrease in rural population as a result of its mass emigration to the city (which is usually considered to be the basis of the formation of a labour market formation); an increase in the proportion of the industrial proletariat in the social structure; as well as a number of other factors. However, a demographic analysis of the population of the Russian Empire at the end of the 19th and beginning of the 20th centuries does not exhibit the effects of any of these factors. Moreover, it is impossible to observe even the dynamics of a changing social structure in the expected direction. This was a society in which the industrial proletariat constituted 2% of the population and was roughly equal to the combined class of property owners; in which the number of personnel in state enforcement authorities (army, police, gendarmery) considerably exceeded the aggregate number of both the industrial proletariat and its 'antagonists'; and in which the overwhelming majority of the population lived in rural areas. Only with an excess of imagination and political will can such a society be characterised by one in which exchange relations prevail in production.

It is also difficult to speak confidently about developed economic interests in Russian industry during the pre-Revolutionary period. It was then that the national production model described in the first part of this survey was finalised. Besides, economic data for the three decades prior to the 1917 Revolution highlight the following features of the economy:

- industrial upsurges in Russia corresponded with budgetary investment in state military-strategic and transportation programmes;
- there was no relationship between a) average consumption standards and the structure of consumption, and b) growth in industrial production. From this, one can infer that the final product of the economy was mainly of a non-consumption nature (mainly military) and that it was withdrawn from economic circulation.

  It should be noted that a consequence of the natural Soviet economy, with its centralised pricing system and fixed prices, was the existence of a 'commodity inflation' that in turn devastated the consumer market under the pressure of worthless money. The destruction of the financial system of the USSR progressed through the following stages in the late 1980s: 1) considerable investment in modernising production in 1983-85 gave rise to problems concerning the saturation of the consumer market; 2) the growth of the foreign debt in 1985-87 resulted from attempts to saturate the consumer market with imported consumer goods and thereby mitigate large-scale disasters; 3) the 1987 USSR Council of Ministers Resolution on 'priority export deliveries' led to a massive outflow of raw materials and a drop in domestic production; the 1988 experiments with negotiated prices and co-operatives inevitably resulted in a deep crisis in the centralised provision of consumer goods and led to the uncontrollability of the consumer market.

- the under-developed financial sphere; completely insufficient – on a national scale – non-state sources of investment; the orientation of domestic financial capital toward obtaining and using government credit;
- the embryonic state of regional and all-Russian markets and of genuine trade relations.

Thus, the above-mentioned considerations allow the authors to draw a working conclusion about the absence of both economic interests and their historical tradition in Russia. The interests of social groups in the production sphere have pronounced features that are characteristic of 'khozyaistvennye' interests, i.e. primarily demand interests. The transformation processes involved in the attempts to introduce market relations in Russia can be examined primarily by the revelation of these transformative trends and how they are evolving in the direction of economic interest formation. It is from this point of view that the evolution and current state of social interests in the production sphere should be studied, i.e., as the foundation of direct business interests in Russia.

In this case it is also extremely important to consider another factor – 'khozyaistvennye' interests in Russia during the Soviet period – since this relates directly to understanding the specificity of the structure of current Russian business.

## 6 The Structure of Economic Interests in Russia during the Socialist Period

The traditional dominance in the Russian economy of the administrative-political Centre (the central organs of state authority and administration) as the main source of essential production and investment resources gave rise to the distribution system described above whereby material and financial resources were moved downwards and upwards along vertical distribution lines. In this connection it was natural, given the peculiarities of social production, which was based on distribution relationships as the dominant force, that the structure of fundamental economic interests reflected the main lines along which materials and resources earmarked for distribution among economic actors flowed.

In very general terms, two vertical (the sectoral and the regional) and two horizontal (the Centre and the Periphery) levels may be discerned in the Russian state-political sphere within which groups of officials operated and in which the main wrangling for control of state economic policy went on.

*The vertical division of interests among the political and economic elite* was determined by the distribution structure described earlier. In the process of fulfilling specific *khozyaistvo* functions, the state through its budget (the treasury) formed a peculiar system of financial distribution, whereby resources were allocated from the top down and revenue collected from the bottom up. Responsibility for the downward movement of resources in the state financial mechanism was traditionally held by the ministries (or departments and so on), which served as a mechanism for state investment and were in charge of economic activity in the provinces. Conversely, the upward movement of resources was traditionally the province of the territorial-administrative organs, which were assigned by the Centre to carry out policing but primarily fiscal functions, ensuring the removal from the economy on the orders of the state of surplus products in the form of taxes.

As a result of this specialisation of state sectors a kind of division of labour emerged in the sphere of economic administration between (relatively speaking) sectoral and regional groupings of officials. The task of each of these sectoral groupings, whose success determined the degree of influence they exerted, was the securing of as great a quantity as possible of resources intended for further distribution. The task of the regional groupings was to maintain a delicate balance between a) the necessity of replenishing the central budget as a matter of priority and b) securing the 'anchoring of resources' in the regions and the creation of conditions for regional accumulation of resources. The former in this case was a condition of loyalty to the Centre and was aimed at ensuring the prolongation of an official's term in office, while the latter determined his degree of influence in local politics.

*The horizontal division of interests among the political and economic elites* was determined by a) the role of the Centre as the chief holder of resources and the main allocator of material wealth and of positions in the state hierarchy and b) by the role of the Periphery as the main source of resources for the Centre and the chief recipient of budgetary allocations. It was this dual role of the Periphery in the country's political and economic structure that determined its traditional willingness to enter into an unconditional union with the central elite as well as its intransigent antipathy towards Moscow (in a broad sense). The relationship between the two tiers of state politics and administration, for all their complexity and variability, could be summarised in a nutshell as a traditional state of antagonism between donor and recipient that is so typical of a distribution system: the Centre tended to regard the Periphery as a parasite and therefore tried to cut its expenditure while preserving the volume of revenue flowing into the central budget; while the Periphery, for its part, was certain that it was the central leadership that was the parasite and it therefore sought to increase the volume of centralised distribution to its own advantage while at the same time trying to reduce its contributions to the budget.

In its turn the Periphery itself was divided into regional and local levels. While military, policing and fiscal affairs were dealt with at the regional level, the local authorities had unlimited control over the lowest link in the sectoral structure – namely, enterprises, or those concerned directly with production.

The division of the political and economic elites just described, which corresponded entirely to the main lines of distribution of material wealth and with the rungs in the distribution hierarchy, determined the position and dominant interests of the main groupings in the power elite. Sectoral groupings, in themselves a concentration of economic interests in domestic politics, traditionally comprised a two-tier structure consisting of the Centre and the localities. The responsibilities of the central sectoral groupings included 'milking' the state budget for the benefit of industrial and other enterprises whose effectiveness was dependent on the degree of influence of ministerial groupings at the local and regional levels.

In state politics sectoral groupings traditionally formed a number of macro-groupings, which were also the bearers of important economic interests on Russia's political territory. The configuration of these interests has changed repeatedly over the past century of Russian history, invariably in accordance with the basic direction of state investment policy. Thus, at the time that the Soviet Union broke up independent economic interests corresponding with the main sectoral groupings included: the military-industrial complex (MIC), the agro-industrial complex (AIC) and the fuel and energy complex (FEC)[3].

The local level represented an organic combination of actors that were directly engaged in economic activity and were oriented towards one or other of the sectoral groupings. The extent to which any particular sectoral grouping dominated in any given territory was determined primarily by the region's economic specialisation and by the importance for the regional economy of a given sector. Moreover, the enterprises and regions in which they were concentrated traditionally served as a political base for the main sectoral groupings, who were forced to take into account their interests in their manoeuvrings and jostling for position in the larger political landscape.

Regional groupings in Russian politics constitute a rather more complex manifestation in a more complex functional environment. If the sectoral vertical, i.e., the descending line in the distribution hierarchy, was a rather lean and structurally simple formation, the ascending line along which material resources moved in the centralised distribution system had an altogether more complex conflictual structure. This complexity stemmed from the dual nature of the regions' chief functions in public life: from a) their function as a link in the hierarchy for the centralised

---

**3** Not long before this, the list had included the transportation sector. However, following the debacle over the construction of the Baikal-Amur railroad the importance of this sector as a distribution channel for state resources dwindled. The other macro-sectors listed had almost continuously since the middle of the last century formed channels for state economic investment. The list thus rather reflects the dominance of particular macro-sectors at various stages of history.

removal of resources from the economy to the central budget (in other words the generation of revenue) and b)their function as the main territorial link in the state system of political administration and control.

As a link in the system for replenishing the state budget the regions found themselves operating within the framework of the political-administrative vertical at the base of which were the local law-enforcement and tax institutions and at the top of which was the Ministry of Finance. The dual position of the regions in this system, in which in addition to replenishing the state budget they were constantly trying to 'milk' it as well, traditionally meant that relations between local leaderships and the country's main financial institution were difficult and conflict-ridden.

In their function as a link in the state system of political administration and control the regions formed a relatively independent grouping. The degree of influence of this grouping stemmed from the decisive role played by regional leaders in approving important political and personnel changes at the Centre and also from its importance as a kind of first reserve pool of officials from which vacant slots at the Centre could be filled. In Soviet history there were at least two occasions on which regional leaders had a decisive say in such matters: the first was the removal from office of Nikita Khrushchev; the second was the appointment of Mikhail Gorbachev as general secretary of the CPSU. The regions thus formed an important link in the political vertical of the Soviet regime.

As a result of historical upheavals and a tacit process of reconciliation of interests, the structural levels of the Soviet political and economic elite listed above together formed a relatively harmonious system of mutual control and division of powers and political influence. The regional link in this system traditionally formed the structural location of mutual agreement and of a compromise between the interests of the central and local levels of the state political and economic mechanism. The regional authorities traditionally kept track of co-operation between the sectoral and regional elites (with the exception of the short period of '*Sovnarkhoz'* policy when the regional elites tried to 'take over' some of the ministerial functions). The regional elites had an interest in drawing the attention of the sectors to their territories, since the ministries were the main source from which resources needed for economic projects could be drawn, while enterprises invariably urged regional elites to lobby for various kinds of regional budgetary privileges ('the northern increments' etc.).

The regional elites strove to preserve their special position and special functions within the economic system by maintaining their own domination in the political system, which gave them essential leverage in localising the already complete omnipotence of the ministries. However, in addition to the co-operation between the economic and political elites at the two levels mentioned, the strategic union of the central and local levels of power in opposition to the regional that was so typical of the country's internal history and that formed one of the main prerequisites for political control by influential regional groupings and for the territorial unity of the state can clearly be traced. The result and guarantee of this union were the efforts of high-ranking government figures to a) ensure the direct financing of enterprises (i.e., the local level) from the central budget, thus by-passing the regions; and b) to carry out a cadres policy based on the principle of rotation from sector to region to sector or from region to Centre to region, thus inhibiting the invariably tendency towards a local concentration of interests among officials belonging to the regional and sectoral groupings and creating an 'imperial elite' whose interests were 'cosmopolitan' compared to those of local officials; and c) to maintain the complex mixture of mutual control and hostility in the provinces between the organs of power and the administration of regional and central subordination.

## 7 The Transformation of the Traditional Structure of Economic Interests in Russia during and after the Break-Up of the USSR

A fact of fundamental importance during the period of *perestroika* was the decentralisation, followed by the liberalisation of foreign trade in the USSR and in the Russian Federation. This development brought about irreversible changes in the structure of economic interests and, correspondingly, changes in the alignment of political forces in domestic politics. For the first time in many years the traditional system for the distribution of material resources and wealth in the domestic economy underwent a serious reconfiguration. The immediate reason for this transformation was the emergence in the economy of a new source of demand and investment resources. That new source was the foreign market, chiefly the markets of the Western industrialised nations.

The immediate impetus for the emergence of this new situation in the economy was the USSR Council of Ministers decree of 1987 on the primary importance and expansion of deliveries of goods for export. In the fairly closed circuit in which resources and material wealth had circulated on the internal market up till then there appeared a sizeable hole through which resources with export value began to flow out of the country. (The personal interests of a number of high-ranking sectoral officials ensured that this flow was scarcely controlled by the Centre.) For the Russian economy, which was experiencing shortages and had a well-controlled system for limiting consumer goods and for its economic elite the leakage of resources abroad had several major consequences.

1. Weak control over exports led to the accumulation in the hands of a very small but fairly influential class of economic officials of a considerable quantity of private wealth. The result was the beginnings of a swift social stratification of wealth (until then differences in individual wealth in the Soviet Union had not been very great and had largely been determined by the state privileges an individual held) as well as changes in patterns of private consumption and in the possibilities for satisfying consumption needs as well as efforts by influential circles among the political and economic elite to maintain their new levels of consumption and consolidate their position.
2. The very nature of the structure of production under the conditions of 'developed socialism' meant that shortages of labour and resources were an inherent part of the system (just as money is scarce in a market economy, so resources are scarce in an economy dominated by distribution). The loss to the domestic economy of a substantial part of the Gross National Product meant that some economic actors now faced not just a deficit of material resources but serious shortages or even a complete absence of resources altogether.

   A category of 'hard-hit enterprises' now began to emerge. Since on the world market, which has a structure for the division of labour analogous to the Russian one (the full production cycle), there exists stiff competition and an incomparably higher technological level of finished industrial and agricultural products, export demand was for products from the technologically least advanced part of the domestic economy – namely, for natural resources and metals. Accordingly, the enterprises that suffered most from the massive export of resources were their immediate producers – enterprises engaged in processing and in the production of finished goods (enterprises involved in agricultural production were also direct victims of this crisis).

   In 1989 the first signs of a slide in industrial production emerged, and in 1990-1991 these took on the character of an economic crisis. A commercial banking structure began to emerge and the efforts of the country's leadership to attract foreign investors together with the decline in the profitability of production and the breakdown of the system of control over the activities of enterprises led the Council of Ministers to issue a resolution in 1990 *On the Suspension of State Investment*, in other words of the allocation of favourable state credits for periods of more than a year. The result of this resolution was that a substantial part of production with a capital turnover cycle of more than a year became unprofitable. This was accompanied by a further fall in the volume of production and a growth in the inflation rate.

3. The substantial growth in the volume of private wealth, the change in the consumption habits of members of the higher strata of Soviet society as well as the emerging supply of fluid hard currency on the consumer market created the prerequisites for a liberalisation of imports. With the easing of restrictions on the import of consumer goods and equipment import capital began to accumulate, and there emerged a new class of economic actors who had at their disposal a swiftly growing money supply and whose prosperity depended directly on the state of Russia's relations with the Western industrialised countries.

Towards the middle of 1991 the shape of a new structure for the distribution of resources and materials in the Russian economy was clearly discernible (see Figure 6). The basis of this structure was formed by two groups whose interests were of differing orientation – importers who were oriented towards the foreign market, and an economic elite that was oriented towards the domestic market as well as a marginal interest group of exporters.

**Figure 6** *Scheme of the main economic interests in Russia after 1990*

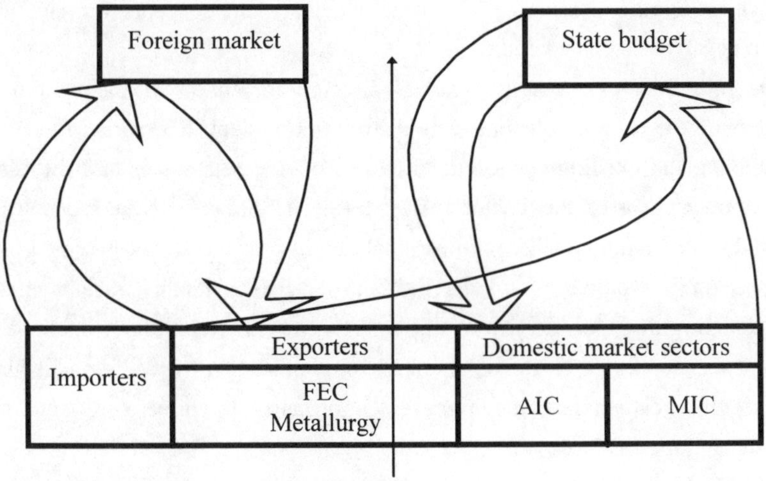

In the group oriented towards the domestic market were concentrated those enterprises that did not have access to hard-currency revenues. These included practically all agricultural enterprises, a substantial number of those involved in industrial processing, medium- and heavy-machine building, and the light and food industries. Having been deprived of the means for development owing to the suspension of state investment, these enterprises were driven to the brink of closure as a result of the growth in inflation and the saturation of the domestic market with imported consumer goods. These factors, namely, made it practically impossible for them to go on existing on the basis of revenues from the market. Towards the end of 1992 the majority of these enterprises were 'hanging by the thread' of budgetary credits – the only basis for their existence. The interests of this group, which had been repeatedly declared throughout all the years of 'reform', as a rule amounted to the full restoration of state subsidies for domestic enterprises and the implementation of a centralised policy of protection of the domestic consumer by means of state protectionism in foreign trade.

The 'importers' consisted in the main of trading companies specialising in large-scale imports of consumer goods. By 1992 this group had been joined by the majority of former state trading enterprises and small private wholesalers.

This situation became a matter of urgent concern to the new generation of politicians who emerged from the realignment of forces at the Centre that took place in the wake of the election in autumn 1991 of Boris Yeltsin and Aleksandr Rutskoi to Russia's top state posts. With the coming to power of the ruling coalition of democratic communists and radical liberals two main concepts for the future of Russia began to be considered.

*The first* of these was the gradual creation in Russia of the conditions for transferring the economy from a state distribution system to a market model. While maintaining the existing economic structures of the state sector and the economic links of enterprises on the territory of the former USSR the private sector was to be allowed to expand on the premise that as it developed and formed its own infrastructure it would draw into its orbit an ever greater number of state enterprises, thus changing their form of ownership and the way in which they functioned. This concept was supported by the democratic communists and by leading officials in the state sector whose interests they represented, primarily the directors of enterprises in the MIC and the FEC.

*The second concept* for the transfer to market relations and the liberalisation of Russian society drew its support mainly from the radical-liberal wing of the ruling coalition, which represented the interests of the new financial-commercial structures which specialised mainly in economic mediation activities. This plan for the liberalisation of the economy, which used as its theoretical basis the Chicago School of political economy, declared as its main political aim during the period of transition the elimination of the threat of a restoration of the 'totalitarian' social order and of the state supply system. Accordingly, the economic aim of the period in question was to bring about the formation and expansion in a short period of time of a sector that would render economic reforms irreversible. This was to be achieved by way of two parallel processes: a) the dismantling of the state distribution system together with a revamping of the structure and principles on which the formation of the state budget was based, the breaking up of the MIC and the FEC and the abolition of the system of state and collective farms in agriculture; b) the creation of market-oriented economic structures, primarily through the elimination of the main pillars of the state distribution system – the State Supply Committee (*Gossnab*) and the State Planning Committee (*Gosplan*) – and their replacement with a system of commodities exchanges and economic middle-men; the curtailment of subsidies to enterprises in the state sector, which would force them to engage in the exchange of goods and capital on the free market; and the subjection of such enterprises to economic regulation by commercial structures. This plan for liberalisation envisaged differing paces of development among the former republics of the USSR and the abolition of its superpower status with the aim of freeing Russia from the burden of its Asian regions.

The plan put forward by the radical liberals, which was unacceptable to the democratic-communist wing of the ruling coalition, was not seriously discussed by the Russian leadership until August 1991. In connection with the departure, or to be more precise the forced resignation, of the then chairman of the Council of Ministers, Ivan Silaev, yet another battle began in the USSR Inter-republican Economic Committee, namely, for the post of head of government to which not only Oleg Lobov, but also apparently Rutskoi himself aspired. All the more so since in its composition his main economic bloc, which included as well as Lobov Yurii Skokov, Evgenii Saburov and others, was close in its views to the vice president. However, the crushing defeat of the conservative wing of the leadership of the Soviet Union and of the political and economic structures supporting it during the period in which part of it (the State Committee for a State of Emergency) attempted to introduce an emergency situation on the territory of the USSR led to the destruction of the balance of forces in the political arena and the emergence of the pre-conditions for the implementation of the radical-liberal concept for the reform of Russian society. These were the fact that their political opponents were now clearly in a state of disarray, which created the illusion that their hands were tied, among others things with respect to their partners in the ruling coalition; considerable international pressure; and the fact that on paper this development concept, which still existed in the framework of Yavlinskii and Shatalin's '500-day program' was at a more advanced stage of preparation. After the liberally oriented supporters of reform who dominated the presidential staff had with the diplomatic support of American government circles defeated Rutskoi and Lobov's group in the battle for (among other things) the right to form a reform government, the selection of such a team was entrusted to the president's associates Gennadii Burbulis and Mikhail Poltoranin and the liberals' reform concept was accepted. The person appointed to draw up and oversee the reforms in practice was a man close to the Chicago theorists of liberal reforms in Eastern Europe (in particular in Poland), Egor Gaidar. The government formed during the months of November and December 1991 was staffed with a significantly smaller number of members of the former reform-communist wing and fewer Russian enterprise directors. Moreover, the approved liberalisation programme failed to obtain their proper consent.

Accordingly, the main bone of contention among the three main political blocs, the radical liberals or Yeltsin's supporters in 1991, the perpetrators of the August coup, and the 'Centrists' who in mid-1992 began to take over posts from the ruling majority as they assumed the role of a 'constructive opposition' in the field of state activity and in the functioning of state institutions, was the question of who was to determine state policy with regard to the implementation of liberal reforms. Having as a result of their 'August victory' obtained a practical monopoly over the elaboration of government strategy and holding the key government posts necessary for its implementation the radical liberal reformers set as the main aim of their policy the creation of a mechanism to make liberal reforms in Russia irreversible and accordingly the expansion of an 'irreversible sector' in the political and economic life of the country, in order that, even in the event of their political defeat, they could force the hand of the most probable victors, namely, the representatives of major state-industrial capital.

The main points of the new economic policy were:

- *financial stabilisation* (in essence the elimination of state distribution mechanisms in the state sector, which would take the form of cuts in government expenditure on production, the army and social programmes; the freeing of prices; and forcing the economy to enter into market-oriented production relations;

- extensive *privatisation of the state sector*, which would entail the simultaneous dismantling of the state sector and the creation of a class of property owners, the natural social basis for irreversible reforms;
- the *liberalisation of foreign economic relations* and the active integration of Russia in the world economy.

It was proposed that these reforms should be carried out using the most drastic methods in the shortest possible time. At the Fifth Congress of People's Deputies of the Russian Federation in the autumn of 1991 Yeltsin promised: „We have a unique opportunity for several months to stabilise the economic situation and to begin the process of recovery… If we take this road we will be seeing real results by the autumn of 1992."

The Centrists, the former partners of the radical liberals in the ruling 'August' coalition of 1991, could not permit the destruction of the state sector not least because of the obvious errors they saw in the reform concept itself, which they considered unrealistic both in terms of the timetable for its implementation and in terms of the strength of the reformers whom were considered incapable of ruling the country single-handedly. They wanted instead to see the transformation of the economy within the framework of state ownership and the creation of the legal conditions for foreign investors to rescue the supply-based flagging Soviet economy and with whose help they hoped to reduce the future of the Russian economy to the market denominator of Von Hayek-Friedman.

This was also understandable given that the state sector and its directors formed the natural economic base for the Centrists during the period 1992–1994 and of the moderate reformers during 1994; their elimination as a class, namely, quite apart from the economic and social impact of the policy in question, would have spelt political death for the Centrists. But chiefly it would have meant the loss of the promising opportunity presented by the forthcoming sharing out of state property by means of voucher privatisation. Incidentally, since the question of who was to oversee the privatisation process had yet to be resolved, enterprise directors and industrial managers were doing their best to delay its getting under way, even though they could not prevent it altogether.

Inasmuch as the main point of controversy at the federal Centre between the Supreme Soviet and the president in 1992–1993 was the amendment of the reform course, its focus shifted to the state institutions responsible for carrying out the reforms, control over which would determine the tempo of the 'irreversible processes' in the social and economic spheres.

The refusal at the beginning of 1992 by the radical liberals lead by the president to co-operate with the 'directors' lobby' and the exclusion of the Centrist leaders from the decision-making process after the Fifth Congress of People's Deputies inevitably pushed them into forming a tactical alliance with the 'uncompromising opposition,' and in so doing deprived Yeltsin and his supporters of control over the highest legislative organs. The radical liberals' disregard for the necessity of fighting for their seats in parliament and engaging in parliamentary debate, in view of the parliament's ability to paralyse the active policy of the presidential and governmental structures, may be explained only by the fact that (in autumn 1991) the president was granted 'special powers' which for the period of one year exempted the head of the executive from any kind of parliamentary control. The authors of the reform plan clearly considered this sufficient time in which to bring about the irreversible destruction of existing economic mechanisms and instruments of political power. It was this bold assumption that moved the authors of the reform to undertake the liberalisation of the economy with only a minimal social and political base and under extreme time pressure. Like any *Blitzkrieg* the essence of this plan was the speed of its realisation.

However, right up until the Seventh Congress of People's Deputies (which took place in December 1992) the Centrists undertook systematic attempts to open a dialogue and engage in co-operation with the government of radical liberals and at the same time to remove Gaidar's economic team from the government. This political situation (the instability of the cabinet of liberal reformers) was also one of the reasons for the suspension of credits by the International Monetary Fund (IMF) (24 billion for democracy – 'liberalisation with privatisation').

After the monetary shock of January–March 1992, the industrialists mobilised sufficient resources to prepare by the time of the Sixth Congress of People's Deputies in April 1992 a retaliatory blow to the most vulnerable element in Gaidar's policy of 'financial stabilisation,' the Russian Central Bank, which was still under parliamentary jurisdiction. While the economy was still dominated by distribution relationships the state bank, which supplied up to 80% of the country's enterprises directly, was indisputably, as Deputy Prime Minister Boris Fedorov admitted, 'somewhere on the grand scale of things, more powerful than the government'[4]. Having forced the resignation of 'the professor' Georgii Matyukhin and secured the appointment as head of the Russian Central Bank of the 'practitioner' Viktor Gerashchenko, the anti-liberal coalition of Centrists and 'the uncompromising opposition,' revealing themselves at this congress for the first time, removed the Central Bank from the sphere of influence of the government of reformers. By organising large-scale monetary emissions and emergency investment in the state sector the bank reduced all the liberals' efforts to bring about 'financial stabilisation' (i. e., their suspension of budgetary subsidies to state enterprises and cuts in government spending) to nil. The only thing that staved off a more serious attack by the opposition forces was the expectation of the possible receipt (and distribution) of Western credits that had been promised by the IMF back in February–March 1992.

On the political level the process of putting a brake on economic reforms was accompanied after the Sixth Congress by a rallying round the 'constructive opposition' or centrist bloc by the 'communist directors' and their organised registration as well as a further strengthening of their informal union with the 'uncompromising opposition' on the basis of their common opposition to the liberal domination of the executive structures. It was from this moment on that the conflict between the executive and legislative branches became manifest that in the autumn of 1992 was to take on the character of an all-out struggle for the seizure of political power.

Even the story of the political conflict between the importers and the budgeteers [byudzhetniki] of the non-export sectors of the Russian economy was in many respects determined by a change in its dimensions and in the tactics and strategy of the 'constructive opposition' during 1992 and culminated in the appointment to leading positions in the government branch of the executive of a compromise economic macro-group, consisting of exporters (representatives of the oil and gas industries headed by Viktor Chernomyrdin), who later found a common language with the importers and resisted attempts by the non-export managers (the MIC, the 'hi-tech' sectors, the producers of domestic consumer goods and the agrarians) to restore a status quo that resembled the economic system of state supply only in a fiscal sense (favourable state credits and subsidies). A tactical compromise was found only with the directors of the AIC, who nonetheless received substantial budgetary resources as well as with the export wing of the metallurgy sector.

---

**4** Interview with Radio Liberty, 12 April 1993.

In this way, the managers of Russia's state industrial sector, having started out as a grouping generally known as the Centrists, emerged as a conglomerate of groups of the political elite that reflected the interests of domestic entrepreneurs and industrial circles closely linked with the state sector of the economy and standing in opposition to Gaidar's laboratory radical-liberals, who were oriented towards supporting the export structures of intermediary trading capital; this grouping now split and was thrown into opposition. Its members, who had never before been notable for their unity, were now forced to present a unified political front. Up till the Eighth Congress of People's Deputies in March 1993 the activities in the state sphere of the groupings making up this political bloc bore a fundamentally negative character, conditioned by their almost complete exclusion from the formulation of government policy as well as by the necessity of offering 'passive resistance' to the destruction by the government of radical-reformers of the state sector and the building up of an 'irreversible sector' in Russian economic and political life.

Nonetheless, the alliance of the two blocs opposing Gaidar's policy (the Centrists and the 'uncompromising opposition') had clearly been formed for tactical reasons, since neither in the economic nor in the political sphere did they, in the words of one of the leaders of the political centre and deputy prime minister in the Silaev Cabinet Saburov, did they have any common ground. In their skirmishes with the radical liberals in December 1992 (when the period in which the president had enjoyed 'special powers' ran out and his constitutional privileges came to and end) the two sides of the alliance were also pursuing different aims. If the aim of the 'uncompromising opposition' was confined to depriving the president unconditionally of his special powers and curtailing the liberal reforms, the leaders of the Centrists who represented the interests of the economic elite connected with the state sector, had a strong interest in preserving a powerful executive and were therefore not inclined to insist on a constriction of Yeltsin's powers. Moreover, in the event of the Centrists' being granted key ministerial posts, as they were demanding, the preservation of the president's 'special powers' would have given them additional leverage. Thus, the aim of the Centrists at this stage was to bring about a change in the government team, even retaining Gaidar as its head.

Returning to the centrist managers it should be noted that the beginning of the new parliamentary session (the fifth session of the Supreme Soviet of the Russian Federation which began in September 1992) brought with it qualitative changes in their activities that resulted in a realignment of forces within the bloc. Following the failure of the autumn negotiations with the radical liberals and after the conflict between the main groups of the political and economic elite had reached a stage of open confrontation (December 1992-March 1993) it was not only the radical liberals but the Centrists too who found themselves in a state of crisis. However, whereas for the liberals this crisis was a time of consolidation, for the political Centre, which by the autumn had begun to predominate both tactically and politically, the Seventh Congress (December 1992) signalled a process of collapse.

Given the narrow, by Russian standards, economic base of the radical liberals (chiefly import firms) the political Centre and the Civic Union, which articulated its interests, should, in theory, have occupied a political niche that guaranteed stability and the continuity of policies directed at economic liberalisation. By the autumn of 1992 after the change in the government team the broad mass of the country's economic elite was convinced of the need for continuity and for certain policy correctives that would take greater account of the demands of other economic groups and of the state sector as a whole. That part of the economic elite whose interests were represented by the policies of the Centrists gravitated towards four main interest groups.

The first of these was the group of *new entrepreneurs* formed from the ranks of Komsomol functionaries and members of co-operatives, some importers and representatives of intermediary trade capital who were concentrated chiefly around the Russian raw materials trade and the Moscow commodities exchange, who after August 1991 had been cut off from state assistance.

This first group exerted influence at the political level in 1992–1993 through part of the All-Russian union 'Renewal' (led by Aleksandr Dolgolaptev) as well as to some extent through the Party of Economic Freedom and its leader Konstantin Borovoi. Having no fundamental disagreement with the economic policy of the radical liberals, this group concentrated on demanding greater consistency in the implementation of economic reforms and in trying to get its people appointed to government posts.

The second group, the *raw materials exporters*, consisted mainly of enterprises in the FEC and their regional structures. Their leader on the political level was Chernomyrdin who in 1992 swiftly gained the support of the elites of the regions involved in raw materials exploitation. Having received, on Chernomyrdin's coming to power, significant export privileges together with the practical domination of the 'sectoral' bloc of the government and having become the object of state capital investment in 1992 and at the beginning of 1993 the majority of its members came out in support of both the president and the government. Their main demand was economic reform and political stability. Their differences with the radical liberals were mainly in the economic sphere, where the activities of the main Russian exporters threatened to destroy the economic base of the Komsomol group – the importers. Their political negotiations with the radical liberals, which were otherwise fairly unproblematic were complicated to a significant degree by their demands for a share of export revenues.

The third group of the economic elite brings together part of the MIC (referred to henceforth as *MIC-1*), mainly its export branch, who were reaping substantial dividends from trading in arms and from the production of components for export during the final years of Gorbachev's *perestroika.* After December 1991 they lost their influence in state politics but managed to become shareholders in the course of the Gaidar's liberalisation policy. Their political leaders were the leaders of the All-Russian Union of Industrialists and Entrepreneurs, Arkadii Vol'skii, Aleksandr Vladislavlev and Mikhail Yur'ev.

This economic group by virtue of the nature of the production that it was involved in was also closely linked with the raw materials exporting elite (the *Uralmash* plant, which had a monopoly on the production of many kinds of oil extraction equipment, whose managers were closely connected with, let's say, Yurii Petrov). As adherents of the policy of immediate liberalisation of the Russian economy, this group was unhappy at being cut off from state support and aspired to membership of the group of importer-entrepreneurs who controlled economic access to the state Olympus (among other things the distribution of foreign investment).

They are generally in agreement with the reformers' policy for the liberalisation of the economy, although they would like to see some correctives made to take account of the interests of industrialists. Yur'ev, the vice president of the All-Russian Union of Industrialists and Entrepreneurs, indicated as much in the following statements: „Today the entire banking system is the enemy of industry. One has the feeling that the banks are operating in the interests of an enemy state, for they are totally paralysing the work of the large industrial enterprises. The small and medium-sized enterprises are still all right. They can, albeit illegally, go over to working in cash. But what am I supposed to do? Cart billions of roubles in cash through the streets? The taxation system dates from the Soviet era. It is structured in such a way that taxes can be collected only from the large industrial enterprises, and from no-one else. The industrial trading sector pays practically no taxes at all. And the reason for this is not that it is less patriotic, but that taxes cannot be collected from it."

Nevertheless, with the appointment of Chernomyrdin as head of government and the adoption of a government programme for foreign economic activity, some degree of compromise was reached with this group as well, the result of which was the appointment to Chernomyrdin's government in the spring of 1993 of Oleg Soskovets as first deputy prime minister.

The fourth group of the economic elite, with the largest membership but the weakest in terms of political influence, brings together the *non-export branch of the MIC* (henceforth referred to as MIC-2); medium machine-building enterprises and the non-export branch of the metallurgical sector; the structures of the former Agro-industrial Committee and the newly formed private farming sector; and domestic producers of consumer goods. The leaders of this group, whose fate was to represent its interests, were Rutskoi, Ruslan Khasbulatov, Skokov and Gerashchenko. The group found itself in a difficult position: while bearing to the same extent as the FEC and the MIC the brunt of economic reform they were cut off both from the fruits of foreign economic activity and from centralised investment. In the political arena MIC-2 in 1992–1993 came out against the president in office, wishing to see Rutskoi in this post instead, and in favour of a coalition government, regarding this as the only kind of government that would allow it a share of power.

Moving on to the intensification of the political conflict in the spring of 1993, the main actors in the radical-liberal bloc considered that the intensification of the political conflict beyond the boundaries of reason and the threat of the systemic failure of the liberally oriented wing of politicians and their constituents among the economic elite would on the whole much more quickly undermine the mellow centrist bloc than it would their own. They gambled on the disintegration of this bloc, which they believed would come about as a result of its members' differing degrees of willingness to reach a compromise with the radical liberals. The radicals only had to wait for an aggravation of the conflict and to maintain the state of mobilisation of its supporters and to revive the ruling coalition, drawing into it parts of the right wing of the Centrists. To paraphrase Yur'ev's commentary on the power struggle: „…everything that is happening now closely resembles the game of speculating on a fall on the stock exchange. All the players know that as a result of these actions, confidence will fall, in other words confidence in all branches of power will fall. But each player hopes that it will fall more quickly for his opponent than for himself. And accordingly he stakes his money on this."

The radical liberals' strategy of trying to draw into the ruling coalition members of the exclusively lucrative sectors of the economy, which generally coincided with the intentions of their potential allies, is based on the concept of 'focused support of industry' as a fundamental part of the revamping economic structures ranking second only in importance to 'financial stabilisation.' The essence of this concept is to concentrate the main investment resources of the state and of private investors in sectors of the economy capable of earning hard-currency at the expense of the loss-making sectors, which would either be allowed to stagnate, have their production cut, or even be partially eliminated altogether. By focusing resources in lucrative parts of the economy the authors of this concept and their supporters hoped to reap hard currency returns from the activities of the exports sector and to use these to revive the domestic market and the stagnating sectors of the economy.

The liberals' gamble on the disintegration of the Centrists proved to be tactically correct, all the more so since the right wing of the 'constructive opposition' was not at all willing to enter into a coalition with partners whom it had earlier written off as political-economic losers. The split was already evident at the Seventh Congress and had become a fact by the Ninth Congress of People's Deputies during the voting on the impeachment of the president – about half of the bloc constituting the 'democratic centre,' which included the majority of the Civic Union faction voted against the impeachment, even though the bloc had already declared Rutskoi as its candidate for the presidency. The result of this and other votes at the congress demonstrated the existence of serious disagreements within the Civic Union as well as a clear reduction in the potential for consensus in the political conduct of its allies.

And thus the split in the centrist bloc and the absorption of the political Centre by the radical flanks of the political front of Russia became manifest.

In late spring 1994 [sic] a certain compromise was reached at government level between the radical liberals and right-of-centre groups regarding the necessity of continuing the liberal economic reforms. This occurred after some degree of consensus had been obtained from the two main opposing groups among the economic elite whose interests ran directly counter to one another – namely, representatives of the largest Russian export structures on the one hand, and on the other intermediary trading capital, which specialised in the supply of goods for import. The specific interests of the two sides that had now reached an agreement determined Chernomyrdin's orientation in identifying the base of his regional support: these were the regions in which the Peripheral structures of the FEC and the export branch of the MIC were based as well as, in part, regions dominated by the AIC.

Chernomyrdin's intention to support only some enterprises in the state sector and his general policy of identifying focal points for investment was illustrated in a statement he made at the Eighth Congress of People's Deputies of the Russian Federation in March 1993: „The task at hand is to move away from the mechanism for the administration of state property. Efficient, economic, market mechanisms ensuring the formation of discipline of a new sort. As soon as we hand out money or advance credits we must ask where they are going, what the aim is, how much and what will be produced, so that it doesn't turn out as it did last year when the government, the President and the Supreme Soviet were squeezed from all sides, demands were made and the money was granted."

The intentions of the main parties to the grand compromise for implementing the concept of supporting selected sectors became fully evident in April 1993 when the press published the first excerpts from the government degree that had just been signed by Chernomyrdin: *The Main Positions and Criteria of the State's Selective Policy*. This document, which had been prepared in absolute secrecy had been seen, apart from the signature of the prime minister, only by his aide Boris Pashkov (former deputy to Nikolai Ryzhkov). As authors of the decree were named the director of the Centre for Economic Trends and Forecasting Yakov Urinson and his deputy Leonard Vid (who in the past had held the post of deputy chairman of the State Planning Committee). The only concession that the government opponents of the document were able to obtain was the postponement of the date for its implementation from April to the summer, when in August when the eclectic government document *A Working Programme for Reform* was adopted that was the product of a grand compromise.

The decree identified as the key element in state structural policy the idea of 'state entrepreneurship' (read 'state capitalism') which 'should give first priority to the production of goods and services essential to society.' It also defined as an aim not only the stabilisation of production but also a growth in the output of products that the authors consider important: oil, goods wagons, bearings, fertilisers and so on.

The main driving force in the implementation of this policy was to be the central state organs. Within the government this work was to be headed by the first deputy prime-ministers (whose appointments only needed Chernomyrdin's signature in order to be ratified). They were to be charged with 'supplying specific enterprises with joint centralised resources, so that enterprises falling within the sphere of influence of the selective structural policy would know exactly where to turn for supplies.' It was envisaged that the Russian Central Bank would make one-time payments to selected enterprises, the State Property Committee would not permit the bankruptcy of enterprises not selected for state investment, and the Ministry of Agriculture would ensure feedback from agricultural producers.

The programme also left room for compromise with private entrepreneurs. 'Here there is no conflict with the interests of private entrepreneurs, since an increase in private companies replenishing the country's tax base, will also have a positive effect on the economy and society as a whole.' Thus this government document incorporated the ideas of the 'structuralists' in the concept of 'focused support of the economy.'

Taking into account the regional factor the concept of 'resource kulaks' in the government, its main facility for the economic linking of the regions, was to be reviewed. Chernomyrdin was willing to make major concessions to the regional elite in the formulation of policy, calculating that in so doing he would gain time and free his hands for economic activity, which with any degree of political sovereignty would with time allow the implementation of unitary principles in economic relations with the Periphery. This calculation was posited on the utilisation of state credits by interested regional economic structures on a market basis, which would also determine the policy of the subjects of the Federation and inter-regional associations.

Responsibility for designing such a mechanism was to be put in the hands of state economic corporations, such as the State Investment Corporation headed by Yurii Petrov, which in the spring of 1994 had tried to create in the form of sub-corporations inter-regional economic associations such as *Ural* and *Bol'shaya Vol'ga* and is now engaged in creating a third *Severo-Zapad.* The Russian Central Bank and other structures were also assigned an important role.

With the break-up of the centrist bloc and its supporting structure the Civic Union, which began after the Seventh Congress of People's Deputies, that part of it primarily oriented towards the MIC-2 found itself in a very difficult and unstable position. The economic groups which form its basis (non-export production of the MIC, practically all medium machine-building, the production of construction materials, agro-industry and private farmers) are forced in their search for political partners to orient the 'centrists' towards a closer co-operation with the 'uncompromising opposition'. In the final analysis, the polarisation of the interests of the budgeteers of non-export sectors and the compromise between 'importers' and 'exporters' led to a deepening of the conflict and its violent eruption in October 1993.

Such were the political circumstances surrounding the creation and consolidation of the Russian business of the 'second (post-Soviet) wave'. The events of 1994, although they did not lead to a political clash between competing economic and political groupings of the 1992-1993 kind (mainly because of the violent gutting of the former political niche of non-export budgeteers – the parliament), still sharpened the contradictions between all economic groupings, which became most visible in the battle for the 1994 state budget, and the analogous campaign for the 1995 budget.

## 8 The Further Corporatisation of Russian Economic Elite Groups and the Political Context of Lobbying.

The spread of lobbying (understood in this context to mean any of various forms and methods that industrialists, entrepreneurs and other public groups use to influence members of the legislative and executive branches power in order to solicit adoption of a decision advantageous to them or the rejection of a disadvantageous one) is directly connected with the use of the entire might of the government machine to implant business institutions 'from below' yet under its control. This led to the formation of a special kind of Russian business 'from the bottom-up,' which can be called a political type of business. This is because it is the state – itself a particular type of political formation – establishes special relations with business, all the while reinforcing the latter with production units and institutions from its own economic sector.

In this way, a corresponding political process is developed (i.e., the forms and mechanisms that elites and masses can use to represent their political interests, as well as the ways that state management decisions are made and implemented by those who hold power). This political process is ideocratic, in that ideological doctrine (in this case, the ideas of strong presidential power with elements of representative democracy, a market economy, and the idiom of Russo-centric national interests) is a principal algorithm of activity. This doctrine enjoys nation-wide consensus (a practical example is the April-May 1994 signing of the Agreement on Civic Accord for two years).

The results of this include the ideological lobbying of state actors primarily on behalf of state entrepreursnip, legal protectionism of the circulation field, and a competitive environment for financial and property markets. This supports free enterprise to a limited extent, primarily for Western nations willing to give money for Russian reforms (mainly for the privatisation of state property and the development of the free enterprise sector, particularly involving small and medium-sized business).

At present, there are four major social groups in the free enterprise arena: representatives of the 'shadow' economy; independent entrepreneurs who began their activities without initial capital; members of the party nomenklatura; and directors of state-owned enterprises, who are participating in privatisation and in turning their enterprises into joint stock companies. It should be noted that state enterprise directors have become increasingly engaged in business activities since the implementation of the privatisation programme[5]).

The specificity of such a business structure and the considerable influence of state enterprise directors in it determines the reasons for the general problems plaguing the entrepreneurial environment (which has united in powerful lobbying structures which are crystallising their general interests in the form of public associations). Since 1987, after the passage of the USSR laws *On the State Enterprise (Association)* and *On Co-operatives in the USSR*, income has been increasingly passing from the hands of producers to those of enterprise managers now independent from the state (and partially to work collectives). This is because economic managers now have the right to engage in business initiatives (i.e., selling some of their output at negotiated read 'free' prices and spending the resources gained in an unrestricted fashion). Now, they are the ones mainly responsible for the turnover and accumulation of capital (that was once and still is advanced by the government for the production funds of plants and factories and for the training of qualified labour). The market value of all this will only be known as the market economy develops.

Under these new conditions, the formation of a commodity market and a market infrastructure has begun to take shape. Raw material and commodity exchanges have become a means of commercialising a part of the social product sold freely at the market. According to Konstantin Borovoi, the founder of the first Russian

---

5 *Rossiyskoye predprinimatel'stvo: opyt sotsiologicheskogo analiza* [Russian Entrepreneurship: Results of a Sociological Analysis]. Moscow 1993: 8-9.

commodity and raw materials exchange, the stock market allowed two different systems to co-exist – the state system and the market system[6].

Regardless of the fact that entrepreneurship in Russia began with small and medium business, Russian entrepreneurs now represent a traditional type of businessman by combining the owner of the means of production and the manager of a company in one person. Initially, these people were oriented to achieving success in business through individual effort. They have are property owners and occupy a special place in the organisation of labour; in particular, as de-statisation processes gain momentum, entrepreneurs feel more and more a part of the new elite that is distinctive in its personal independence and individual freedom.

The largest and most efficient part of the private sector developed as a distinctive form of mixed entrepreneurship, in which the CPSU nomenklatura and Komsomol actively participated. Depending on the specific situation, this process can be regarded as the formation of directly private activity or as the de-statisation of state-owned enterprises. This process of generating entrepreneurship has proven to be successful, and is developing further on the basis of the power levers, personal connections, initial finances and resources (start-up capital), and real estate that the nomenklatura had at its disposal.

The first commercial entities started to appear as early as 1987, under the patronage of the CPSU Central Committee and Young Communist League (Komsomol) Central Committee. These were Youth Centres for Scientific-Technical Endeavours, which acted as middlemen and traders. Many major commercial banks developed from such co-operatives (*Menatep*, *Inkombank* which was established with the participation of the Komsomol Central Committee, the 'Russia' bank which was founded by the Leningrad Regional CPSU Committee, *Glavmosstroibank* which was established by the Moscow City CPSU Committee). According to an assessment of businessmen themselves, about 10% of all commercial structures were founded by the party and Komsomol nomenklatura.

The CPSU backed the first joint ventures with foreign partners and representatives of foreign parties. By August 1991, there were 60 party firms of this kind in the former USSR and another 300 of them located abroad[7].

---

6 Borovoi, K.N. „A New Businessman: What Is He Like? (Interview)." *Mirovaya ekonomika i mezhdunarodniye otnosheniya* (1992), no. 5: 38.

7 Pluzhnikov, S. and S. Sokolov. „Golden Adviser to the President." *Komsomol'skaya Pravda* 5 February 1993: 2.

For the hundreds of thousands of businessmen who started from nothing and had no support from state organs, being a trader or middleman became the only means of acquiring initial capital. Many firms managed to accumulate funds through sales of computers and audio and video equipment, which allowed them to grow into big commercial entities – stock exchanges, banks, finance and investment companies, etc. Firms established 'from the top' (i.e., with money from the CPSU, Komsomol, trade unions and public organisations) were given the opportunity to cash enormous sums.

During the transition period, the old system of personal connections has been preserved and has even grown stronger, as it has turned out to be impossible for all kinds of businessmen and enterprise managers to take entrepreneurial risks with them.

Therefore, the lion's share of business lobbying activities takes place within the framework of informal contacts that are 'free' from institutional and procedural limitations. Formalised relations as such determine the right of access to and the protocol involved in dealing with low- and high-level state officials, on the basis of which opportunities to deformalise essential contacts are made.

At the same time, Russia has developed a distinct type of proprietor-manager-administrator or directorate, in the sense of a special social group of economic executives or state enterprise managers. These persons have received extensive rights to conduct business activities using public funds. This is a rudiment of the idea of market socialism which was rather popular in the late 1980s, i.e., an attempt to commercialise state property.

During that time, after the law on co-operatives had been adopted and mass privatisation began in 1992, one of the main ways private enterprise developed was by the establishment of commercial entities under the aegis of state enterprises. Thus, in 1991, 80% of all existing co-operatives had been established at state enterprises, received raw materials and leasing capital assets from them[8].

Those co-operatives and small ventures were closely linked with a parent company, a state enterprise, but were legally independent from it. Many of them were personally headed by enterprise directors or their agents. Using the capital and circulating assets of state enterprises, commercial structures 'helped' their parent companies sell their output at market prices, thus earning considerable profits. At the next stage, several enterprises of this kind would establish a new, more powerful

---

**8** Barbashov, V., and I. Chebatkov „The Cooperative Sector: Problems and Prospects.“ *Ekonomika i Zhizn'* 5 (1991), no. 20: 20.

structure (i.e., a joint venture, stock exchange or investment company) that permitted the 'pumping' of state financial and material resources into the emerging private sector. Eventually, many of these state enterprise co-operatives managed to develop into autonomous entities, buying out capital assets from the parent company. Many continue to work independently up to the present day, earning income primarily from speculative operations and only partially from the output of needed quality production. At the same time, this model of market formation promoted the destruction of the state distribution economy and laid the groundwork for the appearance of new market actors.

In reality, this form of entrepreneurship led to a large-scale plundering of state-owned property and the formation of quasi-market structures. Accordingly, under Russian conditions, this form of business promoted the corruption of the whole upper stratum of economic-administrative leaders, who got rich in the process.

Especially after the liberalisation of prices and wages in 1992, state enterprise directors and heads of work collectives promoted the outflow of capital from material production to their own personal interests. An unpublicised de-statisation of capital took place and, at the same time, its rapid outflow from material production started. State capital continued to be advanced to industry, agriculture, construction, transportation and communication and quickly started to turn into commercial-speculative and financial-usury capital (especially with the appearance of commercial banks).

As a result of this 'pumping-over' of capital, enormous personal fortunes were made, while the gross income (profit and amortisation) that was created by state enterprises, directors and their agents, speculators, bureaucrats, middlemen, financiers, etc. was very profitably invested in spheres apart from material production. Naturally, group funds have developed, which hardly anyone at present is trying to reinvest in the modernisation and revival of production. This is especially the case since it is possible to start a private and profitable business of one's own that, moreover, would promote the further privatisation and 'pumping-over' of state capital from factories still in operation, especially those dealing with raw materials.

The state – keeping itself increasingly aloof from the investment process, from determining the profile of a particular enterprise, from problems of supplies and sales in material production, and from worrying about establishing the conditions of the support and expansion of material production – tries to control prices and wages at plants and factories which formally belong to it. For all that, part of the revenue from the productive activities of the latter goes to small non-state ventures, joint ventures, co-operatives and other commercial entities. When they resale goods produced by state enterprises, they increase their capital by the uncontrolled raising of prices.

In most cases, state property was transformed into private or group property in the following way: a medium-sized or small enterprise was turned into a co-operative, and the work collective bought it from the state at rock-bottom prices. Then the co-operative was re-registered as a joint stock company whose founders, as a rule, were the enterprise itself:; some kind of commercial bank; possibly an investment company; the district, city, region, territorial or republic administration; as well as a number of partner enterprises (in most cases, those from the technological chain). After that, the joint stock company was reorganised. As a result of that reorganisation, the co-operative shares of the employees were converted into preferred stock (with no voting rights, but with the right to receive dividends), while the management of the joint stock company got a controlling block of shares. As a rule, this marked the end of the stage in which state property was virtually transformed into group property. The future hope is to buy such an enterprise de jure and legalise this property as one's own private enterprise or as a mixed-form of enterprise – during the period of monetary privatisation or widespread bankruptcies that is anticipated.

In this way, even before the 1992 price liberalisation, huge amounts of capital had been transferred from the public sector of the economy to private hands. This was also accompanied by a mass outflow of human resources from the public sector – primarily specialists and qualified workers attracted by higher salaries and wages in the private sector.

This is also connected with the unwillingness on the part of enterprise directors to pay for deliveries of raw materials – especially fuel and energy – as well as for transportation, salaries and wages (at least at an agreed-upon time), and taxes (which are impossible to pay in full, since otherwise production itself would have to stop). It is more attractive to invest money received from the sale of goods in commercial banks at a high interest, in the short-term government bonds so popular nowadays, or in some other business that provides for the quick return on one's investment and high income per rouble expended. Examples of the latter include businesses related to the export of oil, diamonds, non-ferrous metals, etc. or the import of highly profitable foreign goods (consumer goods, computers, cars, housing and other real estate).

The interference of the state can make no substantial changes in this area. Moreover, financial infusions in any form to support factories which are falling into disrepair will only promote the further outflow of the state capital that still exists into private hands. Thus, these infusions will remain outside of the bounds of material production. Paying wages to employees of state-owned enterprises out of the Treasury rather than from earned revenues extends the life of these enterprises and permits a narrow circle of industrial entrepreneurs to continue making enormous private fortunes at the expense of state capital.

The de-statisation of capital and its outflow from material production are facilitated by the convertibility of the rouble, the non-repatriation of hard currency earnings by non-state exporters that goes on with impunity, and the potential to export huge amounts of capital abroad joint ventures, commercial banks and enterprises, evading decrees and resolutions.

Inflation also destroys production potential and contributes to the critical condition of production capital, in particular, by quickly depreciating amortisation.

Hardly anyone would risk investing his capital (which is now virtually private) in long-term capital construction without government guarantees. This is because it is impossible to calculate estimated costs even several months in advance in view of rapidly rising prices for construction, materials, and equipment. Rather, people opt for investments with quick recoupment of expenses and those that don't involve large outlays on technical re-equipping; the reconstruction and expansion of an enterprise; or the construction of new enterprises with unknown prospects in a market economy.

Voucher privatisation of state property facilitates the complete appropriation of state capital and its outflow from production. This is because former state enterprise directors, work collectives and new co-owners of plants and factories most frequently try to turn all enterprise revenues into personal income rather than investing them in the development of production. Typical in this respect are data on the most recent revaluation of fixed assets, according to which the degree of depreciation in the means of production increases commensurably with the number of years since enterprise privatisation. Thus, the fixed assets of enterprises that were privatised in 1993 show 41% deterioration; for enterprises privatised in 1992 – 53%; and in 1991 – over 64%.

Voucher privatisation began when state enterprises had already considerably depreciated in a market sense. This was when state-owned property and fixed assets could hardly be considered to be fixed capital capable of yielding substantial profits within a more or less protracted period of time and of ensuring the competitiveness of domestic production.

The state, by refusing to dispose of capital that had been advanced for material production while retaining substantial property rights to so-called state-owned enterprises, has provoked the practical blending of capital and of property as its temporary carrier. Capital is invested in concrete assets basic to production, in specific equipment, machinery, tools, and buildings. These make it possible to produce output that is in demand and is needed by society, over a more or less extended period of time. The sale of such output allows for the eventual reimbursement of and increase in advanced capital. Whoever disposes of income is the virtual owner of capital – he or she controls the source of its reimbursement and accumulation and determines what should be done next with it. Any means of production that is not physically and qualitatively renovated eventually ceases to yield profit.

The intensity of personal enrichment going on at the expense of former state capital – as well as the outflow of the latter from production and its loss – can be approximately measured by the value of capital underinvested in material production. An enterprise is economically sound if it maintains a definite level of investment from all sources of financing and if the renovation of fixed assets in comparable prices is lower than 10-12 % per year on the average (i.e., the ratio of bringing in new fixed assets to their aggregate value as of 1 January). In this case, one can speak of the beginning of capital outflow from production. The carriers of capital do not wish to have anything to do with the given enterprise in the future and find more profitable and promising uses for their revenues.

From 1986-1993, the approximate outflows and losses of state capital advanced for fixed assets in industry alone amounted to 40 trillion roubles (in prices used to re-evaluate fixed assets as of 1 January 1994). This is equal to approximately 21% of the fixed assets that should optimally be put into operation in industry for this period.

The rate of renovating fixed assets in industry has dropped to below 4% and the share of relatively new means of production (i.e., up to 13 years in operation) is decreasing rapidly. Moreover, insufficient levels of investment in modernising fixed assets lead to their loss in an amount that exceeds the underinvestment by many times.

Another critical factor is the permanent outflow of labour. The number of workers employed in industry dropped by 6,7 million in 1993 alone. This represents a loss of capital equivalent to 26 trillion roubles at current labour rates. From 1987-1993, experts estimate the total losses of this kind to be approximately 100 trillion roubles. So far we have discussed only those who voluntarily leave industry without intending to return, or who leave to find a more profitable application of their abilities in other places.

Certainly, a description of the outflow and loss of all kinds of capital in industry (i.e., in production capital) is not limited to the above discussion. A considerable portion of the state's payment of enterprise debts to employees, suppliers, and creditors; the lion's share of preferential credits; a certain share of direct investment; and some losses related to the delayed repayment of debts and transfer of credits to state enterprises only add to that process.

Private capital is leaving industry, given current inflation rates, the present taxation system, and the virtual absence of the rule of law. Thus one cannot count on it returning to production (including capital deposited in foreign banks). It will be more likely used for limited capital investments, when one can buy an operating enterprise for next to nothing – especially if the enterprise is backed by state subsidies and investments. But as a whole, attempts to attract domestic private capital into production in hopes of it taking root there are completely groundless.

The most attractive spheres of private entrepreneurship still remain those which do not require high capital investment and have quick capital turnover. It is for this reason that those entities that have been engaged in production ever since private business emerged are those which have production capacity at their disposal, i.e. co-operatives located at state-owned enterprises or new joint stock companies.

Private businesses need to be engaged in commercial activity for a relatively long period of time, and they need to diversify as much as possible. The alternative – being engaged in production – is guaranteed to lead to bankruptcy. Due to the existing taxation system, only state or partially-state economic entities can be engaged in production.

Under conditions in which domestic private capital is reluctant to return from abroad and continues to leave the production sphere, while foreign capital is waiting for better opportunities, the only hope is the state and its business activity. At present, state economic actors are making increasing lobbying demands to not extend financial resources through private capital 'which is able to appropriate any state financial infusion'. Moreover, through their public associations and other lobbying groups, directors are insisting that the state should save production not only through indirect means (through taxes, preferential credits and subsidies), but should also directly interfere with its restoration and development. (Naturally, they argue that the government shouldn't do this in the way it did before under a planned economy, but as a player in a capitalist market as a holder of large-scale capital.) They point out that it is imperative to restore and confirm the right of state capital to exist, capital that was in fact finished off in 1987. The main point of this great lobbying and political struggle is the issue of who will directly dispose of state capital and how they will do it, and what the role of economic departments, ministries, committees, local authorities, special government agents, and state entrepreneurs upholding the public interest will be in the management of official capital.

For this business stratum, it is important that organisations or subjects representing the state should have the same rights to capital as private persons under a market system. It is also important that they: receive a certain amount of income from it (no less than 12-15% a year in comparable prices); pay income tax; determine how their capitalised profit should be spent; influence the profile of and development strategy for production depending on their share in the aggregate joint stock capital of the enterprise; and have the right to withdraw their capital in order to invest it into other more promising and more profitable sectors and industries or use it for modernisation of the given enterprise in which state capital has already been engaged. According to them, state capital (protected by the law) should be formed not only at the expense of state investment from the federal budget but also through assessing the market value of remaining state property.

Thus, a stratum of economic managers (of enterprises which have already undergone de-statisation enterprises by turning them into joint stock companies without being privatised) has been formed. This stratum is closely connected with governmental ministerial structures – ministries, state committees, local administrations and authorities. Also closely connected with them is a stratum of managers of economic entities which have undergone de-statisation followed by privatisation. At the same time, this group is rather closely linked with financial capital, primarily commercial banks. There is also a special social niche that is comprised of a stratum of economic managers and their clientele who have de facto privatised the capital assets of state enterprises without their de-statisation. In a legal sense, this in fact a criminal stratum, and is closely linked with state enterprise directors and finance capital.

In view of the specificity of the above-mentioned processes, the sectoral clans of industrialists and central and regional bureaucrats connected with them undoubtedly play a decisive role in the formation of various co-operative ventures. The latter are based upon super-monopolies and groups of enterprises connected with each other regionally, sectorally and technologically which are gradually transformed into financial-industrial groups, financial associations and companies, and large concerns and corporations capable of accumulating financial and other resources to be invested in the political sphere with rather tangible consequences.

The traditional and supposedly 'highest' form of participation by sectoral industries in the former USSR and in present-day Russia are 'direct participation structures.' These comprise the skilled side of sectoral management bodies. They are ministry collegia supplemented with relatively new (for post-communist Russia) governmental bodies such as the Council for Industrial Policy and Entrepreneurship in the Russian government, various inter-governmental commissions, the Council for Foreign Economic Policy at Russia' Ministry of Foreign Economic Relations, and others.

The configuration of business lobbying in Russia is not a classic analogue to Western tradition due, at least, to the fact that it is concentrated primarily on influencing governmental and other executive authorities rather than parliamentary bodies (as is the case in representative democracies). This is due to many factors, and most importantly, to the fact that the practical model of state decision-making is, to a considerable extent, controlled by executive authorities who are also well-represented in the legislative branch. The importance of a presidential decree or act is considerably higher and weightier than that of a law.

The Cabinet's power resources (which are considerably greater than those of the legislature), the monarchical powers of the President, and the virtual absence of a practical separation of powers, in no way encourage the 'Americanisation' of lobbying activity. As a rule, in America the main object of influence is the Congress and, accordingly, the key lobbyists working there.

The focal points of competition are the issues of sectoral subsidies (the trough is too small for everybody) and customs tariffs, and the strategic question about how tough the anti-inflationary fiscal policy will be – a policy that reduces the level of government credits.

As a rule, conflicts on these and other private issues are discussed at top-level meetings between sectoral and finance capital, on the one hand, and between leading sectoral complexes in the country (energy and fuel, agro-industrial and military-industrial), on the other hand, as well as between sectors within these complexes.

In a transitional economy which remains to a large extent non-commercial, capital assets of state enterprises are exposed to attempts by financial capital to capitalise their financial resources. This process is opposed by the industrial establishment and units of the state apparatus that are controlled by it. These conflicts increasingly produce a stratum of directors who have transformed their enterprises into joint stock companies and privatised them and who can therefore dispose of both capital assets and finance capital.

At the same time, finance capital, now competitive in the Russian economy (thus, for example, it is engaged in a strategic struggle to bring a 'government of banks' to power and terminate the activities of the 'cabinet of sectoral leaders' headed by *Gazprom* patron Victor Chernomyrdin), nevertheless, has had to take part in internal 'squabbles' between sectors of production capital rather than defend its own corporate interests.

At the governmental level, sectoral production groups are supported by cadre-nomenklatura complexes: the complex of industrial capital is headed by Vice Prime Minister Oleg Soskovets and that of agro-industrial capital is led by Vice Prime Minister Aleksandr Zaveryukha. Financial capital leans on the State Property Committee headed by Vice Prime Minister Anatolii Chubais and the State Antimonopoly Committee with Leonid Bochkin at its head, but which is controlled by Chubais. These cadre-nomenklatura groupings try to influence the following governmental bodies: the non-corporate Ministry of Economics (that develops the basic principles of economic policy and relations between sectors) and the Ministry of Finance (which is responsible for financing governmental programs).

Lobbying by directors of state enterprises which have been forcibly commercialised (i.e., state authorities give them standards for de-statisation and the management of fixed assets) is aimed at exerting pressure upon federal authorities in order to expedite the de-statisation of enterprises technologically connected with them. Moreover, pressure is aimed at ensuring suitable standards for existing under non-commercial conditions (subsidies, tax exemptions, etc.). The state, in turn, imposes administrative and tax restrictions on the activities of managers whose enterprises have undergone both de-statisation and privatisation. The latter then try to shift tax and other burdens to mangers of state enterprises that are directly subordinated to them and that have been transformed into joint stock companies without privatisation. It is becoming more and more common that directors of new joint stock companies who privatise together with entrepreneurs in finance capital have similar lobbying interests.

A similar organising of industrial and entrepreneurial entities has lead to establishment of a whole group of influential public associations of both a national and trans-sectoral as well as of a sectoral nature. These entities are interested in increasing their 'influence resources' in state decision-making, as well as their 'action resources' in their chosen sphere of business activity. Their main efforts are concentrated on strategic issues, on institutionalising themselves in the system of state decision making, and in the development of recommendations together with ministries and the government as a whole, as well as with local authorities. These associations are not purely lobbying structures, but since their functions include the organisation of lobbying activities, they can be regarded (though rather narrowly) as lobbying organisations.

This is all the more topical as the corporate nature of the current Russian economy is also predetermined by the domination of centralised public financing from the federal budget and thus by the domination of the state machinery – the holder of major financial means and resources.

Most likely, lobbying by associations of industrialists and entrepreneurs is a phenomenon of political business operating 'from below.' (The latter is understood to be entrepreneurial activity determined by political motives.) This type of business is based on the need to organise and regulate society's vital functions for the benefit of the specific interest groups in industrial and business circles that are represented by these associations. These associations concentrate their economic lobbying activities primarily on the federal level, including top-level state bureaucrats.

The specific legal and economic business conditions in Russia (e.g., taxation pressure, insufficient state credits for business programmes, the extensive rights of authorities in the business sphere) force business circles to consolidate along narrow sectoral interests within the framework of informal groups. The latter are organised mainly at the city or regional level, or in a group of sectoral industries; they are club-like groups which bring people together (including bureaucrats) who know and trust each other perfectly well. However, the increased politicisation of the business environment (i.e., its near-total dependence upon official decisions and the informal wishes of bureaucrats from the state machinery) inevitably push these small and narrow unofficial formations toward co-operation on a broader scale – at the sectoral level, or in economic and business spheres at the national and trans-sectoral levels.

As voluntary societies of business 'interest groups', these associations differ from parties in the sense that they do not directly take part in the general political will. Representing individual societal strata, they do not seek political responsibility but try to formulate their political-economic interests on a nation-wide scale in order to influence the political will.

The active formulation of such interests means that the actions of the members of public associations are included – as specific demands – in the political process and in both official and unofficial business negotiations with government representatives. Moreover, in all cases a relatively unified political line is necessary since it increases the chances of effectively influencing politics. On the other hand, the generalisation and formulation of fundamental interests and demands by such large societies as associations – irrespective of the wishes and perceptions of specific government bureaucrats – prove to be important. This is because such articulation promotes the comprehension by state authorities of the scope of demands by numerous business circles, as a rule reducing them to a small number of alternatives. It is also important insofar as the state is able to satisfy only a limited number of demands, lest it should be too overloaded with them.

Practical experience, no matter how negative it may be, makes leading groups of such public associations of entrepreneurs and industrialists certain that they must create a 'hierarchy of interests' which rates the various demands of specific groups according to their perceived current relevance. An overly one-sided selection of demands may lead to a situation in which state authorities are deprived of their authority or end up make selections themselves, which is by no means the most desirable course of events.

This is all the more important as the co-ordination of interests may, to a great extent, be complicated by the divergent orientations of specific member groups of an association. The system of informal lobbying of various state organs by economic groups that developed in 1992 was the fundamental way they realised their interests: from ordering appropriate legislative bills and governmental and local administrative decisions to the illegal official registration of business deals. Mass corruption at all levels of the state apparatus, as well as the widespread participation (both official and unofficial) of bureaucrats and legislators in managing commercial entities, resulted in a very complicated and intricate system of ties between various groups of economic elites and state and political organs. These ties often had nothing to do with the officially declared ideological postulates and political attitudes of those involved.

Neither the attempts to create nor the activities of national political parties of entrepreneurs and industrialists has been very successful to date. The direct bribing of legislators – as well as the unofficial lobbying of governmental and presidential organs including that on a co-operative basis, i.e., through public associations of industrialists and businessmen – have been more effective. The influence of public associations of industrialists and entrepreneurs depends on how effectively they can fulfil the following fundamental tasks:

- the relatively smooth formulation, at the corporate level, of key demands and interests of member industrial-entrepreneurial groups;
- effective representation in the state apparatus, the legislature, and in political parties;
- maintaining unity in the business environment itself, which is rationally imperative;
- offering various types of information, consultative and intermediation services to their members;
- in the foreseeable future, developing a strategy of mutual relationships with employees.

In reality, such associations should and often do practically ensure the following levels of involvement in state decision making:

- access to the central echelons of power through contacts with top state officials and ministries, and consultations on issues that affect the interests of specific corporations of entrepreneurs;
- the development of a political policy within the framework of a structure in which organisations of businessmen and industrialists officially participate in working out key decisions side by side with state officials;
- the implementation of that policy with the direct participation of representatives of organised business interests;
- attempts to the acquire the necessary powers from the government and to take responsibility (with the support of state enforcement mechanisms) for the decision making process.

At the same time, business groups (i.e., national, trans-sectoral and sectoral associations) as well as the aforementioned 'direct participation structures' are the connecting links of economic lobbying in Russia. The lowest link consists of specific production and business units. The top of this giant pyramid is at present represented by the government of the Russian Federation, the presidential administration, and the Federal Assembly where, in fact, conflicts of interest between various economic elites in modern Russian society actually take place.

Naturally, at the centre of the social forces organised directly by entrepreneurial and industrial groups there are national trans-sectoral associations which claim to represent the interests of, if not all, than at least the overwhelming majority of all types of Russian industry and business. At least four associations have made a bid for that role: the Federation of Commodity Producers of Russia, the Russian Union of Industrialists and Entrepreneurs, the Association of Enterprise Managers, and the Chamber of Commerce and Industry of Russia. Practically speaking, these are associations of an inter-sectoral nature as they include, to a greater or lesser extent, enterprises of a significant number of sectors and many private factories. As a rule, membership in such associations is open; hence anyone who wishes to can potentially join.

Sectoral associations (or those belonging to one sector of the economy or entrepreneurial activity) to some extent carry on the traditions of the sectoral trade unions of the All-Union Central Council of Trade Unions (AUCCTU). Those unions included practically all managers and employees. In this case, it is a union of entrepreneurs and industrial managers.

Only by analysing the dynamics of their specific activities can we understand the role and significance of current lobbying activity by the largest associations. This activity is turning into a political struggle to realise corporate interests under conditions of an imminent socio-economic crisis. Analysing these dynamics is important because the one to three years of practical experience these associations have had are the main indicator we have of their activities, that have developed from specific campaigns for survival or for obtaining benefits. The absence of a number of factors (settled traditions; stable, structured schemes for developing these public associations; the legal means to regulate them; and the general criminalisation of business – as well as politics) encourage these associations to take part in radical actions which promote the crystallisation of corporate interests and entail the cultivation of appropriate lobbying targets.

According to the Institute of Sociology of the Russian Academy of Sciences, business circles see the activities of public associations under current conditions as making sense in the following ways[9]:

- 57% in activities which protect business from state corruption;
- 54% in support in the struggle against bureaucratism;
- 48% in assistance in organising foreign economic activities;
- 47% in assistance in receiving reliable information concerning market conditions and political forecasting;

---

**9** Simonyan, R. „Entrepreneurship and Power.“ *Dialog* (1993), no. 5-6: 31.

- 47% in assistance in the selection of business partners;
- 43% in assistance in the selection of associates;
- 41% in protection against unfair competition on the domestic market;
- 39% in protection against unfair competition on the foreign market;
- 37% in assistance in arbitration;
- 33% in assistance in personnel training and consulting;
- 27% in the promotion of exhibitions and fairs.

Thus, the first task in lobbying is establishing the rule of law and curbing the tyranny of bureaucrats. At the same time, the results of this research reflect the interests of mainly small and medium businessmen. Large, established structures are more concerned with more high-profile issues such as obtaining credits and subsidies for all sectors and developing the state's general economic policy. The vectors of rivalry and partnership in Russia's business environment are correlated with their political orientations.

The profound economic context of the political struggle which has been in its most critical phase since December 1992 has played an important role in the crystallisation and definition of political orientations in Russian business[10].

One can interpret the actions of contending political forces primarily by the attempts of various business and industrial circles to forecast the potential loss of its dominating position in various economic spheres, especially in foreign economic activity. In this regard, the degree of influence wielded by economic groupings on government levers of power (in other words, on the direct management and disposal of state property and finances) is especially important. This emphasis on retaining influence on the state machinery and government is based on the key position of the public sector in Russia's economy. This position makes the public sector and naturally the government (like the Supreme Soviet was previously) the main holder of the country's material and financial resources.

When commercial entities received permission, with insignificant exceptions, to finance electoral campaigns for the Federal Assembly in October-December 1993, this helped to legalise the open investment of capital in politics. In an October 1993 commentary by popular journalist Rustam Narzikulov published in the *Segodnya* newspaper, it was pointed out that the success of a commercial enterprise depends on the vigorous actions of 'pressure groups' and the 'lobbying' of that economic group

---

**10** This political struggle has been exacerbated during such political campaigns as the 'political crisis' of March 1993 and the dissolution of the Russian parliament in September-October of the same year.

in state bodies of power: 'The riskiness of politics is higher than that of ordinary short-term investments due to the uncertainty of reimbursement, but for present-day Russia, it is the most important kind of long-term investment...' According to the well-informed *Kommersant Daily* newspaper, a place on a party list in the elections cost 300-400 million roubles in November 1993.

During the feverish 'October' struggle between politicians for the right to represent anyone's economic interests, negotiations were temporarily frozen between such groups as the Russian Union of Industrialists and Entrepreneurs (or RUIE, which supports the economic programme of first Vice-Prime Minister Oleg Soskovets in the form of the Council for Industrial Policy headed by RUIE vice-president Michael Yur'ev); the association 'Entrepreneurs for a New Russia'; the Russian Party of Free Labour (whose chairman Ivan Kivelidi presides over the influential Council for Entrepreneurship under the Council of Ministers, which is also monitored by Oleg Soskovets); and the Party for Economic Freedom. Unity on the necessity of a 'zero option' was achieved at a session of the co-ordinating council of the association 'Entrepreneurs for a New Russia' on 27 September, 1993, with the participation of the RUIE, the All-Russian Union 'Renewal' (ARUR) and the Federation of Commodity Producers. At this session, consultations on the establishment of a single electoral bloc in the light of new realities which emerged on 3-4 October, 1993 began, but this did not result in the joining of forces of 'business people'.

The main ways that the 'captains of business' and 'generals of industry' got into the new Russian parliament were in the single- and two-mandate districts in elections to the State Duma and Council of the Federation. Especially interesting – in the sense of the formation of all-Russian lobbying and party-political structures by 'old' industrial and 'new' financial capital – are the seats filled by party lists in the elections.

Needing protection of their economic interests by political means and at the same time being rather openly blackmailed by the democratic establishment in order to obtain money for its electoral campaign, private business – along with local executive heads – has become the key resource for expanding the political base of pro-government blocs as well as a number of opposition election blocs. However, efforts by radical and moderate democrats to attract associations of entrepreneurs and industrialists to their blocs have run into contradictory processes within Russian business itself. Business, except for that part most dependent on the current government (the All-Russian Association of Private and Privatising Enterprises –

'the party of the State Property Committee'; the Association of Farmers and Agricultural Co-operatives of Russia; the League of Lessees and Co-operators), did not express particular confidence in the ruling radical and liberal group. At the same, it demonstrated reluctance to 'put all its eggs into one basket'.

During the entire election race of 1993 there were quite a few examples of capital investment of one and the same financial group in the election campaigns of a whole range of politically opposed candidates. Thus, the financial group *Most* financed both the Party of Democratic Initiative with Pavel Bunich at the head and Grigorii Yavlinskii's bloc. The inter-bank association *Menatep*, according to Vyacheslav Sen'ko, a member of the Central Committee of the Russian Liberal Democratic Party, was willing to promote Zhirinovskii's party financially in case of an effective election campaign (which proved to be the case). Both groups, as well as *Promradtekhbank*, *Alfa-Bank*, *Olbi-Diplomat* and others also subsidised the elections of *Vybor Rossii* [Russia's Choice]. According to various sources, the Union of Oil Industrialists of Russia supported both the centrist Party of Consolidation headed by Aleksandr Tikhonov and the moderate patriotic bloc *Otechestvo* [Fatherland], which was also financed by such financial groups as *Unikombank;* while the *Olbi* banking group supported, in addition to *Russia's Choice*, the Party of Economic Liberty and the Consolidation party.

*Entrepreneurs for a New Russia*, public in form and political in content, headed by Konstantin Zatulin, gradually changed its orientation in 1993 from finance minister Boris Fedorov to the politician and economist Grigorii Yavlinskii. After breaking with him (according to entrepreneurs because of his exaggerated ambitions which they claimed to be in sharp contrast to his real potential), 'Entrepreneurs for a New Russia' entered into an alliance with the Party of Russian Unity and Concord (PRUC). Zatulin argued in favour of that step because „entrepreneurs cannot but cooperage with authorities and members of the government"[11]. In his opinion, the policy of destroying the rouble zone „may lead to further disintegration of the CIS, establishing new border and customs barriers, which will result in a contraction of Russia's market for raw materials in the near abroad in a situation when we are not ready for substantial trade with the West". Such decisions „run contrary to the interests of a new business which at present can successfully develop only on the basis of firmly established economic contacts within CIS, economic federalism and democracy in Russia itself", and, according to

**11** Statement at the PRUC constitutent conference, 16 October.

numerous statements by leaders of the Civic Union (CU) and the Russian Union of Industrialists and Entrepreneurs (RUIE), they agree with PRUC on this issue.

Zatulin also believes that entrepreneurs share Shakhrai's attitude to the solution of national question, the orientation to „social market economy, federalism, local self-government, and economic paternalism of a strong state during the reform period". In his opinion, the President himself „has begun to change his priorities in the field of economy too, where he considers it strategically important to have a more optimum correlation between liberal principles and state regulation, enhancement of the Russian market by means of restoration and expansion of production. The president is not inclined to make a fetish of monetarism as a panacea for Russia. And on this issue, he is in fact on the side of our bloc and other centrist associations". Another reorientation took place a little later – Zatulin did not find a common language with PRUC in the State Duma, and left the political coalition because of competition for leadership.

The saturation of the electoral lists of big blocs with primarily representatives from the 'political class' and their common orientation to gain victory for one of the contending *nomenklatura* and political groupings, the disparity between economic elites interests and direct representation's criterion already in October 1993 resulted in entering the political scene by business parties proper: the Party of Economic Liberty (PEL) (Konstantin Borovoi, Irina Khakamada), the Party of Consolidation (PC) (Aleksandr Tikhonov, president of the *InterUral* concern, Valerii Neverov, president of the *Hermes* concern), 'the Party of the State Committee for State Property' – the Association of Independent Professionals (Peter Filippov and Michael Kharshan, president of the First Delivery- voucher fund), the 'Transformation of Russia' movement (Victor Korovin, general director of 'Uralmash' amalgamation Kakha Bendukidze). The most radical of all business political organisations, it came out for a 'one and indivisible Russia without sovereignties since they only hide the blood and ambitions of local princelings', as Bendukidze said in a TV discussion held by RIA on 4 November.

The fact that the 'political class' overwhelmingly dominates the electoral list of the *Russia's Choice*, a party claiming to represent the interests of the new bourgeoisie, made Peter Filippov, one of the most radical ideologists of the new Russian capitalism, head of the Analytical Centre for Socio-Economic Policy at the Administration of the President of the Russian Federation, announce his withdrawal from the bloc and the foundation of the Association of Independent Professionals (AIP). The Association was also headed at that time by Andrei Nechayev, president of the Russian finance corporation, Evgenii Yasin, director of the RUIE Expert institute, as well as Andrei Makarov, a well-known lawyer. It declared the need to nominate to the Federal Assembly not 'representatives of small parties' or people having no profound economic knowledge, which would threaten the election of a 'parliament analogous to the second Georgian one'[12], but 'people with funds: entrepreneurs, stock-owners, all those who can and should finance an election campaign', primarily businessmen and leaders of executive bodies of power[13].

The interests of voucher investment funds, united into the Voucher Investment Funds Association (VIFA) under the patronage of the State Committee for State Property of the Russian Federation, became an economic precondition for the foundation of the AIP. As Sergei Shoiko, VIFA vice-president, stated at the All-Russian conference of voucher investment funds (VIF) held in Golytsino on 27-28 October, the failure of all draft law proposals related to the VIF, which the funds proposed to the authorities, demonstrated the failure of the concept of close interaction between the funds and existing authorities. This made them start an active election campaign. Initially, they were going to support *Russia's Choice*, whose ideology coincides with that of investment firms, but then it became clear that this party had little chance for success in conservatively disposed regions. Michael Kharshan (First CIP), Sergey Shoiko, Bessmertnyi (*National* voucher fund), Merkulov (*Aviation-Nautical* voucher fund) and Alekseev (*Investment Funds Promotion League*) became leaders of the CIF independent political organisation.

Konstantin Borovoi, the leader of the 'August' electoral bloc and of the Party of Economic Liberty (PEL), made his anti-bureaucratic rhetoric one of the main features of the election campaign. That the leader of one of the most popular business parties, and director of the Russian commodity and raw material exchange (RCRME), could assume such a stand, has been attributed to the fact that, to all appearances, neither he nor his party succeeded in a number of large-scale lobbyist actions (with a doubtful exception of the right received by Aleksei Vlasov, one of the RCRME administrators, to continue the trade in imported grain, purchased in the USA). In an interview to PEL newspaper *Srochno v Nomer*, Borovoi demonstrated his personal political inclination by saying that for him „there is no difference between Travkin and Gaidar. There is little difference in their concepts, but in fact – it is the same bureaucracy, the same *nomenklatura*, the same preservation of a centralised state. As for me, there is no difference between Gaidar and Yavlinskii

**12** Filippov's interview to Post Factum Press Agency of 7 October.

**13** Another interview with Filippov, 11 October.

either, because they are bureaucrats fighting for power and constantly making up programmes popular for a certain period... First of all, I mean *Russia's Choice*, that claims to play the role of a ruling party... It is simply a group of government officials who declared themselves a party". The refusal of *Russia's Choice* to put entrepreneurs, lawyers, bankers, and administrators of voucher investment funds at the top of the list was the reason why they established an electoral association of their own.

According to *Kommersant-Daily*, the aggregate capital controlled by Konstantin Borovoi and the administrators of *Yalosbank*, *Olbi Concern*, and the ASKO Corporation, who were among PEL top ten nominees, amounts to 0.8-1.1 trillion roubles (note that the PEL 'fathers', exchange circles in the Russian commodity and raw material exchange and RINAKO Corporation, did not provide active support to the party).

The fact that the PEL programme provisions and the *Russia's Choice* programme were identical (the rule of law as the only guarantee against violence and tyranny, inviolability of a person, unity of economic and political freedoms, demand for the state to renounce its economic functions and attend to its direct duties – protection of citizens and their property), left the party little chance for independent success in the last election campaign. As a result, Konstantin Borovoi, who had not managed to collect a sufficient number of signatures for PEL's registration as an electoral association, called on the electors to vote for the very *Russia's Choice* he had sharply criticised a week before.

The failure of 'business parties' to collect a sufficient number of signatures during the Federal Assembly election campaign has demonstrated the political under-development and lack of consolidation of Russian business and banking capital. As a result, the role of representing their interests was assigned to the same ruling *nomenklatura* grouping whose monopolism they had so strongly criticised a month before, i.e. *Russia's Choice*. However, as Irina Khakamada aptly remarked in one her interviews , entrepreneurs „had lost an opportunity to give the new parliament a serious face. Nevertheless, they have enough money to bribe separate deputies, what they used to do before. In this sense, they rather quickly understand the situation, quickly find the necessary people, quickly establish small agile gatherings".

The economically subordinate and dependent role of new business with respect to executive power, which frequently acts as a subject of its formation and development, manifested itself in the inability and unwillingness of the *nouveaux riches* to act in the elections on behalf of themselves and to openly impose their interests, as general and national interests, on the society. As was stated by the Presidium of 'Entrepreneurs for a New Russia' on 15 October 1993, „the class interests of the Russian entrepreneurs are higher and broader than the interests of the party, they are nation-wide interests – what is good for Russia is good for entrepreneurs". Those who had the courage 'to swim alone' were forced to do so, as they had failed to find acceptable allies among 'pure politicians'.

Protection of the interests of sectoral economic groupings which had also taken an active part in the election campaign was the responsibility of a number of parties and blocs, including those affiliated with one or several specific financial-industrial-trading groups (the Party of Consolidation, the Union of Oil industrialists, 'Transformation of the Urals' movement) or claiming to represent the interests of entire social strata or even all citizens (the blocs 'Fatherland', *Civic Union*, the Agrarian Party of Russia).

A considerable number of state enterprise administrators, primarily those of the defence industries, who are politically and ideologically oriented toward the sectoral bloc of state industry, were included into the electoral list of the '*Civic Union*': Nikolai Bekh, director of KAMAZ plant and deputy chairman of the Council for Industrial Politics at the Government of Russia; Peter Semenenko, general director of the joint stock company *Kirovskii Zavod*, Piskunov (*Almazy Rossii-Sakha*), Goryachev (concern *Goryachev*), Koveshnikov (scientific and production association *Avangard*), etc. The political representation of the agro-industrial complex was monopolised by the Agrarian Party of Russia. The Party of the Russian Unity and Concord became a major political stake of the *Gazprom* concern.

The situation of the Party of Consolidation (PC), which has shown itself as a protector of interests of the 'firm business closely connected with national industry', is typical. The political status and expected success of the PC in the elections considerably increased after its chairman Aleksandr Tikhonov announced on 22 October 1993 that the electoral list of the party would be supported by the oil and gas concern *Hermes* (its president Valerii Neverov was running for deputy on the PC-list), by the inter-sectoral scientific and technical complex *Nefteotdacha*, the Foreign trade association *InterUral*, the Union of Oil Industrialists of Russia, and the banking group *Olbi*. Altogether, according to the assessment of *Kommersant-Daily*, PC's financial basis may amount to 0.5-0.7 trillion roubles.

It should be noted that party documents emphasised 'state and regional orientation' (the major field of activities of the *InterUral* association are import-export operations from the Ural, and a number of newspapers pointed out the close ties of Aleksandr Tikhonov with the ex-governor of Sverdlovsk region Eduard Rossel and first vice-prime minister Oleg Soskovets. As for the political interests of *Hermes*, they are closely connected with the transformation of oil industrial enterprises into joint stock companies (the concern utilises their credit and other services for its financial operations), and the continuation of an anti-inflationary policy with targeted state support for industry.

The interests of the defence industry (the League for Defence Enterprises) and those of domestic market sectors, the main body of the Federation of Commodity Producers (FCP), became politically exposed during the election campaign. The refusal of the FCP to take part in the elections was caused by its lack of organisational skills, of available financial resources, and of political consolidation with outsider enterprises. Businessman Yurii Gekht, the former chairman of the parliamentary group 'Industrial Union', who is close to the Federation's leader Yurii Skokov, acknowledged the unpreparedness of the FCP for the elections by declaring in October 1993 that „to hold elections in December is unrealistic, these are not normal conditions. A parliament elected on such terms would only increase people's resentment against the authorities. A normal parliament can be elected no earlier than March".

For the same reasons as in the case of PEL, the Association of Independent Professionals, the 'Transformation' movement, the Party of Consolidation and the 'Fatherland' bloc failed to even approach the decisive stage of the election marathon. As for the Civic Union and, partially, the Agrarian Party, their rooted political orientations, and not their identification with specific social and professional strata, turned out to be crucial for their results in the election campaign: for the CU it was a centrism temporarily devoid, since October, of political attractiveness and lacking Aleksandr Rutskoi's charisma; for the Agrarian party of Russia (APR) – it was the uncompromising opposition to the ruling groups of radical liberals.

The outcome of the elections of 12 December, 1993, the interim results of the government's inner struggle of January, 1994 and the legalisation of a new important centre of political decision making – the Federal Assembly – created preconditions for the transition to a qualitatively new political and economic situation in the country, and stimulated the search for adequate channels of influencing state government bodies by the economic elites. By February 1994, the well-beaten lobbying tracks, as well as those who use them can, generally speaking, be divided into pro-government and pro-parliament groups.

As of today, the predominantly sectoral groupings whose representatives make up the main body of Chernomyrdin's cabinet, as well as the economic groupings that are not represented with their own or politically allied deputies in the parliament, prefer to solve their problems through the Cabinet of Ministries and government agencies.

The interests of the metallurgy sector are defended by first vice-prime minister Oleg Soskovets himself who initiated the development and approval of the Federal programme of technical re-equipment and development of metallurgy for 1993-2000. He also deals with a considerable part of defence industry requirements, the official patronage over which were entrusted last autumn to the Security Council of the Russian Federation (Secretary Oleg Lobov), the Inter-Departmental Commission for Scientific and Technical Policy at the Security Council (Chairman Mikhail Malei) and, partially, the Defence ministry (first deputy minister Andrei Kokoshin).

State enterprises directors, who took the lead in the wave of strikes in January-February, addressed their demands to the government and the president.. Thus, on 2 February 1994, the conference of industrial enterprises representatives of the Perm region, with participation of the chief of the region's administration, addressed the supreme executive power with a demand to introduce government regulation of the economy. Prior to that, similar addresses to the president, the prime Minister, the chairman of the Council of the Federation and the chairman of the State Duma were adopted by administrators of enterprises of the Novosibirsk region who demanded increased government control of prices for basic fuels and electricity, basic goods and services as well as an urgent package of measures in regard to carrying out spring field works, to pay unpaid money for delivered grain and defence products, and to limit taxes imposed on producing enterprises to a level of 35-40% of proceeds.

Public associations of industrialists and entrepreneurs as well as their politicised formations, concentrated around the government, represent, first of all, the Russian Union of Industrialists and Entrepreneurs (vice-president Mikhail Yur'ev – the leader of the Council for Industry and Business at the government, patronised by Oleg Soskovets, the author of the 'Industrial Politics Conception' submitted to leaders of the Cabinet for consideration), which was defeated at the elections to the new federal parliament; and the public association of enterprise businessmen headed by Ivan Kivelidi, the co-ordinator of the association 'Round-table of the Business of Russia'. The latter believes that „a full-fledged, working parliament... has failed to be established, there are too many people there who are far better accustomed to addressing meetings than doing a specific job", but then, „Chernomyrdin has a firm footing, he knows perfectly well the needs of production, and effectively tackles any radical extremes. For me, he seems by far the most preferable figure for a crisis period".

Another well-known organiser of production activities in the field of free enterprise, as well as of import transactions, the president of the International Association of Enterprise Administrators Mark Masarskii, declared himself a representative of 'national capital' in his January interview with the newspaper *24* and strongly criticised Egor Gaidar for abandoning the government. In his opinion, „the objective result of his activities was a sharp consolidation of the comprador bourgeoisie, which is creating jobs abroad rather than in the home country. The very bourgeoisie that is trading in non-replenishable resources, without developing domestic production, and by whose pressure, with the help of restrictive customs measures, imports have practically ceased. Speaking before his resignation, Egor Gaidar mentioned export liberalisation among his achievements, but he did not mention strengthened government control over imports. He spoke about the slow-down in inflation rates but did not mention the continuing suffocation of our economic potential. After all, since 1 January, 1994, a new taxation method has been in effect for legal persons that has increased profit tax from 32 to 38 per cent. The retail sales tax has increased as well, which in this country for some reason is called value-added tax. Local authorities have been given unrestricted rights to impose local taxes. Meanwhile, all serious economists say, and nobody has proved the opposite yet, that an aggregate tax collection exceeding 50 per cent of profit can block production completely".

The ousting of major leaders of the *Russia's Choice* bloc from the government and into State Duma, and the related shift of the centre of activities of the radical-liberal bloc into representative bodies accelerated the reorientation of a considerable part of the industrial and business structures to newly elected deputies, a reorientation that started since they had been elected.

Thus, on 25 October 1993 it was decided at a session of the Council of the Association of Russian Banks (ARB) to „fight for the creation in the new parliament of a professional lobby, whose representatives could be advocates of various political parties and tendencies". The affiliation of a candidate with some political structure will not be of any significance, the main emphasis will be put on his pragmatic qualities and their willingness to defend professional interests.

One of the main requests of the ARB was the strict observance of the presidential decree *On the Activities of Foreign Banks, Created with the Participation of non-*

*Residents on the Territory of the RF*, which de facto prohibits the entry onto the Russian market of foreign banks. On 26 November the Association of Russian Banks and the Moscow Banking Union expressed their strong disagreement with the chairman of the Central Bank Viktor Gerashchenko, who „strongly advocated the broad distribution of foreign banks throughout Russia, despite the obvious impossibility for Russian commercial banks to compete with them on an equal footing for at least 2-3 years. It is also hard to understand, why the chairman of the Central Bank accuses the President and the government, who, in his words, are succumbing before the individual Russian banks and prepared the decree during the electoral campaign. By doing so, the CB accuses all Russian commercial banks, who are interested in the strengthening of the national banking system, in the stabilisation of the rouble and in the protection of national interests."

On the November meeting with the leadership of the Association, the leader of *Russia's Choice*, Gaidar was forced to give assurances that he would not admit any further liberalisation of entry of foreign banks into Russia. With the support of the ARB, the ex-minister Boris Fedorov assumed the chairmanship of the Subcommittee of the State Duma on Banks and Banking Legislation. In that capacity, Fedorov is assumed to continue the fight for control over Russia's Central Bank, in which the forms and limits of foreign banks' economic activity will be one of the main directions. In December 1993, the ARB and the MBU prepared a series of new draft legislative acts regulating banking activity, and a draft for a corresponding decree was transmitted to the President of Russia.

At the same time, the position of the Central Bank of Russia in the discussion about the presidential decree is supported by the leaders of the Moscow Currency Exchange Market – the banks *Optimum*, *Vozrozhdenie* [Rebirth], *Tokobank*, Moscow International Bank, and others. As a result of the protectionist measures, the opening of foreign offices of a number of banks (*Stolichnyi*, *AvtoBAZ-Bank*, *Industria-Service*, *Natsional'nyi Kredit*, etc.) was put into doubt.

One of the deputies from *Russia's Choice*, the president of the Union of Leaseholders and Co-operators Pavel Bunich presented his own version of a programme for the legislative defence of business interests in January 1994. For him, the main priority is tax reform, which should alleviate the tax burden which has been put on entrepreneurs: „the overwhelming majority of entrepreneurs today do not have the one thing for the sake of which we implemented a change in property relations: they do not have sufficient means for accumulation, for building new enterprises, for production. Yet that was precisely the reason why the economic structure of our country was reformed, and certainly not to allow a small segment of the population to bask in luxury". According to Bunich, a 20-30% decrease in taxes would stimulate growth in non-capital intensive and non-fund intensive industries: light industry, food industry, private agriculture, construction material industry.

Bunich is of the opinion that the new parliament will have to adopt legislation that will give entrepreneurs some surplus profits. If this surplus will then be aimed at accumulation and at new production, this will not only stop the decline in production, but will also lead to a stabilisation and even growth. In order to obtain success in carrying out reforms, it is necessary to observe the principle of congruence between prices and income, but not in general, for society as a whole, but for its main segments: for individual workers, farmers, the intelligentsia, the youth, the military, and even for individual unemployed people. Touching upon the issue of privatisation, Bunich said that the non-state sector of the economy, in which already more than 30 mln. people have found employment, is starting to play an ever increasing role. Privatisation has not yet lead to the creation of a middle class, which forms the basis for any civilised state. But the creation of a stock market has already occurred, which leads to a changing of hands and concentration of stocks. As a result of this, a solid group of property-owners will emerge, which will have real ownership over factories and land.

The main task of the activities of the sectoral groupings in the Federal Assembly, as they see it, is to provide parliamentary support for their delegates in the government and to avoid turning the parliament into an arena for the clash of interests between various competing economic groupings and nomenklatura-political groups. This is characteristic for the agro-industrial lobby (the Agrarian Union of Russia and the parliamentary fraction of the Agrarian Part of Russia).

The primary interests of the FEC require the coupling of the financial systems of Russia and the CIS countries to allow for the continued payment of delivered oil, gas and energy; an increase in energy prices to world standards, and the reanimation of the domestic production of oil-extracting equipment. The aim of the creation of an 'oil-lobby' in the Federal Assembly, in the words of Shafrannik, is to counteract the plan to freeze energy prices: „There are people today, like A. Sobchak for instance, who think that it is necessary to 'freeze' energy prices, to implement a 'weak' reform in other sectors of industry instead, and to allow the FEC to reform itself afterwards. I beg your pardon, but at that blessed date, there will be no longer be an energy base in Russia. For the time being, this sentiment is very strong on *Staraya Ploshchad*, and it is not easy for us, for common sense, to convince them." As far as impact on the financial-credit policy is concerned, according to him, the energy-people „were not terribly successful. Here I turned out to be in a minority as a minister in the government.“

Similarly, that same Yuriy Shafrannik commented in that same January interview with *Sibirskaya gazeta* on the creation of a parliamentary oil-lobby on a non-party basis under the aegis of the Union Oil Industrialists in the following way: „For all, today is the time for choosing. We too, having consulted with the presidents of other companies of the fuel and energy complex, and not only oil ones, have decided to put our people in the State Duma and the Federation Council as representatives of the enterprises – to create our own 'energy'-lobby. A whole group from the FEC ended up in parliament. At the same time, we came to the conclusion not to enter into any party grouping, so that we would not be ruled by politics.“ There is in fact such a grouping today under the name of 'New Regional Policy'.

The protection of the interests of powerful lobbyist groupings lead to the creation of a whole range of such organisations, which at the same time compete and cooperage with each other. One can already discern certain 'leaders' among them, who try to take over the cabinet's economic policy ever more energetically.

1993 was remarkable for the clash between the main corporative groupings of the sectoral industrialists: the AIC and the oil group of the FEC with the MIC group over the budget allocations for 1994. Of all groups, the agricultural directors, united in the Agrarian Union of Russia, were the most successful in realising their operational and long-term interests. The directorate of the MIC, in guise of the League for Co-operation between Defence Enterprises and the Russian League of Armaments Producers, partially succeeded in receiving the requested budgetary means. The 'oil generals' of the FEC (the Union of Oil Industrialists) were left in a deplorable situation, having become the victims not only of chronic non-payment, but also of insufficient patronage on the part of Prime Minister Chernomyrdin, who was forced because of political expediency to manoeuvre between all the sectors and the international community, which is financing Russia's debts and the privatised state sector. One can observe a de-facto merger into one lobby group of Goskomoboronprom and the Ministry of Defence with the League for Co-operation between Defence Enterprises, of the Ministry of Agriculture with the Agrarian Union of Russia, and of the Minister of Fuel and Energy with the Union of Oil Industrialists.

The attempts by some deputies of the State Duma and Moscow experts to renew the process of adopting a law on lobbying to a large extent derives from the demand of business actors in the sphere of free enterprise, in as far as their resources at the state level are clearly insufficient to solve their problems. This is clearly illustrated in the not very successful struggle between the Association of Banks of Russia and the Central Bank on the issue of allowing foreign banks onto the Russian financial market, reflecting the failure of the same Round-Table of Russian Business and the Council on Entrepreneurship of the government to lobby for draft legislation which had been authored by the cabinet.

Thus, the draft law *On Regulating Lobbying Activities in the Federal Organs of State Power* that is being elaborated by a group around deputy of the State Duma Vladimir Lepekhin may deal a heavy blow to the lobbying infrastructure of the state directorate. According to this draft, lobbyism is defined as the activity „of legal and physical entities in relation to the federal organs of state power with the aim of exerting influence on the procedures by which the latter fulfil their mandate, as stipulated in the Constitution and legislation of the Russian Federation“. As forms and methods of lobbying activity are recognised the presentation to the federal organs of state power of draft laws, decrees, regulations or other normative acts which have been developed by the lobbying person or group with expertise in that area. The draft law prohibits „deputies of the parliament, elected officials of the Russian Federation and its subjects, and also organs and officials of the executive and juridical branches of power“ from being lobbyists. Incidentally, former parliamentarians, ministers, judges and other persons are allowed to apply their efforts in the lobbying field, but they have to wait at least a year after having quit their position.

Every person who acts in the capacity of a lobbyist, is obliged to register him/herself with the Ministry of Justice of the RF. That is also the same instance to which the lobbyist has to address her/himself not later than 20 days after the end of half a calendar year or after the termination of his activities with a written account of these activities. The revenues received by the lobbyist will be taxable in accordance with the existing legislation.

The main aim for creating a legal basis for lobbyism as defined by Lepekhin consists of the following elements:

- to separate private entrepreneurial activity from the state
- to provide transparency on the distribution of dotations, credits, licences and other privileges to enterprises
- to ensure the interaction of the federal government exclusively with legitimate structures – unions of entrepreneurs and heads of state enterprises at the federal

level, i.e. that are registered with the Ministry of Justice in Russia and that have delegated the appropriate powers of authority to their leaders.

More detailed descriptions of the activities and organisational structures of various interest groups will be given in the third volume of this compendium.

# 7

## List of Authors

*Chervyakov*, Vladimir Vladimirovich (1966, Moscow region), historian; deputy director at the Russian Center for Political Trend Observation (*Tsentr politicheskoi konyunktury*), Moscow.

*De Spiegeleire*, Stephan (1963, Belgium), political scientist, M.A. from Geneva Graduate Institute for International Studies, Columbia University, Ph.D. Candidate at UCLA; research fellow at the Stiftung Wissenschaft und Politik, Ebenhausen.

*Kordonskii*, Simon Gdal'evich (1944, Gorno-Altaisk), biologist and social scientist, *Kandidat* of philosophical sciences; director of the Center for the Study of Civil Society Institutions, in Moscow.

*Medvedev*, Sergei Aleksandrovich (1966, Moscow), graduated from Moscow School of International Journalism, studies at Prague, Columbia University; senior analyst at the Foreign Policy Association, Moscow; head of section at the Russian Academy of Sciences' Institute of Europe.

*Segbers*, Klaus (1954), Dr. phil. habil., historian, research fellow and head of section at the Stiftung Wissenschaft und Politik, Ebenhausen; head of the current Körber project.

*Shchedrovitskii*, Petr Georgievich (1958, Moscow), president of the Association of Innovative Schools and Centers; chairman of the board of the School for Cultural Politics (*Shkola Kulturnoi Politiki*), in Moscow.

# 8

# Index

## *A*



## *B*

## C



## D

## *E*



## *F*



## *G*

## *H*



## *I*



## *J*



## *K*

## *L*



## *M*

***R***



***S***

---

***W***



---

***Y***



---

***Z***

# 9

# Cumulative Table of Contents